Beechcraft T-34 Mentor Pilot's Flight Operating Instructions

by United States Air Force

This manual is sold for historic research purposes only, as an entertainment. It is not intended to be used as part of an actual flight training program. No book can substitute for flight training by an authorized instructor. The licensing of pilots is overseen by organizations and authorities such as the FAA and CAA. Operating an aircraft without the proper license is a federal crime.

2013 Periscope Film LLC
All Rights Reserved
ISBN #978-1-937684-62-4

www.PeriscopeFilm.com

T.O. 1T-34A-1

FLIGHT HANDBOOK
T-34 A
U S A F S E R I E S

COMMANDERS ARE RESPONSIBLE FOR BRINGING THIS TECHNICAL PUBLICATION TO THE ATTENTION OF ALL AIR FORCE PERSONNEL CLEARED FOR OPERATION OF AFFECTED AIRCRAFT.

PUBLISHED UNDER THE AUTHORITY OF THE SECRETARY OF THE AIR FORCE

THIS PUBLICATION REPLACES T.O. 1T-34A-1 DATED 25 OCTOBER 1956

AND SAFETY OF FLIGHT SUPPLEMENTS T. O. 1T-34A-1H THRU N. SEE BASIC INDEX, T. O. 0-1-1, AND WEEKLY INDEX, T. O. 0-1-1A FOR CURRENT STATUS OF SAFETY OF FLIGHT SUPPLEMENTS.

10 FEBRUARY 1958

AIR FORCE, McACo., WICHITA, KANS., 3-15-58 — 9100 (BEECH ACFT. CO.)

T. O. 1T-34A-1

Reproduction for non-military use of the information or illustrations contained in this publication is not permitted without specific approval of the issuing service (BuAer or AMC). The policy for use of Classified Publications is established for the Air Force in AFR 205-1 and for the Navy in Navy Regulations, Article 1509.

LIST OF EFFECTIVE PAGES

INSERT LATEST REVISED PAGES. DESTROY SUPERSEDED PAGES.

NOTE: The portion of the text affected by the current revision is indicated by a vertical line in the outer margin of the page.

TOTAL NUMBER OF PAGES IN THIS PUBLICATION IS 148

Page No.	Issue
Title and A Page	Original
i thru iv	Original
1-1 thru 1-28	Original
2-1 thru 2-28	Original
3-1 thru 3-18	Original
4-1 thru 4-8	Original
5-1 thru 5-6	Original
6-1 thru 6-6	Original
7-1 thru 7-4	Original
9-1 thru 9-8	Original
A-1 thru A-30	Original
X-1 thru X-6	Original

This manual is sold for historic research purposes only, as an entertainment. It is not intended to be used as part of an actual flight training program. No book can substitute for flight training by an authorized instructor. The licensing of pilots is overseen by organizations and authorities such as the FAA and CAA. Operating an aircraft without the proper license is a federal crime.

* The asterisk indicates pages revised, added or deleted by the current revision.

ADDITIONAL COPIES OF THIS PUBLICATION MAY BE OBTAINED AS FOLLOWS:

USAF ACTIVITIES. — In accordance with Technical Order No. 00-5-2.
NAVY ACTIVITIES. — Submit request to nearest supply point listed below, using form NavAer-140; NASD, Philadelphia, Pa.; NAS, Alameda, Calif.; NAS, Jacksonville, Fla.; NAS, Norfolk, Va.; NAS, San Diego, Calif.; NAS, Seattle, Wash.; ASD, NSC, Guam.
For listing of available material and details of distribution see Naval Aeronautics Publications Index NavAer 00-500.

Revised 10 February 1958

TABLE OF CONTENTS

SECTION	I	Description 1-1
SECTION	II	Normal Procedures 2-1
SECTION	III	Emergency Procedures 3-1
SECTION	IV	Description and Operation of Auxiliary Equipment 4-1
SECTION	V	Operating Limitations 5-1
SECTION	VI	Flight Characteristics 6-1
SECTION	VII	Systems Operation 7-1
SECTION	VIII	Crew Duties (Not Applicable) 7-4
SECTION	IX	All-Weather Operation 9-1
APPENDIX		Performance Data A-1
ALPHABETICAL INDEX		. . . . X-1

Read Carefully...

SCOPE.

This handbook contains all the information necessary for safe and efficient operation of the T-34A. These instructions do not teach basic flight principles, but are designed to provide you with a general knowledge of the airplane, its flight characteristics, and specific normal and emergency operating procedures. Your flying experience is recognized, and elementary instructions have been avoided.

SOUND JUDGMENT.

The instructions in this handbook are designed to provide for the needs of a crew inexperienced in the operation of this aircraft. This book provides the best possible operating instructions under most circumstances, but it is a poor substitute for sound judgment. Multiple emergencies, adverse weather, terrain, etc., may require modification of the procedures contained herein.

PERMISSIBLE OPERATIONS.

The Flight Handbook takes a "positive approach" and normally tells you only what you can do. Any unusual operation or configuration (such as asymmetrical loading) is prohibited unless specifically covered in the Flight Handbook. Clearance must be obtained from ARDC before any questionable operation is attempted which is not specifically covered in the Flight Handbook.

STANDARDIZATION.

Once you have learned to use one Flight Handbook, you will know how to use them all — closely guarded standardization assures that the scope and arrangement of all Flight Handbooks are identical.

ARRANGEMENT.

The handbook has been divided into 10 fairly independent sections, each with its own table of contents. The objective of this subdivision is to make it easy both to read the book straight through when it is first received and thereafter to use it as a reference manual. The independence of these sections also makes it possible for the user to rearrange the book to satisfy his personal taste and requirements. The first 3 sections cover the minimum information required to safely get the airplane into the air and back down again. Before flying any new aircraft these 3 sections must be read thoroughly and fully understood. Section IV covers all equipment not essential to flight but which permits the aircraft to perform special functions. Sections V and VI are obvious. Section VII covers lengthy discussions on any technique or theory of operation which may be applicable to the particular aircraft in question. The experienced pilot will probably not need to read this section but he should check it for any possible new information. The contents of the remaining sections are fairly obvious.

YOUR RESPONSIBILITY.

These Flight Handbooks are constantly maintained current through an extremely active revision program. Frequent conferences with operating personnel and constant review of UR's, accident reports, flight test reports, etc., assure inclusion of the latest data in these handbooks. In this regard, it is essential that you do your part! If you find anything you don't like about the book, let us know right away. We cannot correct an error whose existence is unknown to us.

PERSONAL COPIES, TABS AND BINDERS.

In accordance with the provisions of AFR 5-13, flight crew members are entitled to have personal copies of the Flight Handbooks. Flexible, loose leaf tabs and binders have been provided to hold your personal copy of the Flight Handbook. These good-looking, simulated-leather binders will make it much easier for you to revise your handbook as well as to keep it in good shape. These tabs and binders are secured through your local materiel staff and contracting officers.

HOW TO GET COPIES.

If you want to be sure of getting your handbooks on time, order them before you need them. Early ordering will assure that enough copies are printed to cover your requirements. Technical Order 0-5-2 explains how to order Flight Handbooks so that you automatically will get all revisions, reissues, and Safety of Flight Supplements. Basically, all you have to do is order the required quantities in the Publication Requirements Table (T.O. 0-3-1). Talk to your Senior Materiel Staff Officer — it is his job to fulfill your Technical Order requests. Make sure to establish some system that will rapidly get the books and Safety of Flight Supplements to the flight crews once they are received on the base.

SAFETY OF FLIGHT SUPPLEMENTS.

Safety of Flight Supplements are used to get information to you in a hurry. Safety of Flight Supplements use the same number as your Flight Handbook, except for the addition of a suffix letter. Supplements covering loss of life will get to you in 48 hours; those concerning serious damage to equipment will make it in 10 days. You can determine the status of Safety of Flight Supplements by referring to the Index of Technical Publications (T.O. 0-1-1) and the Weekly Supplemental Index (T.O. 0-1-1A). This is the only way you can determine whether a supplement has been rescinded. The title page of the Flight Handbook and title block of each Safety of Flight Supplement should also be checked to determine the effect that these publications may have on existing Safety of Flight Supplements. It is critically important that you remain constantly aware of the status of all supplements — you must comply with all existing supplements but there is no point in restricting the operation of your aircraft by complying with a supplement that has been replaced or rescinded. If you have ordered your Flight Handbook on the Publications Requirements Table, you automatically will receive all supplements pertaining to your airplane. Technical Order 0-5-1 covers some additional information regarding these supplements.

WARNINGS, CAUTIONS, AND NOTES.

For your information, the following definitions apply to the "Warnings," "Cautions," and "Notes" found throughout the handbook:

WARNING

Operating procedures, practices, etc., which will result in personal injury or loss of life if not carefully followed.

CAUTION

Operating procedures, practices, etc., which is not strictly observed will result in damage to equipment.

NOTE

An operating procedure, condition, etc., which it is essential to emphasize.

COMMENTS AND QUESTIONS.

Comments and questions regarding any phase of the Flight Handbook program are invited and should be forwarded through your Command Headquarters to Commander, Detachment No. 1, Hq. Air Research and Development Command, Wright-Patterson AFB, Ohio, ATTN.: RDZSPH.

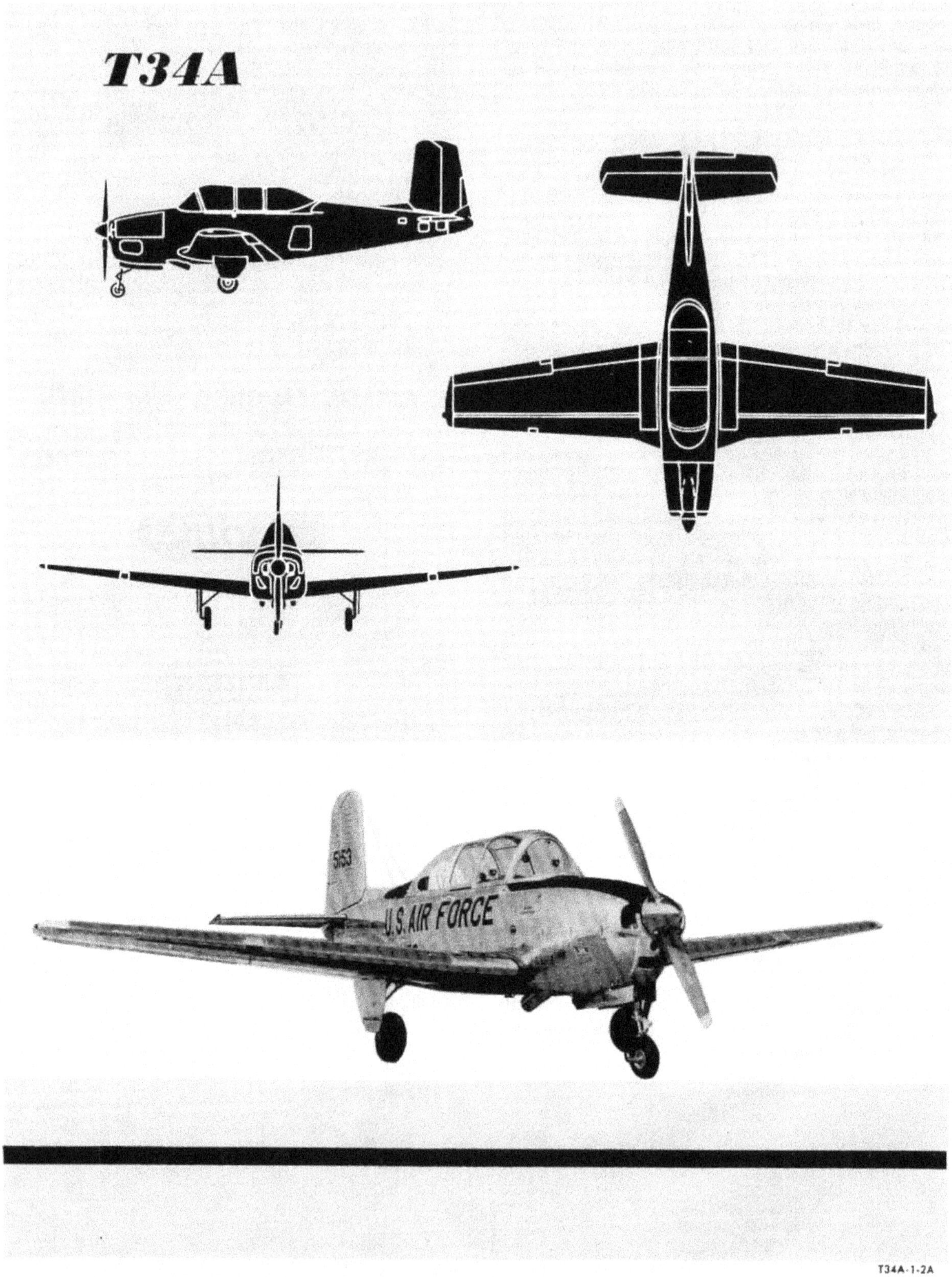

T34A

Figure 1-1

Section 1

Description

TABLE OF CONTENTS

Aircraft	1-1
Engine	1-2
Ignition System	1-7
Priming System	1-7
Starter Switch	1-8
Propeller	1-8
Oil System	1-9
Fuel System	1-9
Electrical Power Supply System	1-14
Flight Control System	1-18
Landing Gear System	1-21
Wheel Brake System	1-23
Nose Wheel Steering	1-23
Instruments	1-23
Emergency Equipment	1-26
Canopy	1-26
Seats	1-28
Auxiliary Equipment	1-28

AIRCRAFT.

The T-34A aircraft is a two-place, single-engine, tandem-seating trainer, built by Beech Aircraft Corporation. This aircraft is designed to meet the requirements of ruggedness and safety demanded of a primary trainer and at the same time prepare the student pilot for the transition to heavier, higher-performance aircraft which he will fly later. Noteworthy features include tricycle landing gear, constant-speed propeller and full instrumentation in both cockpits. Although dual controls are provided for student training, solo flight must be accomplished from the front cockpit only.

DIMENSIONS.

The over-all dimensions of the aircraft areas follows:

Wing Span	32.8 feet
Length	25.9 feet
Height (at rest)	9.6 feet
Tread	9.6 feet

Minimum turn radius and ground clearance are given in Section II.

General Arrangement

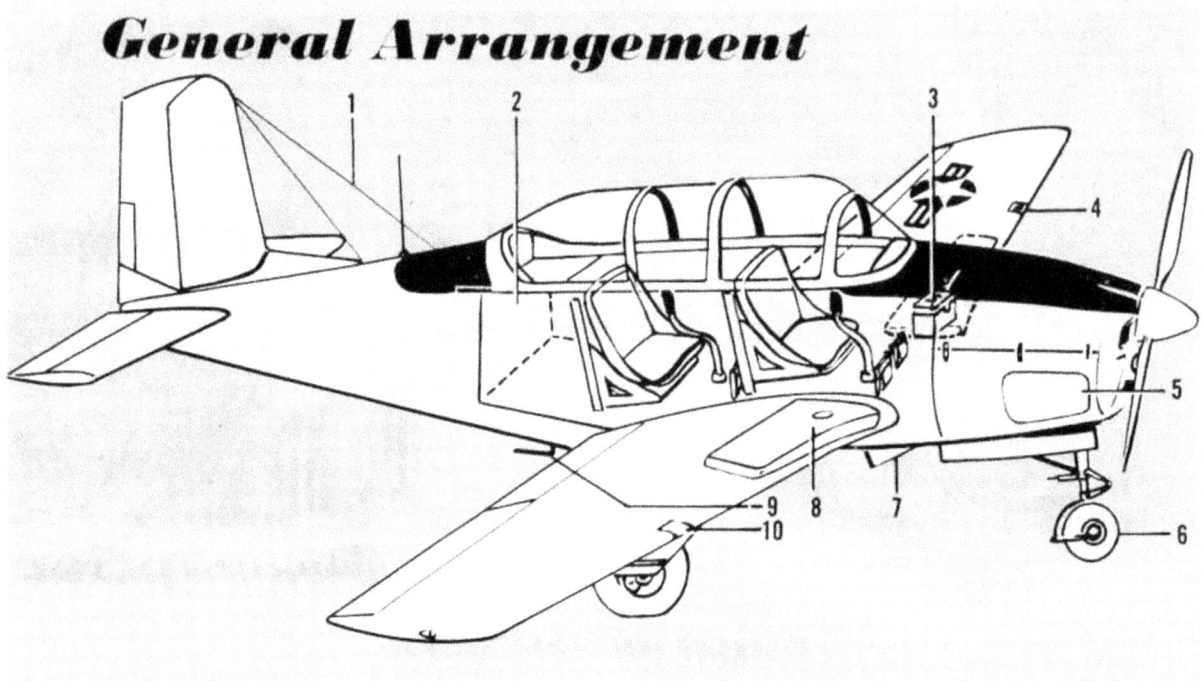

1. Radio Range Receiver Antenna
2. Baggage Compartment
3. Battery
4. Left Landing Light
5. Engine Fire Access Door
6. Steerable Nose Wheel
7. Exhaust Augmentor Tube
8. Right Fuel Tank
9. VHF Antenna
10. Right Landing Light

Figure 1-2

GROSS WEIGHT.

The normal gross weight of the aircraft is 2950 pounds. For alternate gross weights and conditions affecting gross weight limitations refer to Section V.

ENGINE.

The aircraft is powered by a Continental six-cylinder, air-cooled, horizontally-opposed engine which develops 225 horsepower at 2600 rpm at sea level. The engine is equipped with a direct drive starter, pressure type carburetor, and obtains slight additional thrust and greatly improved cooling from an augmentor tube exhaust system. Model designation of the engine is O-470-13 or O-470-13A.

ENGINE CONTROL QUADRANT.

Primary engine controls are conveniently located in the engine control quadrant (5, figure 1-8 and 3, figure 1-10) on the left side of each cockpit. The engine controls are interconnected and can be operated simultaneously from either cockpit.

Throttle.

The throttle (1, figure 1-4) located on the outboard side of each quadrant is CLOSED aft, OPEN forward, and can be placed in any intermediate position for a desired manifold pressure. Two microphone buttons, one for radio transmission and one for interphone operation (2, and 3, figure 1-4), are located in the throttle handgrip. Retarding the throttle to approximately 12 inches Hg. actuates the landing gear warning horn switch which sounds the landing gear warning light at any time any gear is not down and locked.

Mixture Lever.

Fuel-air ratio delivered by the carburetor to the engine is controlled by the mixture lever (6, figure 1-4) on the inboard side of the quadrant. Moving the lever full forward to RICH provides the richest fuel mixture, this position is used for all ground, high power and low altitude operation. Movement of the lever aft toward LEAN progressively leans the mixture. The amount of leaning required varies with altitude. Moving the lever full aft to IDLE CUT-OFF shuts off all fuel flow at the carburetor.

Front and Rear Cockpit General Arrangement

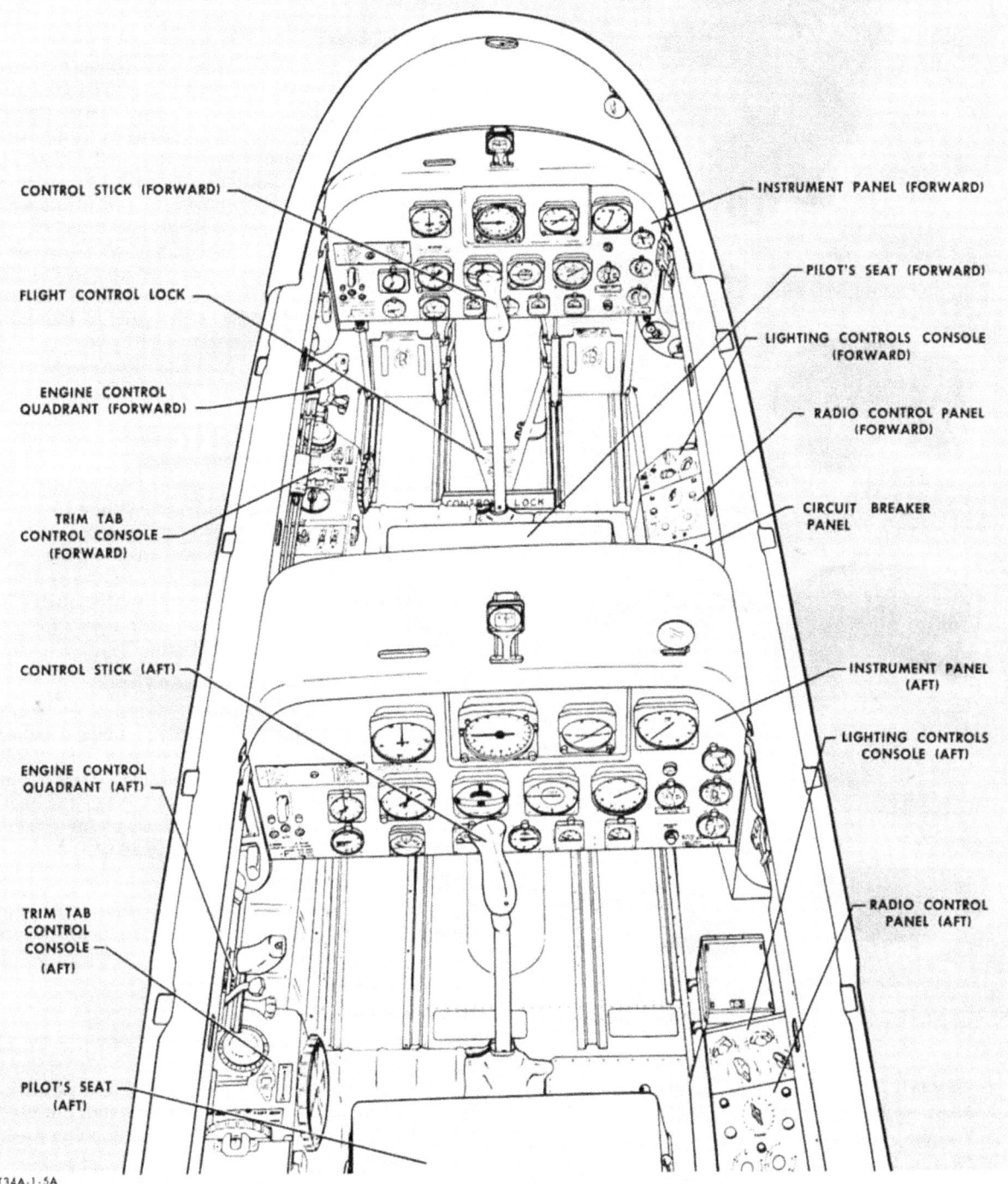

Figure 1-3

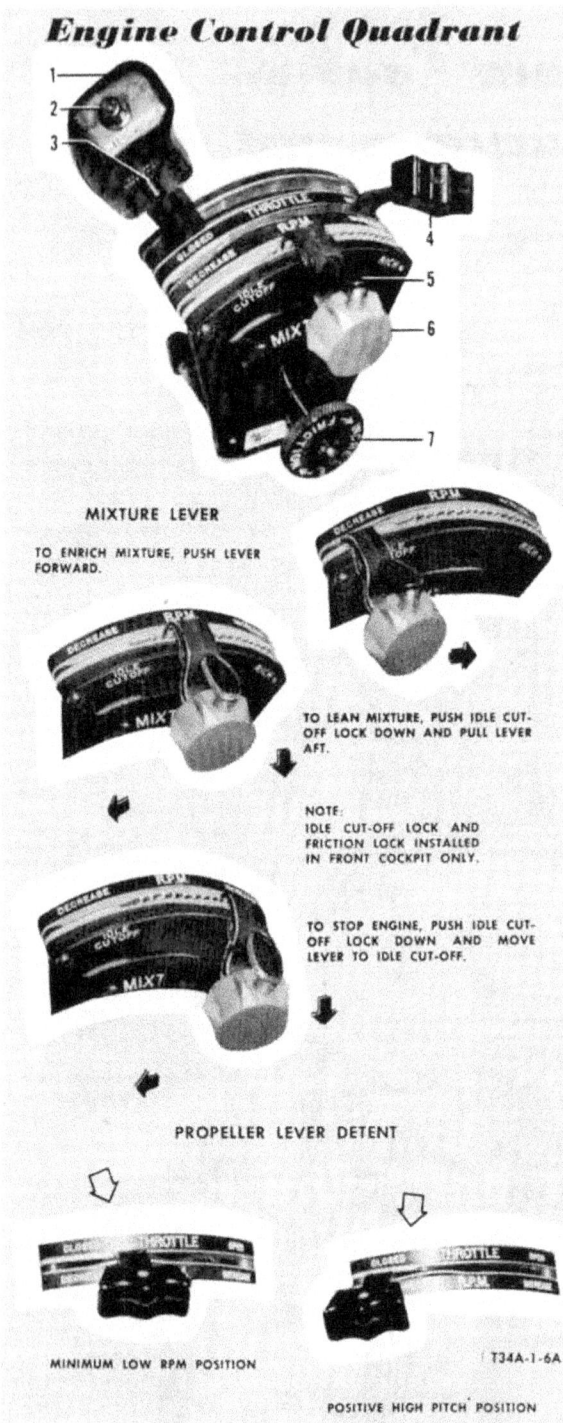

Figure 1-4

Mixture Lever Idle Cut-Off Lock.

The mixture lever idle cut-off lock (5, figure 1-4), located on top of the mixture lever in the front cockpit only, prevents leaning of the mixture or movement of the mixture lever to the IDLE CUT-OFF position from the rear cockpit. For operation of the mixture lever idle cut-off lock, see figure 1-4.

Propeller Lever.

The propeller lever (4, figure 1-4), located in the center of each control quadrant, is used for selection of the desired engine speed. Any engine speed down to the minimum power-on operating speed of 1600 rpm can be maintained by moving the lever aft from the full INCREASE position (2600 rpm). Minimum power-on operating speed is obtained when the propeller lever comes in contact with the detent; see figure 1-4. Movement of the propeller lever past the detent (1600-1650 rpm) results in a positive high pitch and an engine rpm of approximately 700. Movement of the propeller lever past the detent with power on is prohibited in order to avoid the development of excessively high B. M. E. P.

WARNING

Some earlier aircraft were not equipped with a detent in the quadrant; therefore, the minimum power-on operating speed of 1600 rpm must be maintained manually, since further movement of the propeller lever below 1600 rpm will result in the propeller suddenly going into the positive high pitch position.

Engine Control Quadrant Friction Lock.

The engine control quadrant friction lock knob (7, figure 1-4) is located on the inboard side of the front quadrant only. The friction lock knob can be rotated clockwise to increase friction and to prevent creeping of the control levers; counterclockwise rotation decreases friction and allows free movement of the control levers.

ENGINE INSTRUMENTS.

All of the engine instruments (figure 1-6) are located on the right side of each instrument panel and are utilized to provide true indications of engine operation or condition.

Manifold Pressure Gage.

The manifold pressure gage (12, figure 1-6) is located on the upper right hand side of the instrument panel. Manifold pressure, indicated in inches of mercury, is transmitted through a direct line from the intake manifold to the gage on each instrument panel.

Manifold Pressure Purge Valve Button.

The manifold pressure purge valve button (13,

Engine Cooling

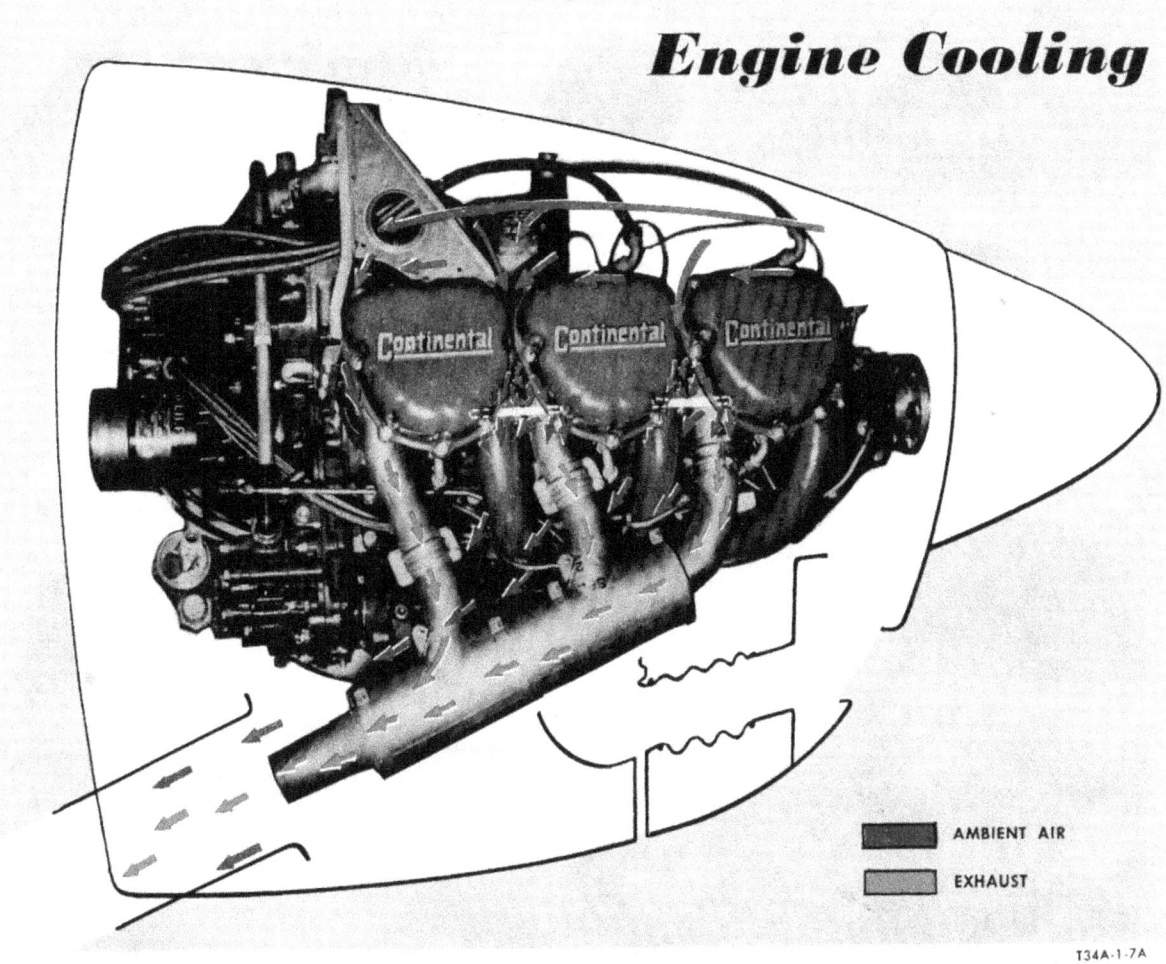

Figure 1-5

figure 1-6) is located on the right hand side of each instrument panel below the manifold pressure gage. Depressing the button actuates a purge valve located in the manifold pressure line between the engine and the gage and allows any accumulated fuel vapor to be purged from the line. The manifold pressure gage should read atmospheric pressure while the purge valve is open.

Tachometer.

The tachometer (11, figure 1-6) is located on the center right hand side of each instrument panel below the attitude indicator. The tachometer indicates engine speed in hundreds of revolutions per minute (rpm) and is energized by an engine-driven tachometer generator, independent of the aircraft's electrical system.

Cylinder Head Temperature Gage.

The cylinder head temperature gage is located on the right hand side of each instrument panel (14, figure 1-6) below the manifold pressure gage. Cylinder head temperature is registered in degrees centigrade which is detected by a flow of dc current through the cylinder head temperature gage. The flow of dc current is varied by a resistance type bulb installed at number one cylinder for the gage in the front cockpit and a bulb at number two cylinder for the gage in the aft cockpit; each acting independently. Electric power for function of the gages is supplied directly from the main dc bus and is controlled by a push-pull 5 ampere circuit breaker on the main circuit breaker panel (figure 1-16).

Carburetor Air Temperature Gage.

The carburetor air temperature gage is located on the lower right hand corner of each instrument panel (18, figure 1-6) below the oil temperature gage. Carburetor air temperature, indicated in degrees centigrade, is detected by a resistance type temperature bulb operated directly from the aircraft's dc bus. The gage registers temperature of air entering the carburetor before it is mixed

1-5

Section I T.O. 1T-34A-1

Instrument Panel

1. Edge Lighted Check List
2. Clock
3. Altimeter
4. Airspeed Indicator
5. Turn-and-Slip Indicator
6. Directional Indicator
7. Magnetic Compass
8. Free Air Temperature Gage
9. Vertical Velocity Indicator
10. Attitude Indicator
11. Tachometer
12. Manifold Pressure Gage
13. Manifold Pressure Purge Valve Button
14. Cylinder Head Temperature Gage
15. Oil Pressure Gage
16. Oil Temperature Gage
17. Radio Call Plate
18. Carburetor Air Temperature Gage
19. Inverter Failure Light
20. Right Fuel Quantity Gage
21. Left Fuel Quantity Gage
22. Fuel Pressure Gage
23. Load Meter
24. Voltmeter
25. Flap Position Indicator
26. Landing Gear Position Indicators
27. Landing Gear Emergency Retract Switch

Figure 1-6

with the fuel. A push-to-reset type 5-amp circuit breaker is located on the main circuit breaker panel (figure 1-16) in the front cockpit only.

Fuel Pressure Gage.

The fuel pressure gage is located on the bottom of each instrument panel (22, figure 1-6) below the vertical velocity indicator. Pressure of fuel at the carburetor pressure chamber, whether developed by the engine-driven fuel pump or an electric boost pump, is indicated in pounds per square inch (psi) by the direct-reading fuel pressure gage.

Oil Pressure Gage.

The oil pressure gage is located on the upper right hand corner of each instrument panel (15, figure 1-6). Oil pressure, indicated in pounds per square inch (psi), is obtained by pressured oil furnished through a restrictor located aft of number four cylinder.

Oil Temperature Gage.

The oil temperature gage is located on the right hand side of each instrument panel (16, figure 1-6) below the oil pressure gage. Oil temperature, registered in degrees centigrade, is detected by a resistance type temperature bulb which operates from the aircraft's dc electrical system. The oil temperature gage registers "oil-in" temperature; that is, oil flowing into the engine. The circuit is protected, in the event of a malfunction, by a push-to-reset type 5-amp circuit breaker which is located on the main circuit breaker panel (figure 1-16) in the front cockpit only.

CARBURETOR.

The aircraft is equipped with a pressure injection, single barrel, updraft carburetor incorporating a manual power enrichment valve. Ram air is admitted at the carburetor air intake below the propeller spinner and is passed through an air filter into a flexible duct leading to the carburetor.

Carburetor Heat Handle.

The carburetor heat handle (2, figure 1-7) is located on the left subpanel below the instrument panel in the front cockpit only. Operation of this handle provides a selection of an alternate source of warm air from the engine compartment to the carburetor. With the handle FULL IN, ram air enters the carburetor through the carburetor air intake below the propeller spinner. Pulling the handle FULL OUT operates a butterfly valve in the duct system, shutting off the normal air flow and admitting warm air from the engine compartment. Intermediate positions between FULL IN and FULL OUT result in a mixture of warm and normal ram air.

ENGINE COOLING.

Cooling of the engine (figure 1-5) is controlled automatically by an augmentor tube exhaust system, which employs the velocity of exhaust gases to vary the flow of cooling air around the engine. Two collectors, one on each bank of cylinders, eject exhaust gases into the mouths of the augmentor tubes. The venturi effect created in the tubes by the ejected gases draws air from the engine compartment through the tubes. Tight baffling controls the airflow around the cylinders. When power is increased, the greater blast effect of the exhaust draws a larger volume of air through the baffled engine, increasing the cooling effect and automatically compensating for the additional heat generated by the greater power being developed. No cowl flaps or other engine cooling accessories are required.

IGNITION SYSTEM.

Ignition is supplied by two magnetos which are grounded individually through the ignition switch. The magnetos automatically provide a retarded and intensified spark for engine starting. The right magneto fires the upper plugs and the left magneto fires the lower plugs.

IGNITION SWITCH.

The ignition switch (3, figure 1-7) is located on the left subpanel below the landing gear handle in each cockpit. The switch has four placarded positions; OFF, RIGHT, LEFT, and BOTH. With the magneto switch turned to BOTH and with the engine turning, an intensified spark is provided to all cylinders. Turning the switch to LEFT (L) or RIGHT (R) positions provides an operational check of either the left or right magnetos, respectively, by grounding out the opposite magneto. Turning the switch to OFF cuts out magneto operation completely by grounding both magnetos.

PRIMING SYSTEM.

The electrically operated priming system consists of a primer solenoid valve; spring loaded to the closed position, an engine primer distributor and a primer switch. The priming system is installed to aid in cold weather starting, but is not normally required except for subfreezing starts. Priming is accomplished by fuel under booster pump pressure which is directed to each cylinder by the primer distributor.

PRIMER SWITCH.

The primer switch (5, figure 1-7) is located at the top of the right hand subpanel adjacent to the starter switch in the front cockpit only. The switch is a two-position ON-OFF toggle type switch, spring loaded to the OFF position, and is equipped with a guard to prevent inadvertent operation. Power for the electrically operated primer solenoid valve is supplied from the main dc bus. Actuation of the primer switch to the

Left and Right Sub Panels

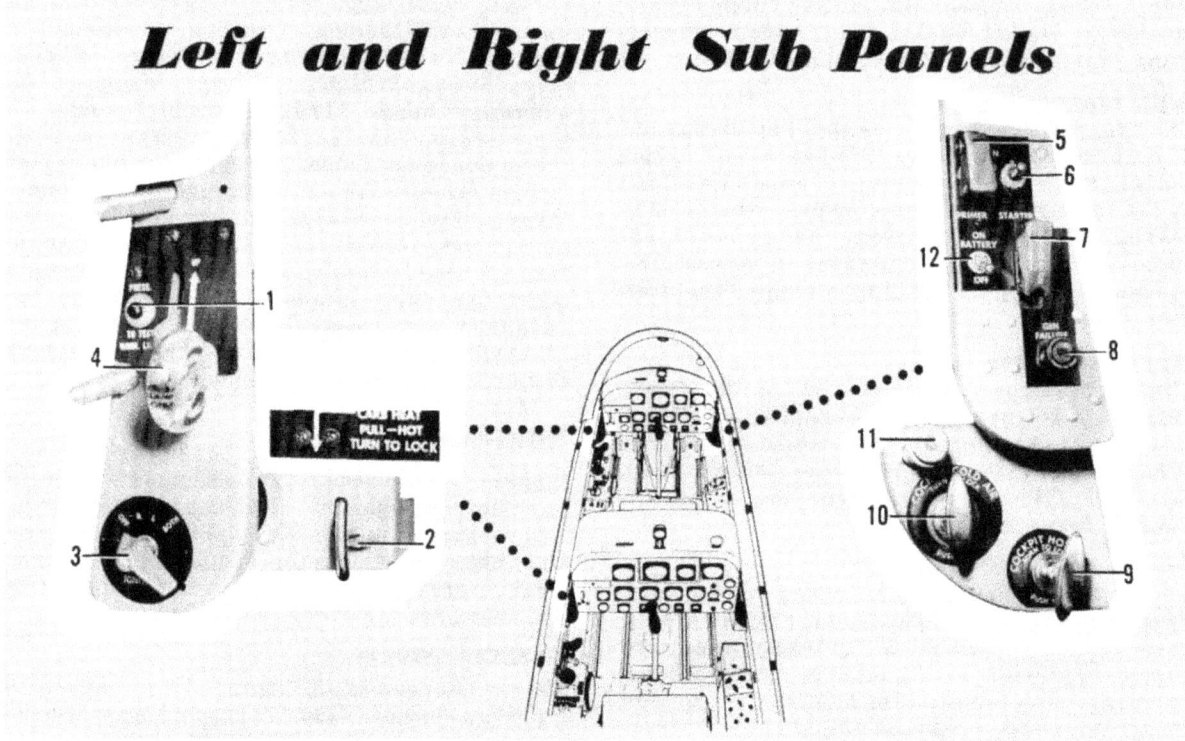

1. Landing Gear Warning Light Test Button
2. Carburetor Heat Handle
3. Ignition Switch
4. Landing Gear Handle
5. Primer Switch
6. Starter Switch
7. Generator Switch
8. Generator Failure Light
9. Cockpit Hot Air Handle
10. Cockpit Cold Air Handle
11. Parking Brake Handle
12. Battery Switch

Figure 1-7

ON position electrically energizes the valve coil and the plunger-type armature is withdrawn, opening the valve, and allows fuel to be directed to each cylinder by the distributor valve. When the switch is returned to the OFF position, the plunger is returned to its seat by a compression spring inside the plunger. A push-to-reset type 5-amp circuit breaker is located on the left hand side of the circuit breaker panel (figure 1-16) in the front cockpit only.

STARTER SWITCH.

The starter switch (6, figure 1-7) is located at the top of the right hand subpanel adjacent to the primer switch in the front cockpit only. The switch is spring loaded to the OFF position. Actuation of the switch to ON energizes the starter relay, which in turn completes the circuit to the direct-cranking electric starter. The starter is automatically engaged when the switch is actuated ON and disengaged when the starter switch is released. Electrical power for the operation is supplied directly by the main dc bus.

PROPELLER.

The engine drives a Beech-designed, hydraulically operated, two-blade, all metal, constant-speed propeller with a blade diameter of either 84 or 88 inches. A governor system maintains a selected engine speed by varying the pitch of the blades to compensate for varying engine loads, regardless of aircraft attitude. A setting introduced into the governor by the pilot determines the engine speed to be maintained and the governor then controls the flow of engine oil, boosted to high pressure by the governing pump, to or from a piston in the propeller hub. Aerodynamic forces acting on the propeller, tend to turn the blades toward low pitch and oil pressure moving the piston forward is translated through linkage into rotation of the blades toward high pitch. The normal operating governed range of the propeller is from 2600 to 1600 rpm. Governor action can be by-passed by overriding a detent in the control quadrant which results in a positive high pitch and a minimum rpm of approximately 700. This positive high pitch increases gliding distance approximately 25 per cent.

PROPELLER LEVER.

The pilot's manual control over the propeller is maintained by a propeller control lever on the engine control quadrant in each pilot's compartment. This propeller control lever, which is connected to the propeller governor, regulates the compression of a speeder spring within the governor itself, which in turn controls the various rpm settings. As the propeller control lever is moved forward, engine speed will increase, if the propeller control lever is moved aft, engine speed will decrease. A detent, near the aft travel limit of the propeller control, marks the normal low operating rpm setting and should never be by-passed with power applied to the engine.

OIL SYSTEM.

The engine employs a dry-sump pressure lubrication system incorporating engine-driven circulating and scavenging pumps, an oil radiator and an oil tank with a capacity of 3 U. S. gallons, plus ½ gallon expansion space. A weighted flexible oil outlet hose, installed in the oil tank, insures a continuous supply of oil from the tank to the circulating pump during inverted flight and when negative G forces are in effect. The weighted end of the flexible outlet hose stays submerged in the oil reservoir due to the effect of gravitational forces. Oil from the tank is directed by the circulating pump, under pressure, to the engine. A thermostatically controlled by-pass valve, at the radiator, begins to open when oil temperature is below 85°C, and is fully open at 65°C, allowing oil to by-pass the radiator. For oil specifications, see figure 1-27. No oil dilution provisions are installed.

FUEL SYSTEM.

The aircraft is equipped with a series-type fuel system (figure 1-12). Major components of the system are two fuel tanks (2 and 6, figure 1-27), an electrically operated, motor-driven, submerged booster pump located in each tank, a fuel tank selector valve located in each cockpit, an engine-driven fuel pump and a pressure-type carburetor. The fuel tanks are filled through individual filler necks located in each inboard wing leading edge (5, figure 1-27). Fuel is pumped from the tank by the engine-driven fuel pump through the selector valve, operated by the pilot, to the carburetor. The engine-driven fuel pump incorporates a pressure relief and by-pass valve which regulates the output fuel pressure of the pump and, in the event of engine-driven fuel pump failure, allows fuel, pumped by the booster pump, to be by-passed to the carburetor.

It is characteristic of any pressure type carburetor that, in its normal operation, a certain quantity of unused fuel and vapor is returned to the fuel tank. The return flow on this aircraft is approximately 3 gallons per hour at cruising speeds and is returned from the carburetor through the fuel selector valve to the tank being used. Refer to figure 1-14 for fuel quantity data and figure 1-27 for servicing and fuel specifications.

FUEL SELECTOR VALVE HANDLE.

The fuel selector valve handle is located on the left console in each cockpit (12, figure 1-8 and 10, figure 1-10). The handle has three placarded positions, OFF, LEFT and RIGHT. Positioning the handle at LEFT or RIGHT tank position, permits movement of fuel from the corresponding tank to the engine and routs return fuel to the same tank. A fuel strainer forms an integral part of the valve body. Turning the handle to OFF position shuts off all fuel flow from both tanks.

FUEL BOOSTER PUMP SWITCH.

The electrically operated fuel booster pumps are controlled by a switch located on the left console in the front cockpit just aft of the fuel selector valve handle. Electrical power for the operation of the fuel boost pumps is supplied directly from the main dc bus. Positioning the switch at LEFT or RIGHT from center, OFF position, operates the booster pump in the corresponding tank and provides fuel to the carburetor under booster pump pressure, providing the fuel selector valve handle is turned to the same tank as the booster pump switch. The booster pumps serve as an auxiliary source of fuel pressure and are used for starting, and in the event of engine-driven fuel pump failure. A 5-amp, push-to-reset type circuit breaker is located on the main circuit breaker panel (figure 1-16) in the front cockpit.

FUEL BOOSTER PUMP OVERRIDE SWITCHES.

Two fuel booster pump override switches (3 and 4, figure 1-12) are located on the fuel booster pump override panel on the left side of the rear cockpit only (11, figure 1-10).

WARNING

Both switches must be set in the FORWARD COCKPIT CONTROL position prior to solo flight.

The switches are placarded LEFT and RIGHT to correspond with the left and right fuel booster

Section I T.O. 1T-34A-1

Front Cockpit Left Side

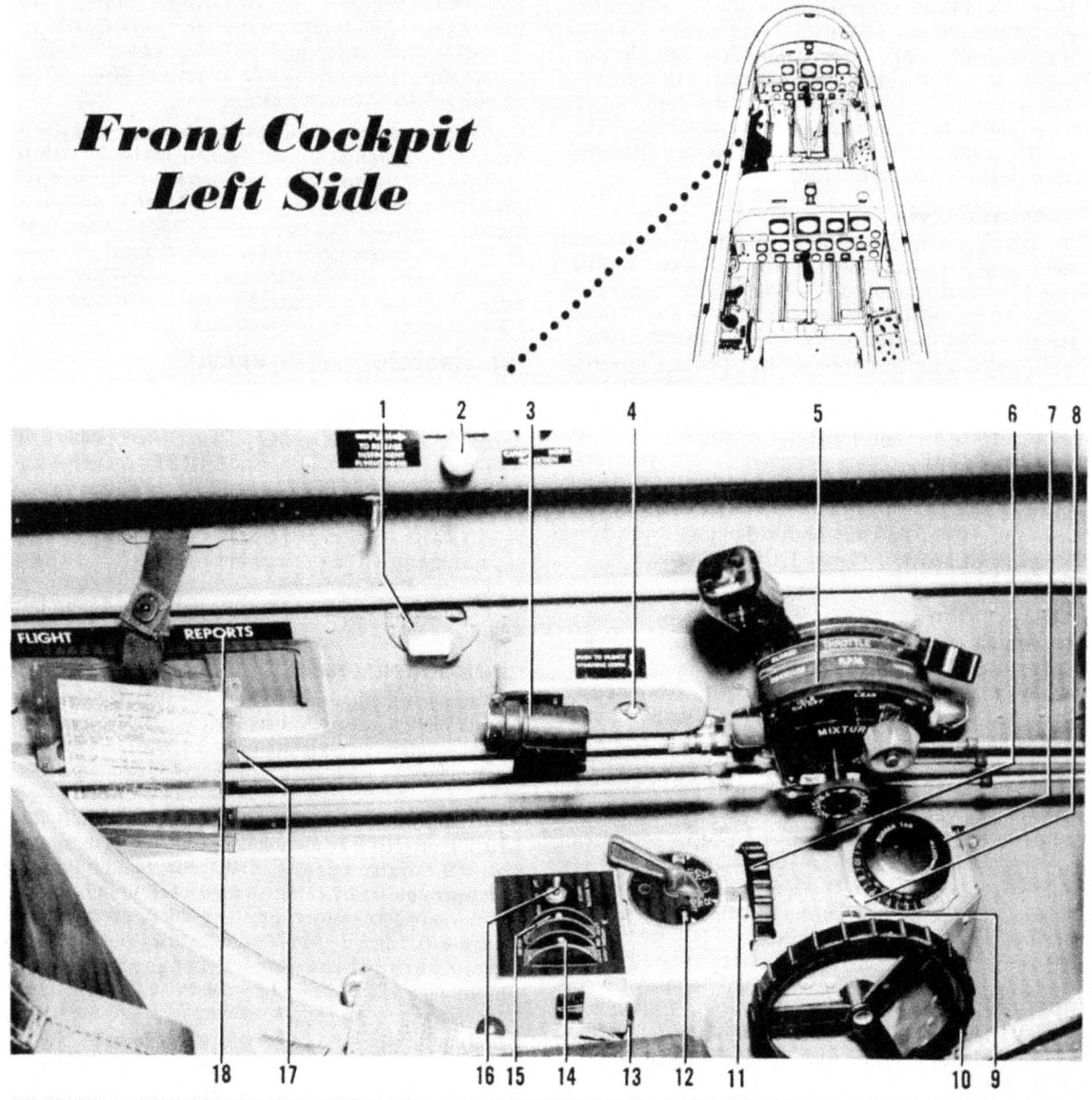

1. Cockpit Air Outlet
2. Instrument Flying Hood Release
3. Console Light
4. Warning Horn Silencer Button
5. Engine Controls Quadrant
6. Aileron Trim Tab Wheel
7. Rudder Trim Tab Knob
8. Rudder Trim Tab Position Indicator
9. Elevator Trim Tab Position Indicator
10. Elevator Trim Tab Wheel
11. Aileron Trim Tab Position Indicator
12. Fuel Selector Valve Handle
13. Wing Flap Lever
14. Right Landing Light Switch
15. Left Landing Light Switch
16. Fuel Booster Pump Switch
17. Pilot's Check List Holder
18. Flight Reports Case

Figure 1-8

Front Cockpit Right Side

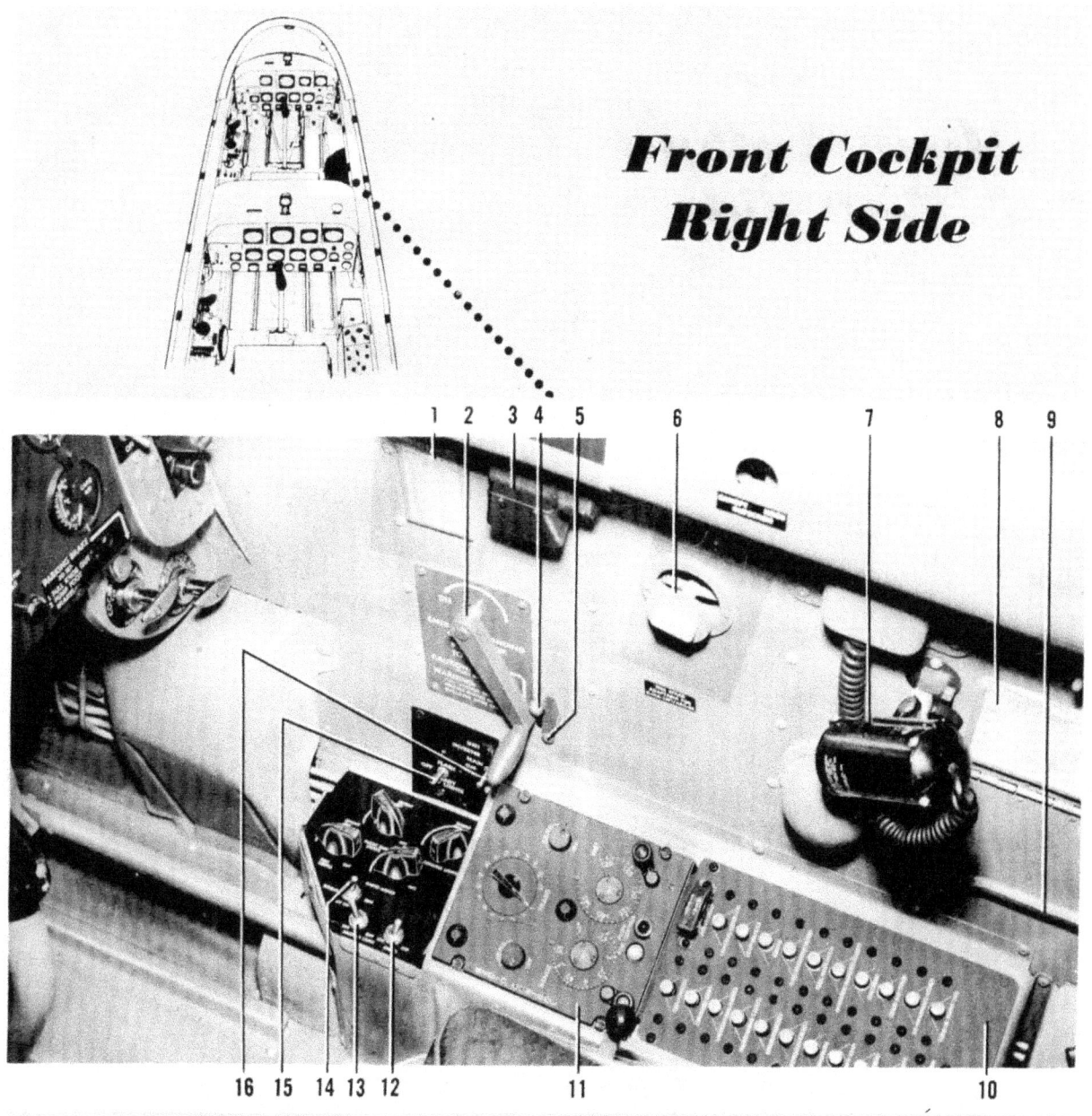

1. Compass Deviation Card
2. Emergency Landing Gear Crank
3. Console Light
4. Emergency Gear Crank Clutch Knob
5. Emergency Gear Crank Clutch Knob Lock
6. Cockpit Air Outlet
7. Utility Light
8. VHF Transmitting Frequencies Card
9. Map Case
10. Circuit Breaker Panel
11. Radio Control Panel
12. Radio Switch
13. Passing Light Switch
14. Navigation Light Intensity Switch
15. Navigation Light Switch
16. Inverter Switch

Figure 1-9

Rear Cockpit Left Side

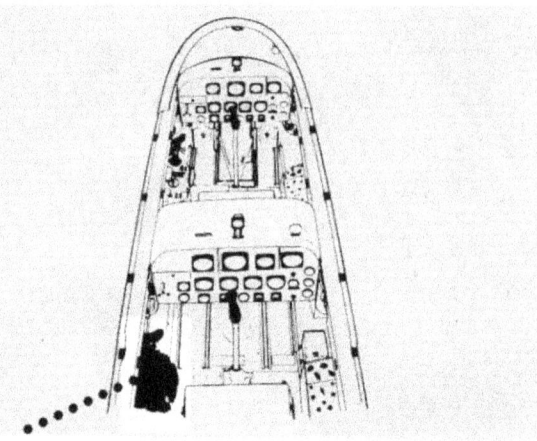

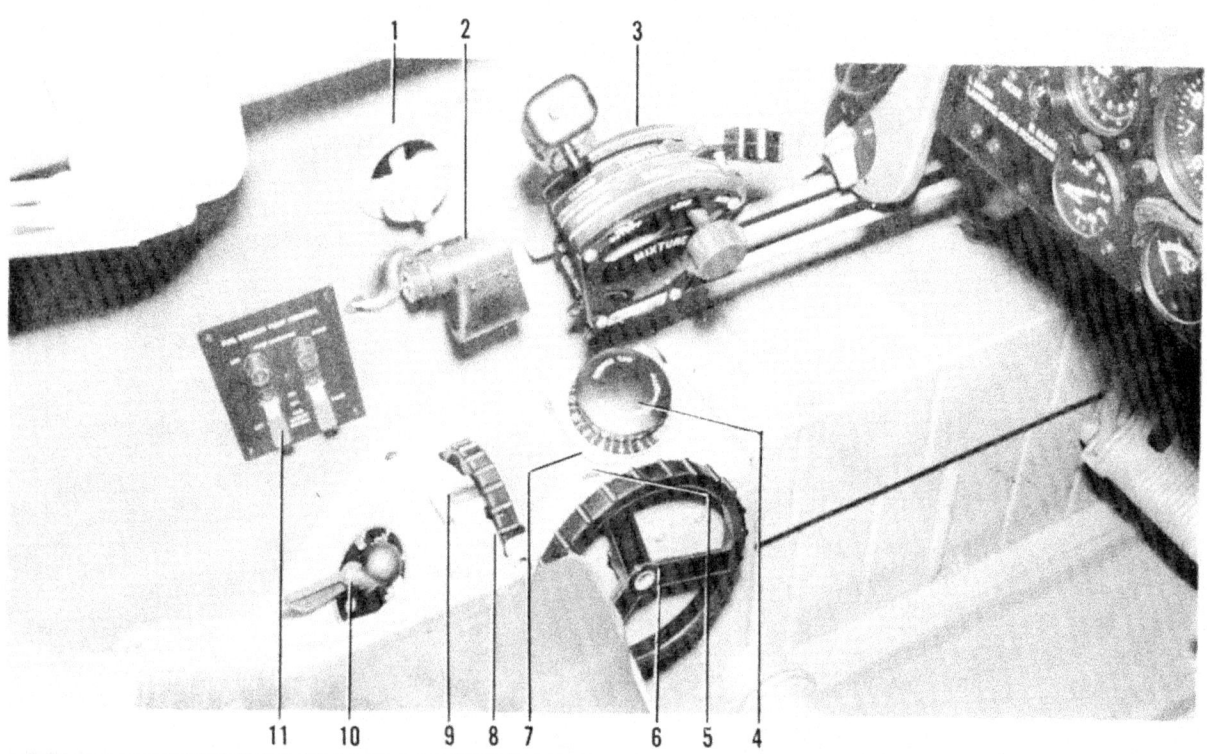

1. Cockpit Air Outlet
2. Console Light
3. Engine Controls Quadrant
4. Rudder Trim Tab Knob
5. Elevator Trim Tab Position Indicator
6. Elevator Trim Tab Wheel
7. Rudder Trim Tab Position Indicator
8. Aileron Trim Tab Wheel
9. Aileron Trim Tab Position Indicator
10. Fuel Selector Valve Handle
11. Fuel Booster Pump Override Panel

Figure 1-10

Rear Cockpit Right Side

1. Generator Failure Light
2. Canopy Emergency Release Handle
3. Canopy Emergency Release Safety Tab
4. Compass Deviation Card
5. VHF Transmitting Frequencies Card
6. Console Light
7. Cabin Air Outlet
8. Utility Light
9. Ash Tray
10. VHF Tuning Dial
11. Range Receiver Tuning Dial
12. Sens (sens) Knob
13. VHF Transmitter Selector Dial
14. Interior Lighting Control Dial

Figure 1-11

Fuel Booster Pump Override Panel

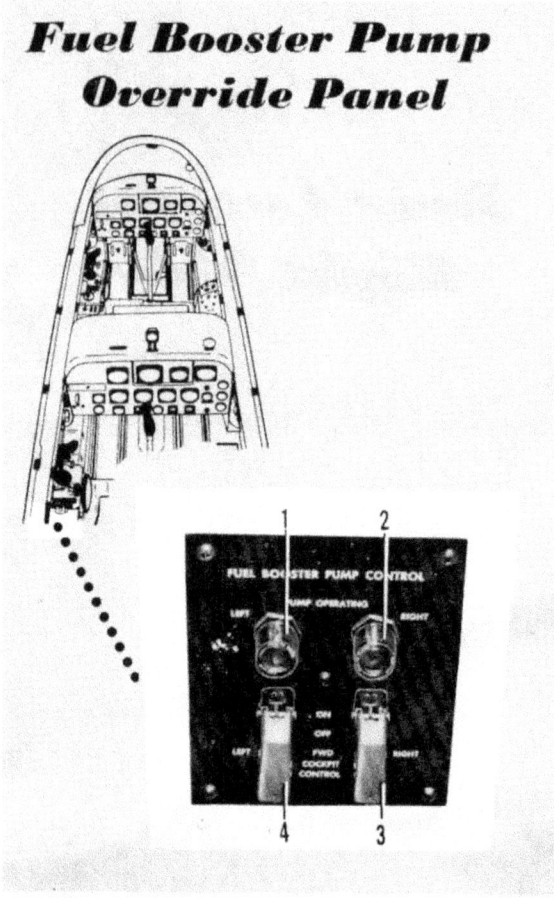

1. Left Fuel Booster Pump Indicating Light
2. Right Fuel Booster Pump Indicating Light
3. Right Fuel Booster Pump Override Switch
4. Left Fuel Booster Pump Override Switch

Figure 1-12

pumps and are provided in order to furnish the instructor with control of booster pump operation, if necessary. Each switch has three placarded positions: OFF, ON and FORWARD COCKPIT CONTROL. When an override switch is placed in the OFF position the front cockpit has no control over boost pump operation, and the boost pump corresponding to the switch is turned OFF. When an override switch is placed in the ON position, the rear cockpit retains control of the boost pumps and the pump corresponding to the switch turned ON. For normal operation, and control of the fuel boost pumps from the front cockpit, the override switches are guarded to the FORWARD COCKPIT CONTROL position.

FUEL BOOSTER PUMP INDICATING LIGHTS.

Two fuel booster pump indicating lights, amber in color, (1 and 2, figure 1-12) are located on the fuel booster pump override panel (11, figure 1-10) and operate as an integral part of the fuel booster pump override switches in providing the instructor with a visual indication of booster pump operation.

FUEL QUANTITY GAGES.

Two fuel quantity gages (20 and 21, figure 1-6) located on the bottom of each instrument panel indicate the quantity of fuel in the two tanks in fractions of tank capacity. The gages operate on electrical power from the main dc bus through a potentiometer type transmitter in each tank. A 5-amp push-to-reset type circuit breaker is located on the main circuit breaker panel (figure 1-16) in the front cockpit.

ELECTRICAL POWER SUPPLY SYSTEM.

The basic electrical power distribution system (figure 1-15) is a 28-volt dc single-wire system, using the aircraft's structure for a ground return. All equipment powered from the aircraft's electrical system is dc except the attitude and directional indicators, which are powered by ac current. All circuits except the starter power are protected by circuit breakers (figure 1-16).

DC POWER SUPPLY.

The dc power supply consists of a 75-ampere engine driven generator and a 24-ampere-hour, 24-volt storage battery. A carbon pile voltage regulator maintains generator voltage at 28.5 volts and a reverse current and generator control relay disconnects the generator from the circuit when generator output drops so low that the battery current would tend to drive it as a motor. The generator will automatically cut in at 900 rpm and reach full rated output at approximately 1200 rpm.

Battery Switch.

The battery is connected to the power distribution system through a two-position ON-OFF BATTERY switch (12, figure 1-7) located on the right subpanel in the front cockpit only. Placing the switch in the OFF position removes battery power from the bus system but does not affect generator operation. The switch should be OFF when external power is connected. Placing the battery switch in the ON position closes the battery relay and furnishes power to the main bus system.

Generator Switch.

The generator supplies power to the system through the reverse current relay which electrically disconnects the generator when output drops below battery voltage. In case of generator failure, the generator can be disconnected from the system electrically by a two-position ON-OFF generator switch (7, figure 1-7) located on the right subpanel in the front cockpit only. Placing

Fuel System

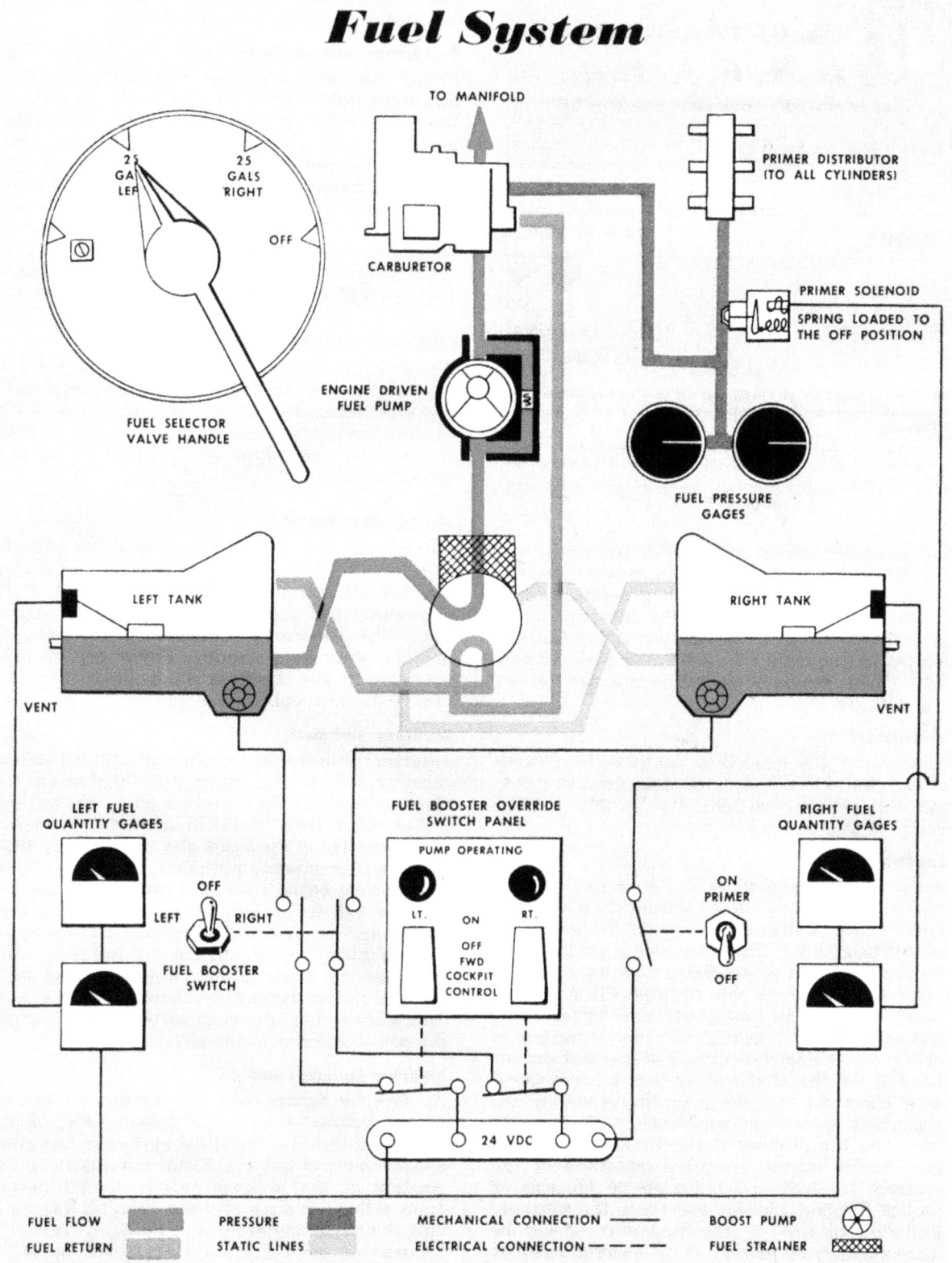

Figure 1-13

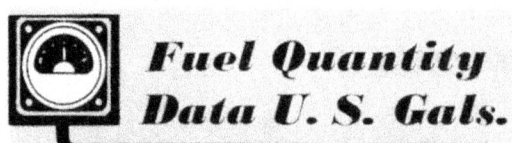

Table Based On Level Flight	Left	Right
Fully Serviced	25.5	25.5
*Usable	25.0	25.0

50 TOTAL USABLE FUEL (GALS.)

*This table is based on level flight and will vary slightly with changes in altitude. Fractional figures have been rounded out for simplicity of reading.

To convert U. S. gallons to pounds, multiply 6 by the known quantity of usable fuel. This conversion provides pound values for standard conditions only.

Figure 1-14

T34A-1-16A

the generator switch in the OFF position opens the generator field circuit and reverse current relay, thereby shutting off all generator power to the system. The generator field circuit is protected by a 5-amp push-to-reset circuit breaker located on the main circuit breaker panel (figure 1-16). The generator switch is guarded to the ON position.

Voltmeter.

A voltmeter, (24, figure 1-6) located on the bottom of each instrument panel, indicates generator output voltage. Normal indication is 28.0 to 28.5 volts.

Loadmeter.

An electrical loadmeter, (23, figure 1-6) marked "LOAD" and located on the bottom of each instrument panel, indicates the percent of generator output being used. The loadmeter is graduated in decimal fractions of generator capacity and indicates the portion of this capacity (75 amperes) being delivered to the system and battery. An indication of .5 would mean the generator is delivering 37.5 amperes or half of its rated output. Loading of the electrical system to correspond with operating limitations of the generator are dependent upon flight conditions, battery condition, and the amount of electrical equipment in use. Under normal operative conditions of the systems involved and following 30 minutes of normal daylight cruising operation, the electrical loading indicated on the loadmeter should be approximately 30 percent of the generator output or between .2 and .4 indicated on the loadmeter. Night operations, however, will constitute normally higher loadmeter readings due to the added electrical equipment being used.

Generator Failure Light.

Proper generator operation is indicated by the generator failure light (8, figure 1-7) located on the right subpanel in each cockpit. When the generator is not running fast enough to generate current and open the generator failure light relay, the relay remains closed and allows the warning light to remain illuminated, indicating no generator output. The generator failure light circuit is protected by a 5-amp push-to-reset circuit breaker located on the main circuit breaker panel (figure 1-16) on the right side of the front cockpit.

EXTERNAL POWER RECEPTACLE.

The dc external power receptacle (1, figure 1-27) is located on the right side of the engine compartment and accessible through an access door. With external power plugged in, the main bus system is energized regardless of the position of the battery switch.

AC POWER SUPPLY.

Alternating current for operation of the attitude and directional indicators is supplied by either of two 100 volt-ampere inverters located in the aft empennage just forward of the horizontal stabilizer. One inverter is installed for normal use and the other as a standby. Power required for operation of the inverters is supplied by the aircraft's dc electrical system.

Inverter Switch.

Inverter operation is controlled by a three-position inverter switch (16, figure 1-9) located on the right side of the front cockpit only. Moving the switch from OFF to MAIN position places the main inverter in operation and connects the attitude and directional indicators to that inverter. In the event of main inverter failure, the standby inverter can be utilized by placing the inverter switch in the STANDBY position. Transfer of the attitude and directional indicators to the individual inverter output circuits instead of a common output bus avoids shorting out the indicators through a grounded inverter even though the other inverter is in operation.

Inverter Failure Light.

An inverter failure light (19, figure 1-6) located on the bottom of each instrument panel illuminates any time the electrical system is energized and inverter is not operating, regardless of the position of the inverter switch. Power output from either inverter opens a relay in the light circuit and extinguishes the light. If the light remains on with the inverter switch in either MAIN or STANDBY position, the corresponding inverter is inoperative.

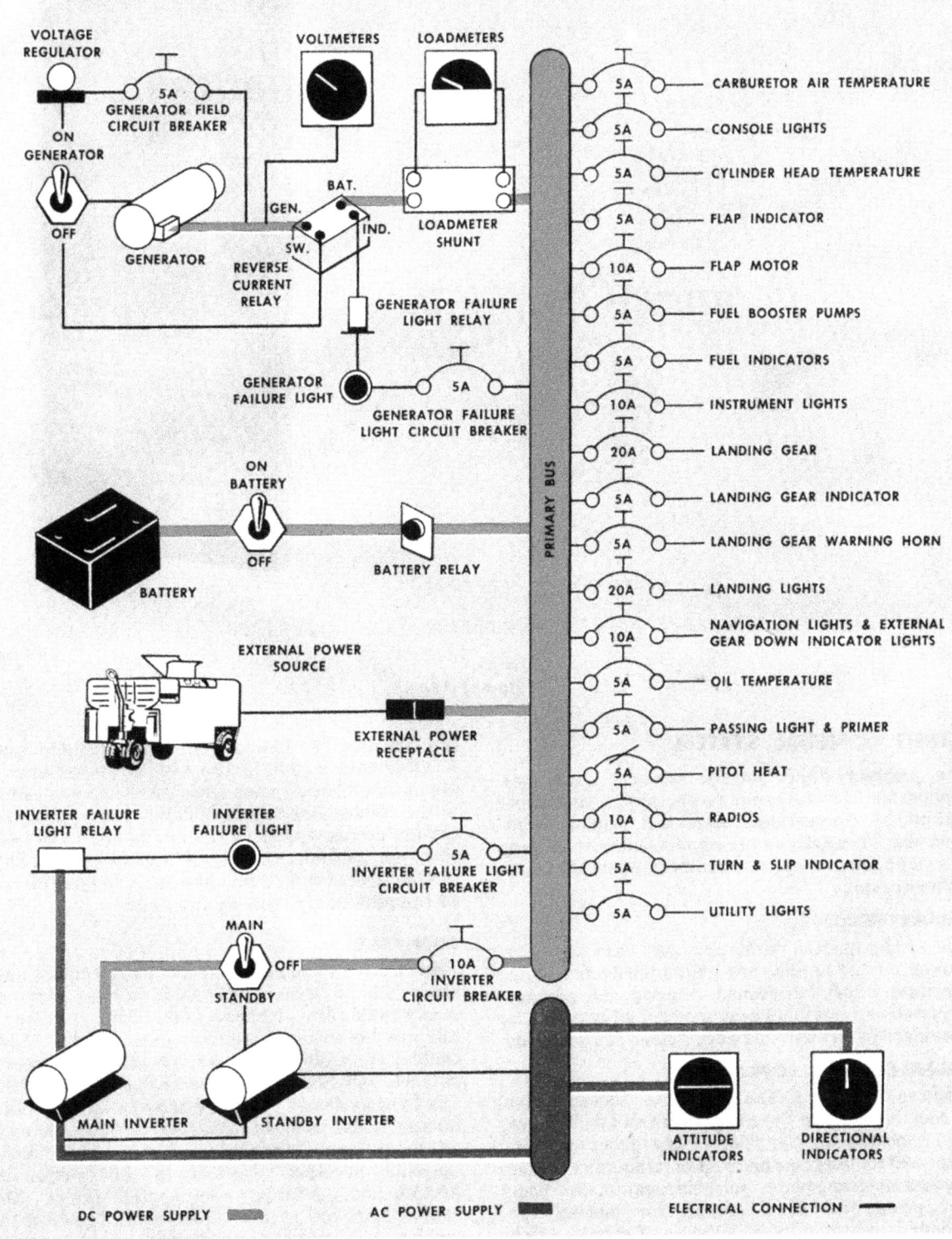

Figure 1-15

FLIGHT CONTROL SYSTEM.

The primary flight control surfaces (ailerons, rudder, and elevator) may be operated from either cockpit by conventional stick and rudder pedal controls. Trim tabs on the control surfaces, except the right aileron, are mechanically operated from either cockpit.

RUDDER PEDALS.

The rudder pedals, which are also used to apply brakes by toe action, are mechanically linked to the nose wheel for ground steering and are not adjustable. Individual seat to pedal adjustment is provided by fore-and-aft adjustment of each seat.

FLIGHT CONTROL LOCK.

Positive locking of the elevators, ailerons, and rudder is provided by a flight control lock (figure 1-17) located on the floor of the front cockpit. The control lock consists of a triangular brace pivoted at two points and held against the floor by spring tension. Provision for locking the rudder is provided by installation of a rudder lock bracket on the side of the lock frame. To lock the controls, the free aft end of the control lock is lifted and a hole in the lock is placed over a pin in the control stick, this also allows a notch in the rudder lock bracket to slip over a pin in the rudder pedals which locks the rudder. The controls are unlocked by first lifting the control lock to free the controls then allowing it to be returned to the stowed position on the floor.

TRIM TABS.

Trim tabs are installed on all flight control surfaces and all, except the right aileron tab, are controllable from either cockpit. The right aileron tab can be adjusted on the ground only. Cable control from either cockpit operates a jackscrew at each tab and the jackscrew is linked to the tab by a pushrod to insure irreversibility. Both aileron tabs incorporate servo action; as each aileron deflects from neutral, its tab moves in the opposite direction, assisting in the control deflection and lightening aileron stick forces. The rudder trim tab is of the anti-servo type; as the rudder is displaced from neutral, the tab moves in the same direction, increasing effective rudder

Circuit Breaker Panel

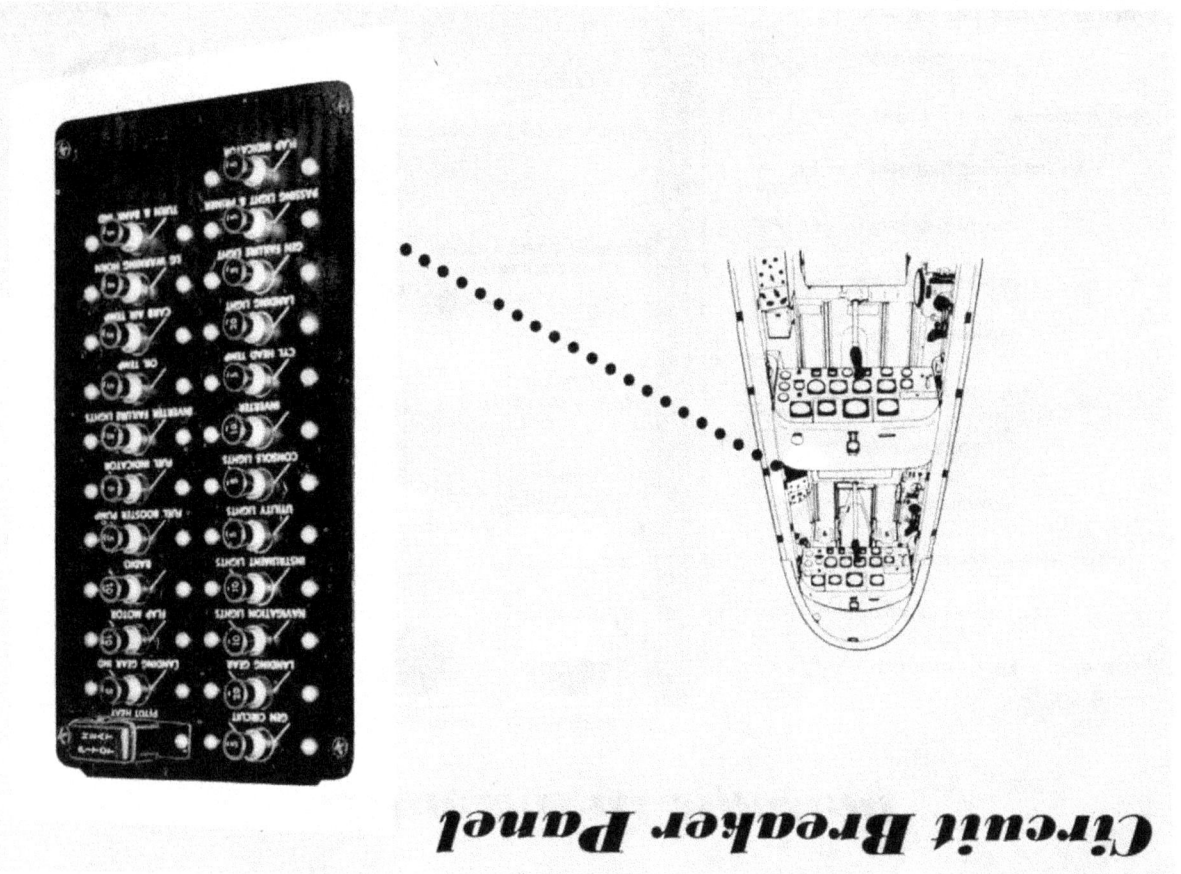

Figure 1-16

T34A-1-18A

area and the force required to displace it. This provision also increases rudder control "feel."

ELEVATOR TRIM TAB WHEEL.

The elevator trim tab wheel is located on the left console (figure 1-18) in each cockpit. Rotation of the wheel forward raises the tab and lowers the nose of the aircraft. Rotation of the wheel aft lowers the tab and raises the nose of the aircraft.

Controls Lock Installation

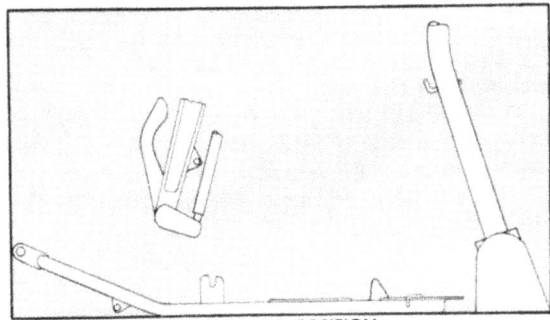
1. CONTROL LOCK IN STOWED POSITION.

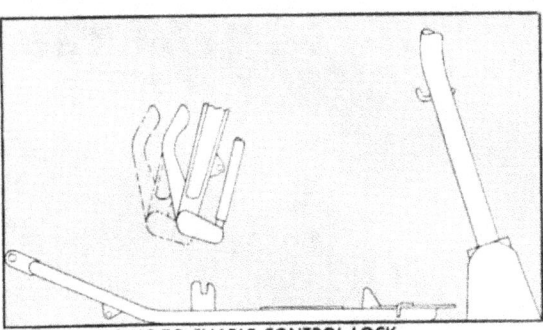
2. ALIGN PEDALS TO ENABLE CONTROL LOCK BRACKET TO ENGAGE PEDAL LOCK PIN.

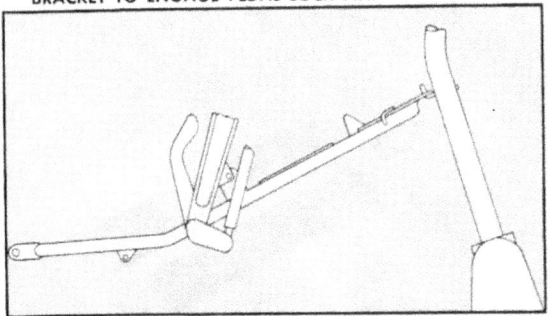
3. PLACE CONTROL LOCK OVER PIN LOCATED ON STICK.

Figure 1-17

Elevator Trim Tab Control Wheel

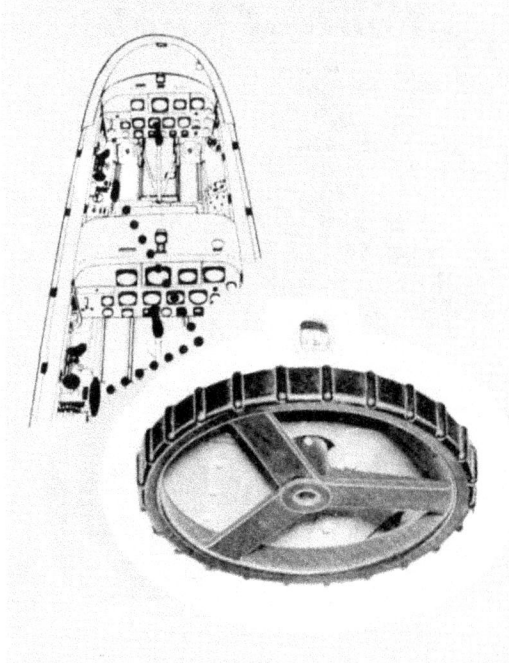

Figure 1-18

Elevator Trim Tab Position Indicator.

The elevator trim tab position indicator is located on the left console (figure 1-18) and operates as an integral part of the elevator trim tab wheel. As the wheel is turned, the amount of tab applied is shown on an indexed scale visible through a window adjacent to the tab control. The indexed scale is calibrated to show the approximate tab deflection in degrees.

RUDDER TRIM TAB KNOB.

The rudder trim tab knob is located on the left console (figure 1-19) in each cockpit. Clockwise rotation of the knob moves the tab to the left and counterclockwise rotation moves the tab to the right.

Rudder Trim Tab Position Indicator.

The rudder trim tab position indicator (figure 1-19) is a part of the rudder trim tab knob. Turning of the trim tab knob directly turns a pointer which moves over an indexed scale to provide a visual reference of the rudder trim tab position. The indexed scale is calibrated to show the approximate tab deflection in degrees.

Rudder Trim Tab Control Knob

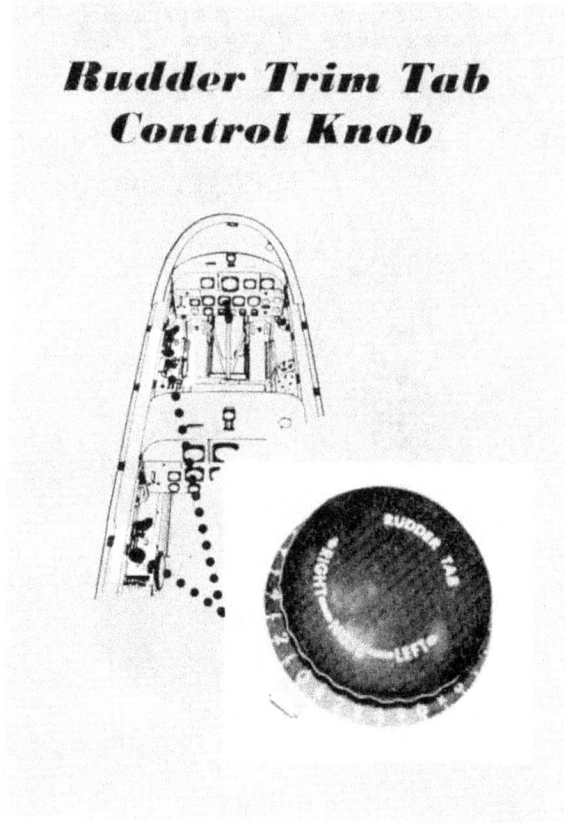

Figure 1-19

Aileron Trim Tab Wheel.

The aileron trim tab wheel (figure 1-20) is located on the left console in each cockpit. Rotation of the wheel clockwise (inboard) raises the tab on the left aileron and counterclockwise (outboard) rotation lowers the tab. The right aileron trim tab is not affected by rotation of the trim tab wheel.

Aileron Trim Tab Position Indicator.

The aileron trim tab position indicator (figure 1-20) is located on the left console in each cockpit and operates as an integral part of the aileron trim tab wheel. As the wheel is turned, the amount of tab applied is shown on an indexed scale visible through a window adjacent to the tab control. The indexed scale is calibrated to show the approximate tab deflection in degrees.

WING FLAPS.

Electrically operated, single slot-type flaps extend from the fuselage to the aileron on each wing. The flaps are operable from either cockpit and a flap position indicator is provided on each instrument panel. No emergency system is provided for operation of the flaps in the event of electrical failure.

Wing Flap Lever.

Flap motor operation is controlled by a three-position lever on the left console in each cockpit (figure 1-21). Lifting the lever UP raises the flaps; moving the lever DOWN lowers them. Moving the lever to the center (OFF) position will stop the flaps at any intermediate point, otherwise, they will continue until full up or down travel is reached, at which time limit switches shut off the motor whether or not the switch is moved to OFF position. The time period required to fully extend or retract the flaps is approximately 10 seconds. A 10-amp push-to-reset type circuit breaker is located on the main circuit breaker panel (figure 1-16).

Wing Flap Position Indicator.

Position of the flaps is indicated in terms of percentage of maximum extension (not in degrees) by a flap position indicator (25, figure 1-6) on the bottom of the instrument panel in each cockpit. Full pointer deflection of 100 percent indicates full flap extension of 30 degrees. A 5-amp push-to-reset type circuit breaker is located on the main circuit breaker panel (figure 1-16) in the front cockpit.

Aileron Trim Tab Control Wheel

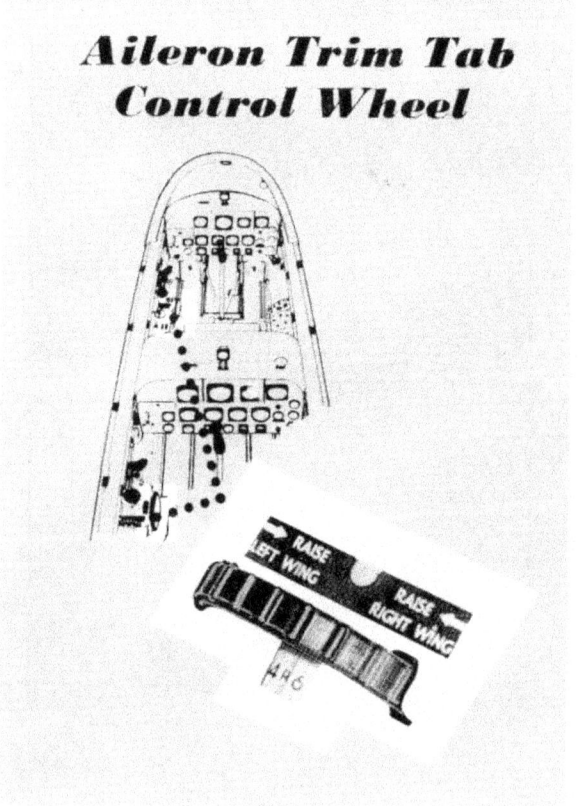

Figure 1-20

Wing Flap Lever

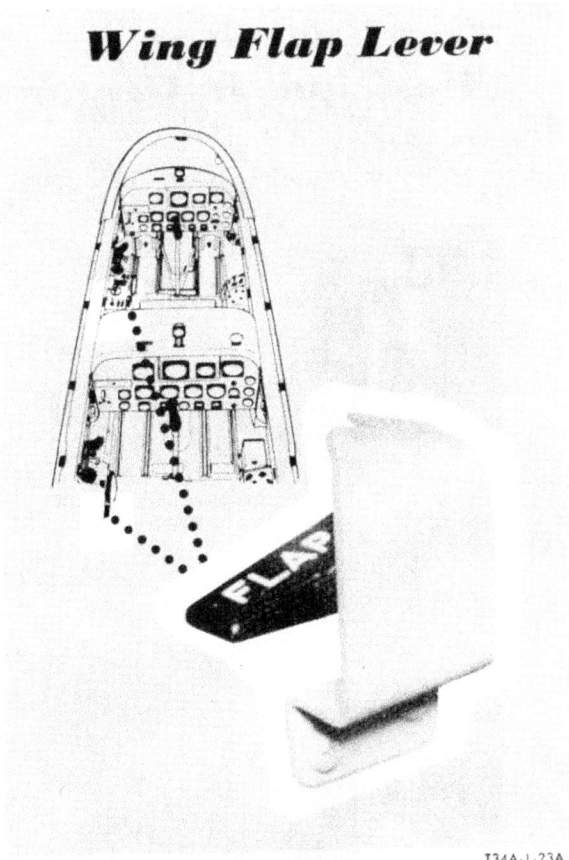

Figure 1-21

LANDING GEAR SYSTEM.

The electrically-operated tricycle landing gear is fully retractable. The main wheels retract inboard into the wings and the nose wheel retracts aft into the fuselage. Fairing doors, operated by gear movement, fully cover all wheels when retracted. The main gear inboard doors open during the gear extension and close again when the gear is fully extended. All gear is actuated by a single dc motor and actuator gear box located under the front cockpit. Individual uplocks actuated by the retraction system lock the gear positively in the retracted position. No downlocks are provided since the offset or over-center pivot of the linkage provides a geometric locking effect when fully extended. The linkage is also spring loaded to the offset position.

The nose wheel steering mechanism is such, that the wheel is automatically centered and the rudder pedals relieved of the nose steering load when weight of the aircraft is removed from the nose gear.

A safety switch on the right main strut prevents accidental gear retraction on the ground, but provisions are made for emergency on-the-ground retraction. In flight, the gear may be manually extended, but not retracted, in an emergency. All landing gear electrical circuits, including warning circuits, are operable only with the battery switch ON or external power or generator output applied. No emergency bus system is employed.

LANDING GEAR HANDLE.

The landing gear handle (4, figure 1-7) is located on the left subpanel in each cockpit. Moving the handle to UP or DOWN, no neutral position is provided, actuates a switch which controls the reversible motor that retracts or extends the gear. Approximately 7 to 8 seconds are required to extend the gear and approximately 10 seconds are required for retraction. The handle is formed in the shape of a wheel and is made of clear translucent material with a red warning light installed inside which illuminates the entire handle any time the landing gear is in any position not corresponding to that of the handle. Weight of the aircraft on the landing gear actuates a safety switch on the right main strut which opens the circuit and renders the gear-up circuit inoperative. A similar switch on the left main strut closes the circuit to the warning horn if the landing gear handle is moved to UP, with the aircraft on the ground, sounding the warning horn. When weight of the aircraft is removed from the strut, as the aircraft leaves the ground, the gear-up circuit is restored and the gear can be retracted. The circuit is protected by a 20-amp push-to-reset type circuit breaker located on the main circuit breaker panel in the front cockpit (figure 1-16).

LANDING GEAR EMERGENCY RETRACT SWITCH.

The landing gear emergency retract switch (27, figure 1-6) located on the left hand side of each instrument panel, is used for emergency retraction of the gear while the aircraft is on the ground. The switch is a two-position UP and DOWN toggle switch and is guarded with a safety wired guard in the DOWN position. When the switch is moved to UP position, the ground safety switch on the right main strut is by-passed and the gear will retract.

LANDING GEAR EMERGENCY HANDCRANK.

The gear may be manually extended (but not retracted) in an emergency by a handcrank (2, figure 1-9) located on the right side of the front cockpit only. The crank, when engaged, drives the normal gear actuation system through a flexible shaft. Approximately 37 turns of the handcrank are required to fully extend the gear. See figure 3-8 for operating instructions.

> **CAUTION**
>
> The landing gear emergency extension system is designed and stressed only for

emergency extension and must never be used to retract the gear.

Landing Gear Emergency Handcrank Clutch Knob.

A guarded knob (4, figure 1-9) located adjacent to the landing gear emergency handcrank is pushed down to engage the crank with the flexible drive shaft for emergency extension of the landing gear. A clutch knob lock (5, figure 1-9) must first be disengaged from the handcrank clutch knob by moving it toward aft end of the cockpit, this releases the crank clutch knob for manual operation. The clutch knob must be returned manually to the disengaged (up position) and again secured with the lock after the gear has been extended.

WARNING

The handcrank must be disengaged from the drive shaft after extending the gear manually; otherwise, subsequent actuation of the gear electrically will cause the crank to spin rapidly with possible injury to personnel.

LANDING GEAR POSITION INDICATORS.

Position of each landing gear is shown by three individual indicators (26, figure 1-6) located on the lower left hand corner of each instrument panel. A simulated strut and wheel appears on each indicator when the corresponding gear is fully extended and locked. Any intermediate position between fully extended and fully retracted, or when the electrical system is not energized, is indicated by a cross hatch pattern. As the gear reaches a fully retracted and locked position, the cross hatch pattern will be replaced by UP appearing in each indicator. Electrical power for the operation of the landing gear position indicators is supplied directly from the main dc bus. The circuit is protected by a 5-amp push-to-reset type circuit breaker located on the main circuit breaker panel (figure 1-16) on the right side of the front cockpit.

LANDING GEAR WARNING LIGHT.

A red warning light, which operates on electrical power from the main dc bus, is located inside each landing gear handle (4, figure 1-7) and will illuminate causing the entire handle to glow red when any gear is in any position not corresponding to the position of the landing gear handle. When the gear handle is moved to actuate the landing gear, the light is illuminated by the same dc circuit that actuates the gear position indicators and remains on until all three gears have reached the full up or down positions. This arrangement serves also on the ground as a warning that the landing gear handle is in the UP position.

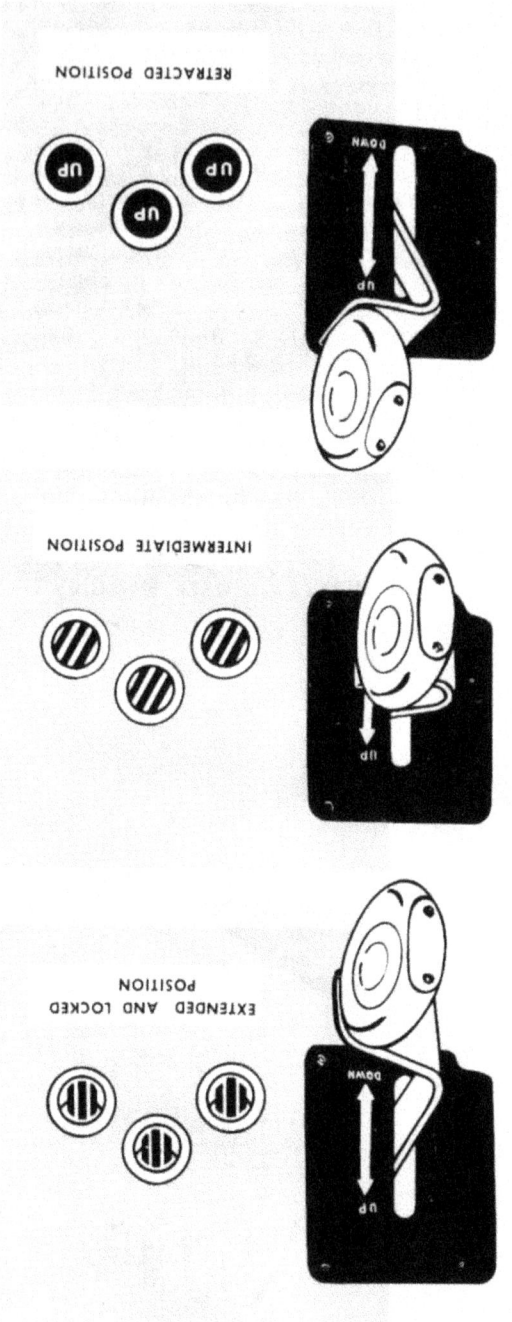

Landing Gear Position Indicator

EXTENDED AND LOCKED POSITION

INTERMEDIATE POSITION

RETRACTED POSITION

13A4-1-24A

Figure 1-22

WHEEL BRAKE SYSTEM.

The main landing wheels are equipped with hydraulic brakes, operated by toe pressure on the rudder pedals in either cockpit. Fluid from a reservoir aft of the firewall supplies a master cylinder at each rudder pedal. Toe action on the rudder pedals actuates the cylinder, and applies brake pressure to the corresponding wheel. For operation of the wheel brake system, refer to Section VII. See figure 1-27 for hydraulic fluid specifications.

Parking Brake Handle.

A parking brake handle (11, figure 1-7) is located on the right subpanel in the front cockpit only. The parking brakes are set by first pulling out the handle, then applying toe brakes. The parking brakes can be released only by pushing the handle in. Pulling the handle out seats a check valve in the system and any brake pressure subsequently applied by the pedals is held. Pushing the handle in unseats the check valve, releasing pressure.

NOSE WHEEL STEERING.

The steerable nose wheel is mechanically controlled by the rudder pedals through a range of 18 degrees to either side of center, which is the limit of rudder pedal travel. Full turning range of 30 degrees to either side requires application of brakes on the inside of the turn. Shimmy dampener displacement permits this additional deflection and permits turns with a 3-foot radius to the inside wheel. The "give" thus provided in the system also dampens nose wheel ground shocks which would otherwise be transmitted through the linkage to the rudder.

INSTRUMENTS.

The instruments described herein are not a part of any complete system such as the landing gear or fuel systems which will have their own instruments. All instruments except the free air temperature gage, at the top of the windshield, are duplicated in both cockpits. A magnetic compass is mounted atop each instrument panel shroud. All other instruments are located on the instrument panels (figure 1-6). Refer to Section V (figure 5-1) for instrument markings.

TURN-AND-SLIP INDICATOR.

The turn-and-slip indicator (5, figure 1-6) is located on the center of each instrument panel below the directional indicator. The turn-and-slip indicator operates directly from the dc power supply system and is utilized to provide visual indication of the direction and coordination of a turn. The indicator is equipped with a pointer which indicates the rate of a turn and an inclinometer tube and ball which indicates slips, skids and co-

In flight, the warning light also illuminates any time the warning horn circuit is energized by retarding the throttle to a position equivalent to approximately 12 inches of manifold pressure with any gear not fully extended and locked.

Landing Gear Warning Light Test Button.

The landing gear warning light test button (1, figure 1-7) is located to the left of each landing gear handle on the left subpanel in both cockpits. If the landing gear handle fails to illuminate when the warning light test button is pressed, the warning light is inoperative.

NOTE

If the light fails to illuminate in normal operation, but illuminates when the test button is pressed, the indicator circuits are at fault and the gear position indicators will not be reliable.

LANDING GEAR WARNING HORN.

The landing gear warning horn, located between the cockpits just aft of the pilot's seat back in the front cockpit, sounds if the landing gear handle is moved to UP and the aircraft is on the ground. In flight, retarding the throttle to a position equivalent to approximately 12 inches of manifold pressure with any gear not fully extended and locked will also sound the horn. The landing gear warning horn operates directly from the aircraft's main dc bus. The circuit is protected by a 5-amp push-to-reset type circuit breaker located on the main circuit breaker panel on the right side of the front cockpit (figure 1-16).

Landing Gear Warning Horn Silencing Button.

The warning horn may be silenced during prolonged throttle-off maneuvers by pressing the horn silencing button (4, figure 1-8) located on the left side of the front cockpit. Subsequent advancement of the throttle will reset the circuit and retarding the throttle will again illuminate the landing gear warning light and resound the horn. When the horn silencing button is pressed, the landing gear warning light will be extinguished simultaneously with the silencing of the warning horn.

GEAR DOWN EXTERNAL INDICATOR LIGHTS.

A white light by each main wheel well provides a ground observer with an external indication of gear position at night. The lights are illuminated automatically when the main gear is down and locked and the navigation lights switch is ON. The external gear down indicator lights operate from the same circuit as the navigation lights and are protected by the 10-amp navigation lights circuit breaker located on the main circuit breaker panel (figure 1-16).

ordination. No adjustment or caging knobs are required to operate the indicator. The turn-and-slip indicator is protected by a 5-amp push-to-reset circuit breaker located on the main circuit breaker panel in the front cockpit (figure 1-16).

DIRECTIONAL INDICATOR.

The Type C-5C directional indicator (6, figure 1-6) is located at the top of the instrument panel below the magnetic compass and is operated by alternating current from either inverter. The indicator is equipped with two knobs; one pointer knob and one combination dial and pointer knob. Either knob can be utilized for a "push to cage" operation and can be rotated respectively in either direction, while the indicator is caged, to set the pointer or dial at a desired heading. Pulling the respective knob out uncages the indicator. The indicator is also equipped with a CAGED indicator flag which appears when the indicator is inoperative. The gyro must be in operation for from 5 to 8 minutes to allow it to come up to speed to provide accurate indications. The directional indicator is normally left uncaged. The directional indicator circuit is protected by the 10-amp inverter circuit breaker located on the main circuit breaker panel (figure 1-16) in the front cockpit.

CAUTION

To prevent tumbling or damage to the mechanism, the heading indicator should be caged before performing acrobatics, or any maneuver exceeding the indicator's roll and pitch limits which are 85 degrees in each axis.

ATTITUDE INDICATOR.

The Type J-8 attitude indicator (10, figure 1-6) is located at the top of each instrument panel, adjacent to the directional indicator, and is operated by alternating current from either inverter. A fixed symbol in front of the face of the indicator represents the aircraft and a movable horizontal bar behind the aircraft symbol represents the horizon. With the aircraft in a level flight attitude, the aircraft symbol is superimposed on the horizon bar. With the aircraft in a nose-up attitude, the horizon bar lowers and in a bank to the right, the horizon bar banks to the left; the aircraft symbol then appears to have lifted above the horizon bar and banked to the right. The aircraft symbol may be adjusted vertically by means of the small knob at the lower left corner of the indicator to correct for variations in level flight attitude at different airspeeds and gross weights.

NOTE

Allow 30 seconds after power is applied to the Type J-8 Attitude Indicator for the gyro to attain speed, then cage immediately thereafter, to prevent unnecessary torque stresses on the instrument mechanism. The J-8 will be caged by means of a gyro centering device operated by pulling the cage knob.

WARNING

A slight amount of pitch error in the indication of the attitude indicator will result from accelerations or decelerations. It will appear as a slight climb indication after a forward acceleration and as a slight dive indication after deceleration when the airplane is flying straight and level. This error will be most noticeable at the time the airplane breaks ground during the take-off run. At this time, a climb indication error of about 1½ bar widths will normally be noticed; however, the exact amount of error will depend upon the acceleration and elapsed time of each individual take-off. The erection system will automatically remove the error after the acceleration ceases.

The attitude indicator is caged by drawing the "Pull to Cage" knob away from the face of the instrument. A momentary stop will be felt when the bank caging mechanism is engaged, and as the caging knob is pulled further, the pitch caging mechanism will engage. As soon as the knob reaches the limits of its travel, it should be immediately released. The knob should be pushed toward the face of the instrument to uncage the gyro. Further travel or precession indicates that the caging mechanism is not releasing properly or that the erection mechanism is not functioning properly. The indicator is designed to operate through all attitudes and need not be caged for any maneuver. The attitude indicator circuit is protected by the 10-amp inverter circuit breaker located on the main circuit breaker panel (figure 1-16) in the front cockpit.

CAUTION

A temporary displacement of the gyro from its normal position during turns, commonly referred to as "turn error," may be introduced into the indicator when normal turns are performed. The caging knob should not be pulled violently and caging of the indicator should be kept to a minimum and never accomplished in flight except when the aircraft is in straight and level flight.

FREE AIR TEMPERATURE GAGE.

A self-contained type C-13B thermometer (8, figure 1-6), mounted on the forward windshield, indicates the temperature of the outside air, which is of prime importance in determining and predicting airspeeds, altitudes and meteorological conditions.

PITOT STATIC SYSTEM.

The airspeed indicator, altimeter and vertical velocity indicators are operated by the pitot static system. This system is composed of an electrically heated pitot tube, mounted on the underside of the left wing leading edge, and static air pressure ports which are located in the skin low on both sides of the fuselage, aft of the baggage compartment.

ALTIMETER.

A conventional altimeter is installed on the left hand side of each instrument panel (3, figure 1-6)

Canopy Locking Handles

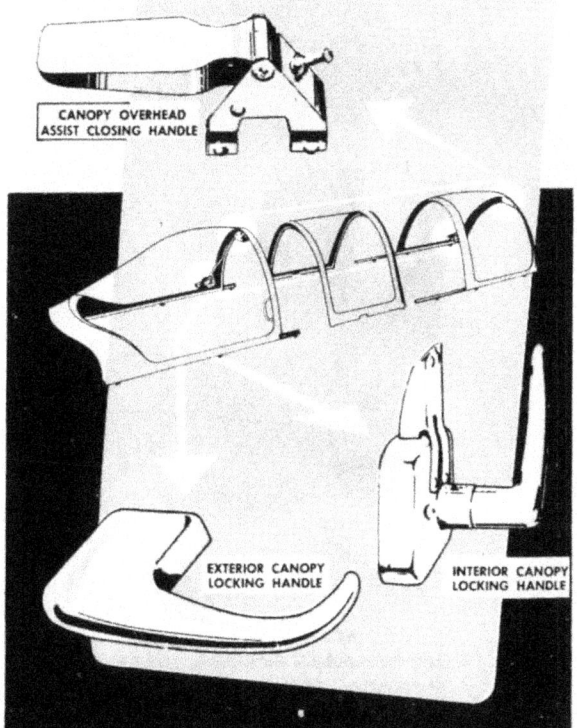

Figure 1-23

Canopy Emergency Release Handles

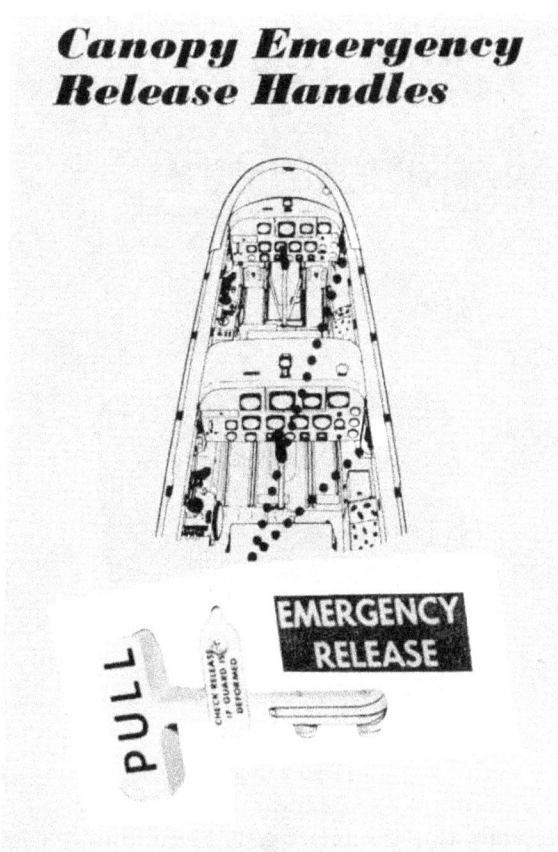

Figure 1-24

for use in determining pressure altitude of the aircraft above sea level. The altimeter functions on static pressure alone and is equipped with three pointers which are used to indicate values of altitude as they pass over a dial graduated in units of feet. A barometric dial is also incorporated in the instrument and may be set in conjunction with the altitude pointers by an external adjusting knob. Adjustment is made with the knob so that the reading on the barometric dial will correspond to the actual barometric condition of the area in which the aircraft is located.

AIRSPEED INDICATOR.

The airspeed indicator, located on the upper left hand side of each instrument panel (4, figure 1-6), operates by pressure differential between pitot tube impact pressure and static pressure, and is calibrated in knots. No external adjusting knobs are provided.

VERTICAL VELOCITY INDICATOR.

The vertical velocity indicator, located in the center of each instrument panel (9, figure 1-6),

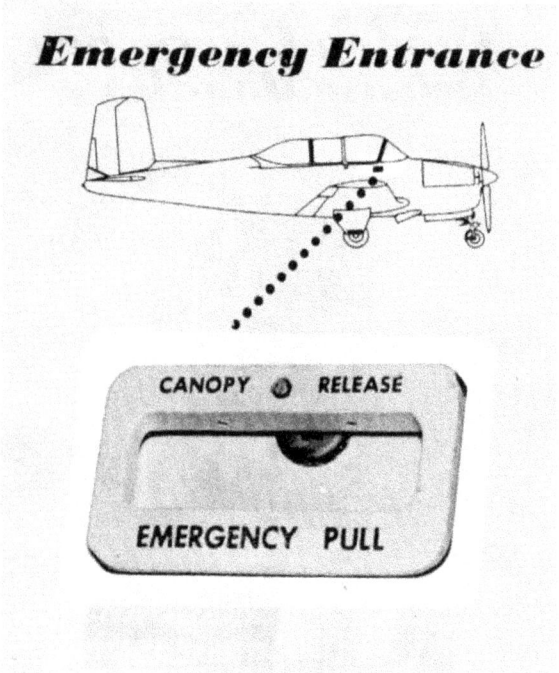

Figure 1-25

CANOPY LOCKING HANDLES.

Interior and exterior canopy locking handles, located on the left side of each sliding section (figure 1-23), are turned to lock or unlock and to assist in opening the canopies from either the inside or outside.

CANOPY OVERHEAD ASSIST CLOSING HANDLE.

To aid in closing the canopies from inside the cockpit, an additional assist handle is provided at the top of each sliding section (figure 1-23); the canopy cannot easily be closed without the assistance of this handle.

CANOPY EMERGENCY RELEASE HANDLES.

A canopy emergency release handle is located in the canopy rail support housing on the forward right hand side of each cockpit (figure 1-24). Normally, the release handles will be positioned full forward into a depression on the canopy rail support housing and will be saftied in this position by a safety plate arrangement. With the handles in the safetied position, the canopy rails are engaged by hooks which secure the canopy assembly to the fuselage. Pulling the handle out and aft, from either cockpit, releases the canopy rails from the fuselage and allows the entire canopy assembly to blow free of the aircraft.

operates on static pressure alone and is calibrated to indicate the rate of climb or descent in feet-per-minute.

EMERGENCY EQUIPMENT.

Emergency equipment carried in the aircraft consists of a first aid kit only. No engine fire extinguishing system is installed.

The first aid kit (figure 3-2) is located on the rear deck (AF Serials 55-190 and after) in the small recess behind the aft seat back and is accessible from the aft cockpit only.

NOTE

Aircraft with AF serials 52-7626 through 55-189 have the first aid kit installed on the left forward side of the rear instrument panel structure, just behind the forward seat back, accessible from either cockpit.

CANOPY.

The canopy is in three sections; a manually-operated sliding section over each cockpit and a rigid center section between. Each sliding section opens aft and can be operated independently.

Seat Adjustments and Inertia Reel Lock

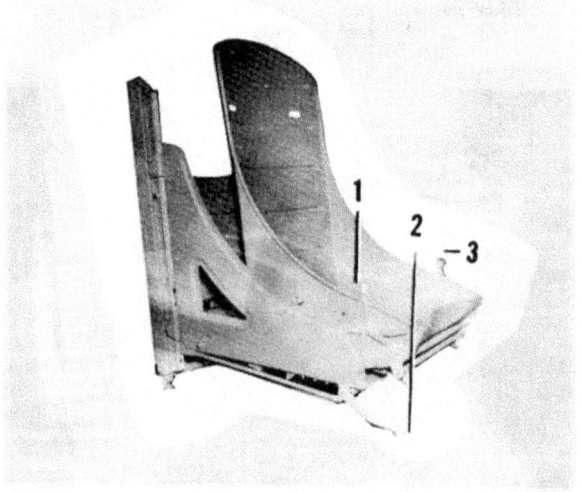

1. Seat Fore-and-Aft Adjustment Handle
2. Seat Vertical Adjustment Handle
3. Inertia Reel Lock Handle

Figure 1-26

Servicing Diagram

SPECIFICATIONS

FUEL   MIL-F-5572, GRADE 80
OIL   MIL-L-6082, GRADE 1065 (BELOW 25°F)
                   GRADE 1100 (ABOVE 25°F)
BRAKE HYDRAULIC FLUID   MIL-H-5606

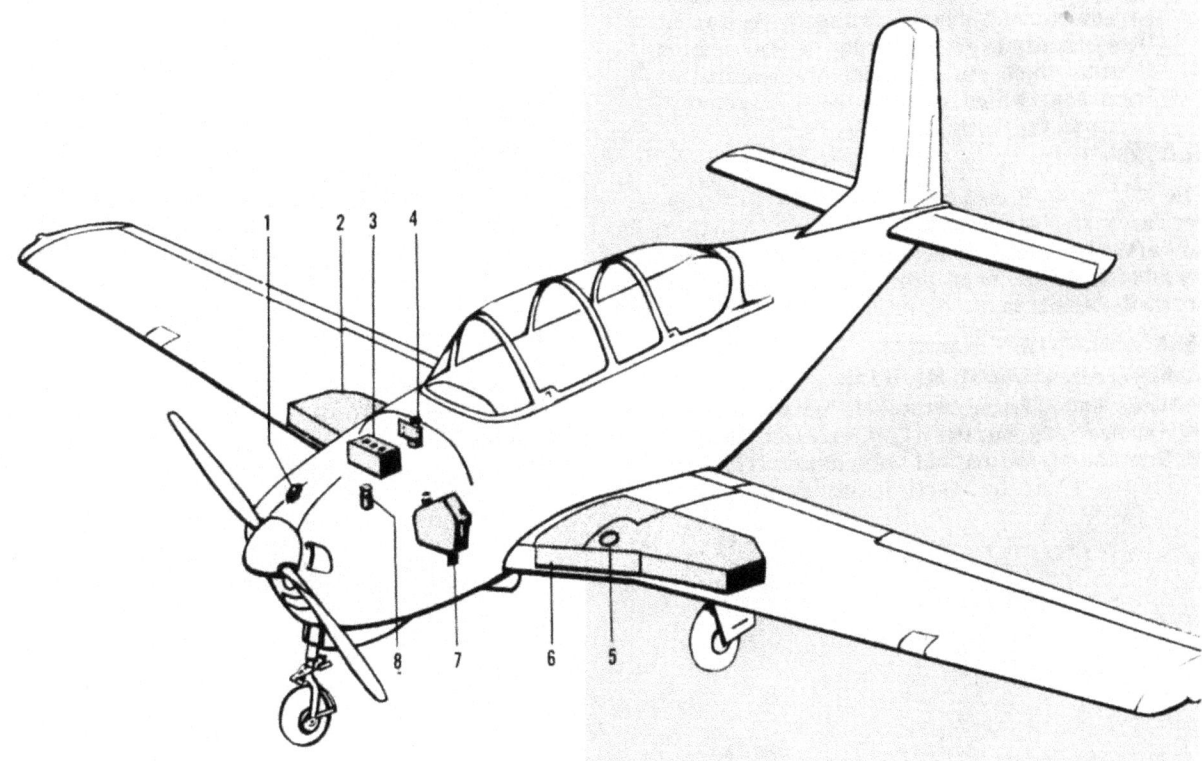

1. External Power Receptacle Access Door
2. Right Fuel Tank
3. Battery
4. Hydraulic Fluid Reservoir
5. Left Fuel Tank Filler Neck
6. Left Fuel Tank
7. Oil Tank
8. Battery Drain Jar

Figure 1-27

EXTERIOR CANOPY EMERGENCY RELEASE HANDLE.

For emergency entrance to the cockpit, an external canopy emergency release handle (figure 1-25) on the right side of the fuselage at the front cockpit releases both canopy rails. For emergency procedures, refer to Section III.

NOTE

The front and rear canopy sections are tied together by cables which provide the additional assist necessary for removal of both sections simultaneously. The cable connection will cause the front section to exert a jerk on the rear section thus exposing it positively to the air stream which will complete its removal from the cockpit.

SEATS.

The seat in each cockpit is adjustable 5½ inches vertically and 4¼ inches fore-and-aft. The fore-and-aft adjustment provides selection of a comfortable distance from the rudder pedals which are non-adjustable.

SEAT ADJUSTMENT HANDLES.

The seats are adjustable by two spring loaded handles, one on the right side of the seat for fore-and-aft adjustment (2, figure 1-26) and one on the front for vertical adjustment (1, figure 1-26). The seat is positioned by pulling up on the appropriate handle, moving the seat to the desired position and releasing the handle which locks the seat in place. A safety belt and shoulder harness with inertia reel are installed at each seat.

INERTIA REEL LOCK HANDLE.

The shoulder harness inertia reel is locked or unlocked by movement of the inertia reel lock handle (3, figure 1-26) located on the left hand side of each seat. A spring-loaded latch in the end of the handle locks the handle in either LOCKED or UNLOCKED position. When the handle is unlocked (aft), the inertia reel maintains a slight tension on the harness but permits the pilot to lean forward to reach the controls. When the handle is moved to the LOCKED (forward) position, the inertia reel locks the harness in successive positions as the pilot leans back. Before the reel can be unlocked, all tension must be removed from the harness by leaning full back in the seat. The reel also locks automatically when the aircraft is under a linear deceleration of 2 G's or more, as in a crash landing.

AUXILIARY EQUIPMENT.

For a complete description and operating instructions covering the following auxiliary equipment, refer to Section IV: heating and ventilation system, pitot heat, communications equipment and instrument flying hood.

Section 2

Normal Procedures

TABLE OF CONTENTS

Preparation for Flight	2-1
Entrance to Aircraft	2-2
Preflight Check	2-2
Before Exterior Inspection	2-2
Exterior Inspection	2-2
On Entering Aircraft	2-4
Before Starting Engine	2-4
Engine Ground Operation	2-5
Before Taxiing	2-6
Taxiing	2-6
Engine Run-Up	2-6
Take-Off	2-7
After Take-Off — Climb	2-9
Cruise	2-9
Flight Characteristics	2-9
Systems Operation	2-9
Descent	2-9
Before Landing	2-9
Traffic Pattern Check	2-10
Landings	2-10
Go-Around	2-12
After Landing	2-12
Post Flight Engine Check	2-12
Engine Shut Down	2-12
Before Leaving Aircraft	2-12
Condensed Check List	2-15

PREPARATION FOR FLIGHT.

FLIGHT RESTRICTIONS.

Refer to Section V for all operating restrictions.

FLIGHT PLANNING.

To determine fuel consumption, airspeed, power settings, ranges, etc., for flight planning, refer to the Appendix charts.

TAKE-OFF AND LANDING DATA CARD.

Take-off and landing data cards as shown in the condensed check list, this section, will be filled out and used for every flight. Refer to the Appendix, Performance Data, for the necessary information.

WEIGHT AND BALANCE.

Refer to Section V for weight and balance limitations and to the Basic Weight Check List, T.O. 1T-34A-5, for loading information. Before each flight, check the following:

1. Take-off and anticipated landing gross weight and balance — check within prescribed limits.
2. Fuel, oil and equipment aboard — check adequate for mission.

ENTRANCE TO AIRCRAFT.

Enter the aircraft from the left side (figure 2-1) since canopy handles and rear cockpit step are on the left side only. The front cockpit is accessible from the wing. A kick-in step on the side of the fuselage facilitates access to the rear cockpit from the left wing. To open the canopy, rotate the canopy handle clockwise and pull canopy aft.

CAUTION

Do not step on the canopy rails. Damage to the rails could prevent proper canopy operation.

Figure 2-1

PREFLIGHT CHECK.

The pilot's preflight inspection is based on the assumption that maintenance personnel have completed the maintenance preflight contained in the Handbook of Inspection Requirements (T.O. 1T-34A-6). Discrepancies noted during the preflight will be recorded in DD Form 781 and the aircraft cleared for flight by authorized maintenance personnel prior to take-off.

BEFORE EXTERIOR INSPECTION.

1. DD Form 781 — check.
2. Battery and ignition switches — check OFF.
3. Aileron trim tab wheel — 0 degrees.
4. Rudder trim tab knob — 0 degrees.
5. Elevator trim tab wheel — 0 degrees.
6. Landing gear handle — DOWN.
7. Landing gear emergency retract switch — OFF and safetied.
8. Canopy emergency release handle seal — undamaged.
9. Flight controls — unlocked.

Rear Cockpit Check for Solo Flight.

10. Safety belt — secure.
11. Shoulder harness — secure.
12. Headset — stowed.
13. Flight controls — free from obstruction.
14. Attitude indicator and directional indicator — uncaged.
15. Fuel booster pump override switches — FORWARD COCKPIT CONTROL.
16. Rear canopy — closed and locked.

EXTERIOR INSPECTION.

Starting at the inboard trailing edge of the left wing, perform the following exterior inspection checks using the inspection route outlined in figure 2-2. During this inspection, check all exterior surfaces for skin damage or other obvious defects. In addition, check beneath the aircraft for signs of fluid leakage.

1. Left wing.
   a. Wing flap — check.
   b. Aileron — check; trim tab for servo action.
   c. Wing tip and navigation light — check.
   d. Leading edge and landing light — check.
   e. Pitot tube — check.
   f. Fuel quantity — check, cap secure.
   g. Air intake — check, screen clean.
2. Left main gear.
   a. Wheel chocks — in place.
   b. Tire — check.
   c. Wheel brake — check puck, hydraulic line, adjusting pin recessed $3/16$ inch maximum.
   d. Strut — check.
   e. Landing gear doors — check.
   f. Wheel well — unobstructed.
3. Nose section.
   a. Left augmentor tube — unobstructed.

Figure 2-2

Exterior Inspection

b. Left cowling — secure.
c. Propeller — check.
d. Passing light — secure.
e. Air intake — check, unobstructed.
f. Strut — check.
g. Tire and static wire — check.
h. Nose landing gear doors — check.
i. Wheel well — unobstructed.
j. Right cowling — secure.
k. Battery and battery retainer bar — secure.
l. Battery sump jar — check.
m. Exterior canopy emergency release handle — undisturbed.
n. Right augmentor tube — unobstructed.

4. Right main gear — check same as left main gear

5. Right wing.
   a. Air intake — check, screen clean.
   b. Fuel quantity — check, cap secure.
   c. Leading edge and landing light — check.
   d. Wing tip and navigation light — check.
   e. Aileron — check; trim tab for servo action.
   f. Wing flap — check.

6. Fuselage right side.
   a. Fuel tank vent — check, 12 degrees forward pitch.
   b. Antenna — secure.
   c. Static air vent — unobstructed.

7. Empennage.
   a. Right horizontal stabilizer — check.
   b. Right elevator and trim tab — check.
   c. Vertical fin — check.
   d. Rudder — check; trim tab for anti-servo action.
   e. Navigation light — check.
   f. Left elevator and trim tab — check.
   g. Left horizontal stabilizer — check.

8. Fuselage left side.
   a. Tail skid — check.
   b. Under side — check.
   c. Static air vent — unobstructed.
   d. Baggage compartment — check, door secured.

WARNING

If aerobatics are to be performed, remove all equipment or other objects from the baggage compartment.

e. Fuel tank vent — check, 12 degrees forward pitch.

ON ENTERING THE AIRCRAFT.

INTERIOR INSPECTION.

1. Seat — adjust and lock.
2. Seat belt and shoulder harness — fastened.
3. Inertia reel lock — check.
4. Parking brakes — set.
5. Flight controls — check freedom of movement and response.
6. Wing flap lever — NEUTRAL.

If flaps are not up, move flap lever to UP; when flaps are up, move lever to NEUTRAL.

7. Landing light switches — OFF.
8. Fuel selector valve handle — LEFT TANK.

NOTE

Each time the fuel tank selector valve handle is moved from one position to the other, the "click and feel" method should be utilized in conjunction with lining up the handle pointer with the marked position on the fuel tank selector. Refer to Section VII for fuel system operation.

9. Fuel booster pump switch — LEFT.
10. Trim tabs — set for take-off.
    a. Aileron trim tab wheel — 0 degrees.
    b. Rudder trim tab knob — 3 degrees RIGHT (R).
    c. Elevator trim tab wheel — 3 degrees UP.
11. Engine control quadrant friction lock knob — adjusted.
12. Mixture lever — IDLE CUT-OFF.
13. Propeller lever — FULL INCREASE.
14. Throttle — cracked ¼ inch.
15. Ignition switch — OFF.
16. Landing gear handle — DOWN.
17. Landing gear emergency retract switch — guard safetied.
18. Carburetor heat handle — IN and LOCKED.
19. Clock and altimeter — set.
20. Attitude indicator and directional indicator — uncaged.
21. Primer switch — OFF.
22. Starter switch — OFF.
23. Battery switch — OFF.
24. Generator switch — ON.
25. Cockpit air handles — as desired.
26. Landing gear emergency handcrank — disengaged (clutch knob UP and LOCKED).
27. Inverter switch — OFF.
28. Light switches and rheostats — OFF.
29. Radio switch — OFF.
30. Pitot heater switch — OFF (guard down).
31. Circuit breakers — IN.
32. Battery switch — ON.

If external power is available, leave battery switch OFF.

33. Landing gear position indicators — check.
34. Landing gear warning light — test.
35. Fuel quantity gages — check.
36. Fuel pressure (booster pump) — check.

NOTE

The use of fuel booster pumps is prohibited except during engine start and during flight when the fuel pressure gage indicates less than 9 psi.

37. Generator and inverter warning lights — check illuminated.
38. Navigation lights — check STEADY and FLASH positions.
39. External gear down indicator lights — check illuminated.
40. Passing light — check.
41. Pitot heat — check.
42. Instrument and console lights — check.
43. Landing lights — check.
44. Flashlight on board and ready for use — check.

BEFORE STARTING ENGINE.

Always make sure a fire guard is posted, the propeller area clear, and wheel chocks in place before starting engine. Set the parking brake and leave canopy open until the engine is running.

STARTING ENGINE.

The engine can be started from the front cockpit only. Start the engine as follows:

1. Starter — engage.

Check for possible hydraulic lock as engine makes first two revolutions. If hydraulic lock is suspected or encountered, discontinue starting attempt and have lower spark plugs removed to drain fluid from cylinders before a restart is attempted.

2. Ignition switch — BOTH (after two engine revolutions).

CAUTION

Primer is very sensitive. Prime ½ to 1 second when engine is cold. Only a rapid momentary actuation is required when the engine is hot. Primer is neither recommended nor required for warm weather starts.

3. Mixture lever — FULL RICH.
4. Starter switch — OFF (after engine starts).

Continue to prime intermittently, if necessary, to keep engine running.

NOTE

If engine does not fire after 10 to 15 seconds of continuous cranking or if

Minimum Turning Radius Diagram

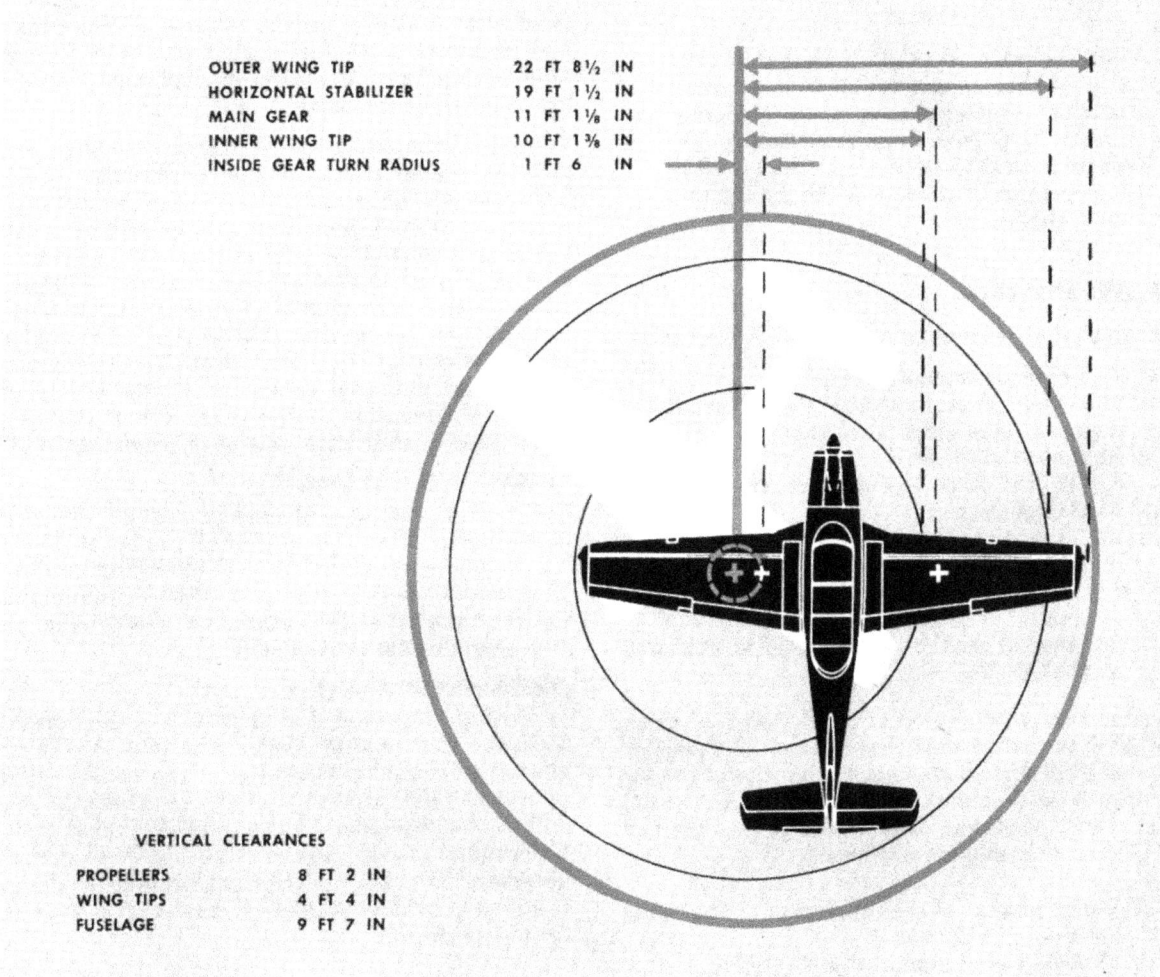

Figure 2-3

engine starts then ceases firing, release starter switch and proceed as follows:

    a. Fuel booster pump switch — OFF.
    b. Ignition switch — OFF.
    c. Mixture lever — IDLE CUT-OFF.

Attempt to clear engine of excess fuel by turning it over several times with starter then repeat starting procedure.

    5. Throttle — 1000 rpm.
    6. Oil pressure gage — check.

If oil pressure does not start to rise within 10 seconds or reach 30 psi in 30 seconds, shut down engine and investigate.

NOTE

For procedure in event of engine fire during starting, refer to Section III.

ENGINE GROUND OPERATION.

    1. Throttle — 1200 to 1600 rpm (for engine warm-up).

Warm up engine at the lowest speed between 1200 and 1600 rpm at which smooth operation is obtained until the oil temperature shows a definite increase or until the oil pressure is stabilized. Do not exceed 1600 rpm until oil temperature has reached minimum operating temperature.

NOTE

When aircraft serviced with grade 1100 oil has been exposed to low temperature weather, ground warm-up of oil temperature to 40°C is recommended to assure warm-up of the entire oil supply. Oil temperature is taken at the oil pump inlet screen.

BEFORE TAXIING.

During engine warm-up, make the following tests:

1. Engine instruments — check.
2. Manifold pressure purge valve button — depress (hold for 3 to 5 seconds).
3. Radio switch — ON.
   a. "SENS" knob — rotate clockwise.
4. Electrical system.
   a. Generator voltage — 28 to 28.5 volts.
   b. Loadmeter — check.
   c. Generator warning light — out at 900 rpm.
   d. Inverter switch — check STANDBY and MAIN.

Set inverter switch to STANDBY position, then to MAIN, to test inverter operation. The inverter warning light should go out when switch is moved to either position and illuminates when the switch is at OFF position. Leave inverter switch at MAIN after completion of check.

5. Wing flaps — check operation, wing flap lever — NEUTRAL.
6. Fuel booster pump switch — OFF.
7. Fuel selector valve handle — RIGHT TANK.
8. Idle speed — check.
9. Ignition switch — check (grounded).

Set throttle at 700 rpm and quickly turn ignition switch to OFF and back to BOTH and note whether engine momentarily stops firing. If engine does not stop firing completely, one or more magneto leads are not grounding properly and the engine should be shut down immediately. As soon as the engine stops, warn ground crew to keep clear of the propeller.

CAUTION

Perform this check as rapidly as possible to avoid backfiring.

10. Radio — check operation.

TAXIING.

1. Area — Check clear for taxi.
2. Wheel chocks — removed.
3. Brakes — check.

Hold feet on rudder pedals, release parking brake and let aircraft roll forward. Test brakes before building up taxiing speed by applying firm toe pressure on both pedals.

Taxiing is simplified by the tricycle landing gear and the rudder pedal linkage to the nose wheel. The good visibility and steerable nose wheel give excellent ground handling characteristics. The initial roll should be straight ahead and turns started while the aircraft is in motion. Turning from a standstill requires more power and shortens tire and brake life. Start turns with rudder pedal steering of the nose wheel. To tighten the turn after full pedal deflection is reached, apply brake on the inside of the turn. When stopping the aircraft, stop with the nose wheel straight.

DOWN-WIND TAXIING.

Down-wind taxiing will usually require little or no throttle after the initial roll is established. To avoid overheating the engine when taxiing down-wind, keep the use of power to a minimum. Rather than ride the brakes, let speed build up and apply brakes occasionally.

CROSS-WIND TAXIING.

In taxiing crosswind, the aircraft has the normal tendency to "weathervane" (turn into the wind) due to the wind force acting on the rudder area, however, the "weathervaning" tendency is not difficult to overcome. The nose wheel linkage from the rudder pedals provides the steering control necessary for safe and efficient ground handling. Hold any rudder pressure necessary to correct for a crosswind.

ENGINE RUN UP.

Before turning onto the runway, turn as near into the wind as practical, stop the aircraft clear of the runway, with the nose wheel straight, set parking brake and perform the following checks:

1. Fuel selector valve handle — fullest tank.

CAUTION

On the first flight of the day, the fuel selector valve handle should be left in the same position used for ground operation. Do not switch to opposite tank just prior to take-off if it has not been used on the ground. If there is an unknown defect in fuel delivery from the unused tank, it would likely not become evident until a critical point in the take-off.

2. Propeller lever — FULL INCREASE.
3. Mixture lever — FULL RICH.
4. Engine instruments — check.
5. Propeller governor — check at 1800 rpm. Note 150-200 rpm drop.

Pull the propeller lever back toward DECREASE until 1600 rpm is obtained (no detent in quadrant) or until contact with the detent is made, in quadrants so equipped. When the desired rpm drop is obtained, return the propeller lever to full INCREASE.

6. Ignition system — check at 2000 rpm, 75 rpm maximum drop.

Turn ignition switch to RIGHT (R), note rpm drop and return ignition switch to BOTH until rpm stabilizes. Turn ignition switch to LEFT (L), note drop and return to BOTH.

NOTE

A marginal rpm drop may be due to fouled plugs resulting from prolonged operation at idle rpm. Advance the throttle to full power for a few seconds in an attempt to clear engine and repeat test.

7. Carburetor heat system — check at 2000 rpm.

Pull carburetor heat handle full OUT and check for approximately ½ inch drop in manifold pressure. Return carburetor heat handle to full IN.

8. Engine power — check (2475 ±75 rpm).

Advance the throttle with a smooth motion to full OPEN (full power) and check to see that the desired rpm is obtained. Acceleration and deceleration during this check should be smooth without backfire, coughing or roughness.

NOTE

Run engine up to full power only on paved areas to avoid damage to the propeller and aircraft from loose gravel kicked up by the propeller. If no paved surface is available, full power and acceleration checks may be made on the initial portion of the take-off run.

BEFORE TAKE-OFF.

1. Wing flaps — up (lever — NEUTRAL).
2. Trim tabs — repeat 10, interior inspection.
   a. Aileron trim tab wheel — 0 degrees.
   b. Rudder trim tab knob — 3 degrees RIGHT (R).
   c. Elevator trim tab wheel — 3 degrees UP.
3. Friction lock knob — adjusted.
4. Mixture lever — FULL RICH.
5. Propeller lever — FULL INCREASE.
6. Engine instruments — check.
7. Flight controls — freedom of movement and proper response.
8. Canopy — position optional.
9. Safety belt and shoulder harness — adjusted.
10. Inertia reel — LOCKED.

TAKE-OFF.

Take-off in this aircraft presents no special problems and is further simplified by good visibility and the use of nose wheel steering. Although this is true, any take-off can be improved by proper technique and careful planning. Plan your take-off according to the following variables affecting take-off technique: field elevation, gross weight, wind, outside air temperature, type of runway, and height and distance of the nearest obstacles. A normal take-off as outlined herein will give the take-off performance covered in the Performance Data in the Appendix.

NORMAL TAKE-OFF.

Release the brakes and roll into take-off position, aligning the nose wheel with the runway, and advance the throttle smoothly to full OPEN (2600 rpm). During the initial roll, maintain directional control with rudder pedal steering of the nose wheel. The rudder becomes effective for directional control at about 35 knots IAS. When you feel good response to elevator control (approximately 50 to 55 knots) apply back pressure to the stick and raise the nose wheel off the runway. When the aircraft is ready, it will fly itself off the ground at 60 to 65 knots IAS.

NOTE

For procedure to be followed in the event of engine failure during take-off, refer to Section III.

MINIMUM RUN TAKE-OFF.

For a minimum run take-off, line up with the runway, set the brakes and apply 75% flaps. Advance the throttle to full OPEN (2600 rpm) and release the brakes. Do not assume a nose-high attitude until reaching approximately 50 knots IAS. Pull back on the stick rapidly but smoothly to assume nose-high (take-off) attitude so that runway may be cleared as soon as minimum flying airspeed (approximately 55 knots IAS) is reached. When clear of the runway, retract the gear and drop the nose slightly to gain a safe airspeed; continue with the normal take-off and climb procedure.

OBSTACLE CLEARANCE TAKE-OFF.

Use the same procedure as given for a minimum run take-off to the point of assuming a nose-high attitude. Do not assume the nose-high (take-off) attitude until reaching approximately 55 knots

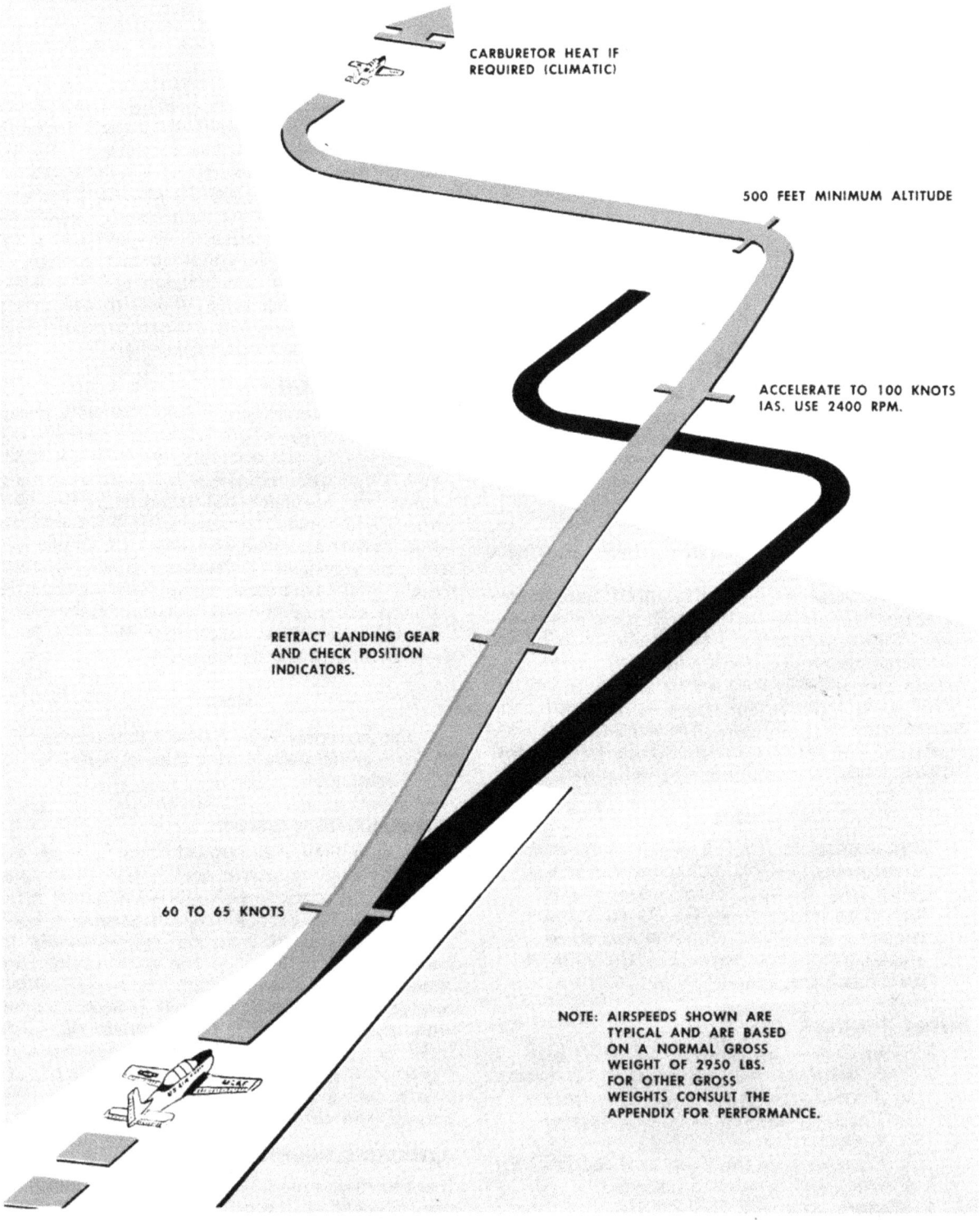

Figure 2-4

IAS. Clear the ground, retract the gear and as soon as a 70 knot airspeed has been attained, hold this airspeed for maximum angle of climb until obstacle is cleared. Accelerate to normal climb speed and retract flaps; continue normal climb.

NOTE

With normal speeds and the engine developing full power (2600 rpm), no particular caution need be exercised in retracting the flaps since acceleration will be sufficient to offset any tendency for the aircraft to sink. Under conditions of minimum airspeed and/or less than full power, caution should be exercised and the flaps raised in increments of 25 to 30 percent.

CROSSWIND TAKE-OFF.

In accomplishing a crosswind take-off, directional control may be more difficult to maintain, therefore, use smooth application of power and attempt to correct for the crosswind by holding upwind aileron and by using rudder pedal steering of the nose wheel. If these are not sufficient at the start of the take-off roll, some use of brakes may be necessary; however, brakes should not be used after take-off roll is underway since every application of brakes on the take-off roll will lengthen the take-off run. Hold the nose wheel on the ground longer than in a normal take-off, using aileron as required to hold wings level. As flying speed is reached, make the pull-off definite to avoid sideskipping as the aircraft starts to become airborne. When definitely airborne, correct for drift by making a coordinated turn into the wind.

NIGHT TAKE-OFF.

Night take-off procedure is similar to normal daytime take-off; however, you should be thoroughly familiar with the location of all switches and controls in the cockpit. Align the aircraft with the runway carefully before starting take-off run, preferably using a sighting point to aid in directional control during the run. After becoming airborne, maintain take-off attitude longer than in normal daytime take-off and gain altitude required to clear obstacles before assuming normal climb attitude.

AFTER TAKE-OFF — CLIMB.

1. Landing gear handle — UP.
2. Landing gear position indicators — check.

Raise flaps before gear and flaps-down airspeed is reached. Aircraft will climb with nose slightly higher.

3. Propeller lever — 2400 rpm (at 100 knots IAS).
4. Carburetor heat handle — climatic.

Climb is normally with full throttle, 2600 rpm. You will note that manifold pressure drops off as altitude increases. Refer to the Climb Chart in the Performance Data, Section X, for fuel consumption, recommended airspeeds and rates of climb for varying altitudes and gross weights. Refer to Section V for power setting limitations.

CRUISE.

After the aircraft has reached cruising altitude, trim for level flight and adjust power as necessary to attain cruising airspeed. Refer to the Appendix, Performance Data, for the necessary information.

FLIGHT CHARACTERISTICS.

For a discussion of the aircraft's flight characteristics, refer to Section VI.

SYSTEMS OPERATION.

For a discussion of systems operation, refer to Section VII.

DESCENT.

1. Carburetor heat handle — climatic.
2. Mixture lever — FULL RICH.
3. Throttle — 15" Hg.

Descent from cruising altitude is best accomplished by letting down in a fast, low-power cruise. During prolonged glides or gliding turns the engine should be cleared at least every 180 degrees of turn, or as often as necessary. Clearing the engine has a threefold purpose: To keep the cylinder head temperature above 149 degrees centigrade, to prevent the engine from becoming "loaded up" due to an excessive rich idle mixture, and to give an early warning of carburetor icing during cold weather operation. The throttle should be applied smoothly and evenly during this clearing process to prevent "killing" the engine in the event an over-rich mixture condition is present.

BEFORE LANDING.

1. Radio — check proper frequency.
2. Parking brake handle — IN.
3. Carburetor heat handle — IN and LOCKED.
4. Mixture lever — FULL RICH.
5. Fuel selector valve handle — fullest tank.

Entry to Pattern.

6. Propeller lever — 2400 rpm.
7. Landing gear warning horn and light — checked.

8. Landing gear handle — DOWN.
9. Landing gear position indicator — check.

Downwind.

10. Airspeed — 100 knots.
11. Canopy position — optional.
12. Shoulder harness — LOCKED.

Base Leg.

13. Landing gear warning horn — silent.
14. Landing gear warning light — out.
15. Propeller lever — FULL INCREASE.
16. Wing flap lever — as required.

Check brake system by depressing brake pedals and noting resistance to pedals. Plan to enter traffic on a downwind leg at 105 to 110 knots and approximately 1000 feet.

TRAFFIC PATTERN CHECK.

Typical landing pattern and traffic pattern checks are detailed in figure 2-5. Although pattern configurations may vary locally, the checks listed apply to all landings.

LANDINGS.

NORMAL LANDING.

Normal landing in this aircraft is made with 100 percent flaps, using either a power-on or power-off approach. In using flaps, lowering approximately 50 percent on the base leg will help to establish a suitable glide angle for approach and the additional flap can then be applied on the approach as determined by wind velocity. Speed should be decreased throughout the pattern to approximately 80 knots for the base leg and to approximately 75 knots as you begin the flare-out. Start flaring-out just over the end of the runway and, if a power-on approach is used, start removing power simultaneously with flare-out. Round out with a smooth, continuous increase of back pressure on the stick and touch main wheels first, holding the nose wheel off with back pressure and maintaining directional control on the runway with rudder. Lower the nose wheel while you still have ample elevator control then use nose wheel steering for directional control. Let speed dissipate as much as practicable before using brakes. Do not hold brake continuously while slowing down, since braking action and brake life are both improved by using short, intermittent applications of brake.

MINIMUM-RUN LANDING.

A minimum-run landing involves touching down at the lowest speed practicable, to cut down the landing roll. Since this is a maximum-performance maneuver and the aircraft is barely above stalling speed, care must be exercised in handling of the flight controls. Abrupt stick movements could cause a stall and allowing the aircraft to yaw will increase the tendency to roll with the stall. To execute a minimum-run landing, lower full flaps after turn onto final approach and slow the aircraft to 50 knots, controlling the rate-of-descent with power. Plan to land as short as possible and start flare-out just over the fence, using very gradual stick pressure. Keep power on until the touchdown, as slower flying speed is possible with power. Immediately at touchdown, cut the throttle, lower the nose wheel smoothly to the runway and apply brakes.

CAUTION

Don't use brakes before letting the nose wheel down; doing so can cause the aircraft to pitch, dropping the nose wheel hard.

CROSSWIND LANDING.

Landing in a crosswind presents no special problems except the elimination of drift correction, at the proper moment, to avoid touching down in a skid. Correction for drift may be accomplished by three methods: crabbing, carrying the upwind wing low (a slip), or a combination of both. Crabbing is most successful for the traffic pattern phase while a combination is most successful for landing. Generally, less flaps should be used, depending on the velocity and angle of the wind since stall characteristics and ground handling characteristics, in a crosswind, are less desirable with full flaps. Approach the runway with crab, but eliminate most of the crab on nearing the runway by replacing the crab with an upwind wing low attitude. Touch down easily onto the low main wheel while flying airspeed remains and allow the aircraft to settle smoothly onto the opposite gear. Lower the nose wheel smoothly to the runway to preserve directional control. If an excessive amount of crab should remain just prior to touchdown, attempt to eliminate it at point of touchdown by use of rudder. If excessive skidding across the runway appears imminent, make a coordinated turn to realign with the runway and drop upwind wing to correct for tendency to drift.

NIGHT LANDING.

Night landing technique is similar to normal daytime landing, except that judgment of distance may be somewhat affected in semi-darkness and with runway floodlights. If runway floodlights are used, avoid looking at the beam of light as

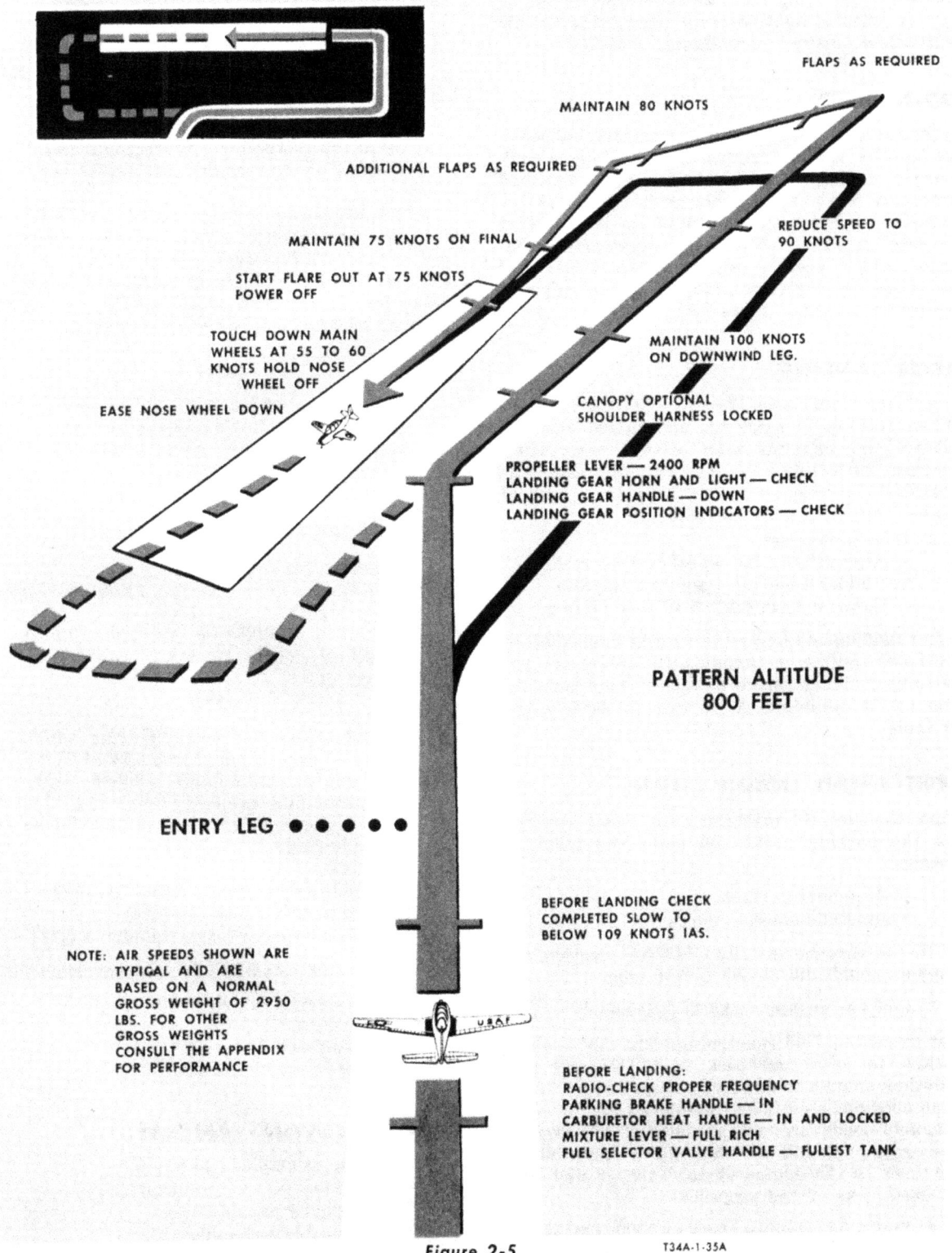

Figure 2-5

there may be a tendency to level off on top of it instead of on the runway. Don't use landing lights until at a low enough altitude for them to be of use and avoid using them in thick haze, smoke or fog, as reflected light from the particles in the air will reduce, instead of enhance, visibility.

GO-AROUND.

Make the decision to go around as early as possible, in the landing approach, to provide a safe margin of airspeed and altitude. The go-around procedure is a normal maneuver and does not become an emergency procedure unless it is started too late. Accuracy of judgment and early recognition of the need to go around are important; these are developed by practice. Go-around procedure is shown in figure 2-6.

AFTER LANDING.

1. Wing flaps — up (lever — NEUTRAL).

When landing is made on unprepared runway, retract the flaps as soon as the nose wheel touches the runway, if practical, to reduce the possibility of damage to the flaps from mud or gravel thrown up by the wheels.

2. Trim tabs — set.
   a. Aileron trim tab wheel — 0 degrees.
   b. Rudder trim tab knob — 0 degrees.
   c. Elevator trim tab wheel — 0 degrees.

After landing roll, clear the runway immediately. Also use caution in taxiing over uneven or soft terrain, avoiding severe bumps or hard braking, and use a minimum of throttle in loose gravel or sand.

POST FLIGHT ENGINE CHECK.

Park the aircraft with the nose wheel straight, set the parking brake and make the following checks:

1. Instruments — check.
2. Engine idle speed — check.

With the throttle in fully CLOSED position, the engine should idle at 600 to 700 rpm.

3. Ignition switch — check (grounded).

Set throttle at 700 rpm and quickly turn ignition switch to OFF and back to BOTH and note whether engine momentarily stops firing. If engine does not stop firing completely, one or more magneto leads are not grounding properly and the engine should be shut down immediately. As soon as the engine stops, warn ground crew to keep clear of the propeller.

4. Ignition system — check at 2000 rpm, 75 rpm maximum drop.

Turn ignition switch to RIGHT (R), note rpm drop and return ignition switch to BOTH until rpm stabilizes. Turn ignition switch to LEFT (L), note drop and return to BOTH.

NOTE

A marginal rpm drop may be due to fouled plugs resulting from prolonged operation at idle rpm. Advance the throttle to full power for a few seconds in an attempt to clear engine and repeat test.

5. Engine power — check (2475 ±75 rpm). Advance the throttle with a smooth motion to full OPEN (full power) and check to see that the desired rpm is obtained. Acceleration and deceleration during this check should be smooth without backfire, coughing or roughness.

NOTE

Run engine up to full power only on paved areas to avoid damage to the propeller and aircraft from loose gravel kicked up by the propeller.

ENGINE SHUT DOWN.

1. Parking brake — set.
2. Ignition switch — check (if not done during post flight).
3. Throttle — 1000 rpm (for one minute).
4. Mixture lever — IDLE CUT-OFF.

NOTE

Should engine fail to stop firing when mixture lever is moved to IDLE CUT-OFF due to one or more magneto leads not grounding properly or if the fuel metering valve is stuck open, accomplish the following:

   a. Ignition switch — leave at BOTH.
   b. Throttle — open slightly.
   c. Fuel selector valve handle — OFF.

After propeller rotation has stopped completely:

5. Fuel selector valve handle — OFF.
6. Throttle — CLOSED.
7. Ignition switch — OFF.
8. Electrical switches — OFF.

BEFORE LEAVING AIRCRAFT.

1. Flight controls — LOCKED.
2. DD Form 781 — completed.
3. Wheel chocks — in place.
4. Parking brake handle — IN.
5. Pitot cover — in place.

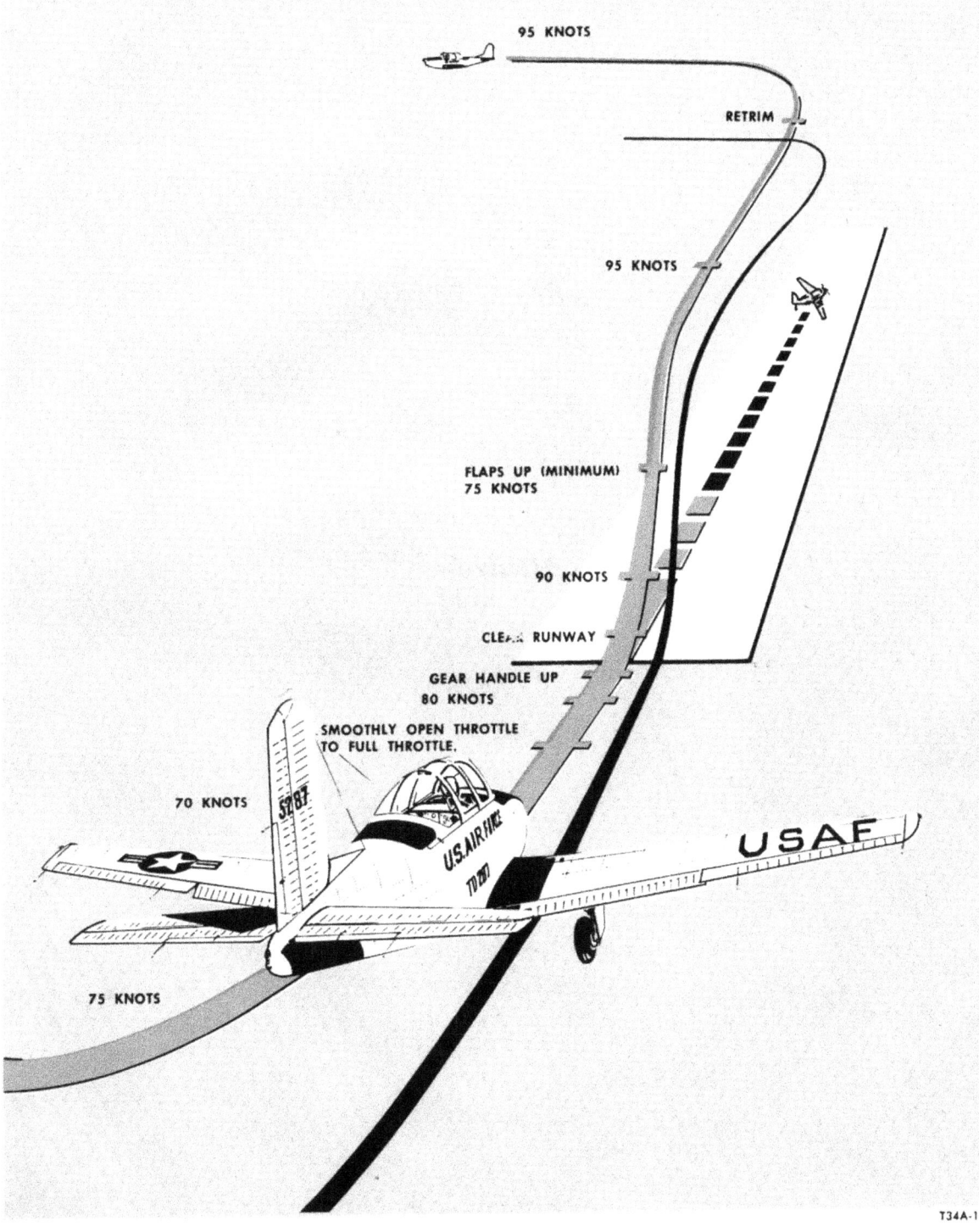

Figure 2-6

Blank

CUT ON LINE

T-34A CONDENSED CHECK LIST NORMAL PROCEDURES

PREFLIGHT CHECK.

BEFORE EXTERIOR INSPECTION.
1. DD Form 781 — check.
2. Battery and ignition switches — check OFF.
3. Aileron trim tab wheel — 0 degrees.
4. Rudder trim tab knob — 0 degrees.
5. Elevator trim tab wheel — 0 degrees.
6. Landing gear handle — DOWN.
7. Landing gear emergency retract switch — OFF and safetied.
8. Canopy emergency release handle seal — undamaged.
9. Flight controls — unlocked.

Rear Cockpit Check for Solo Flight.
10. Safety belt — secure.
11. Shoulder harness — secure.
12. Headset — stowed.
13. Flight controls — free from obstruction.
14. Attitude indicator and directional indicator — uncaged.
15. Fuel booster pump override switches — FORWARD COCKPIT CONTROL.
16. Rear canopy — closed and locked.

EXTERIOR INSPECTION.
1. Left wing.
   a. Wing flap — check.
   b. Aileron — check; trim tab for servo action.
   c. Wing tip and navigation light — check.
   d. Leading edge and landing light — check.
   e. Pitot tube — check.

T.O. 1T-34A-1
10 February 1958

1

f. Fuel quantity — check, cap secure.
g. Air intake — check, screen clean.
2. Left main gear.
   a. Wheel chocks — in place.
   b. Tire — check.
   c. Wheel brake — check puck, hydraulic line, adjusting pin recessed $^3/_{16}$ inch maximum.
   d. Strut — check.
   e. Landing gear doors — check.
   f. Wheel well — unobstructed.
3. Nose section.
   a. Left augmentor tube — unobstructed.
   b. Left cowling — secure.
   c. Propeller — check.
   d. Passing light — secure.
   e. Air intake — check, unobstructed.
   f. Strut — check.
   g. Tire and static wire — check.
   h. Nose landing gear doors — check.
   i. Wheel well — unobstructed.
   j. Right cowling — secure.
   k. Battery and battery retainer bar — secure.
   l. Battery sump jar — check.
   m. Exterior canopy emergency release handle — undisturbed.
   n. Right augmentor tube — unobstructed.
4. Right main gear — check same as left main gear.
5. Right wing.
   a. Air intake — check, screen clean.
   b. Fuel quantity — check, cap secure.
   c. Leading edge and landing light — check.
   d. Wing tip and navigation light — check.
   e. Aileron — check; trim tab for servo action.
   f. Wing flap — check.

T.O. 1T-34A-1
10 February 1958

2

CUT ON LINE

6. Fuselage right side.
   a. Fuel tank vent — check, 12 degrees forward pitch.
   b. Antenna — secure.
   c. Static air vent — unobstructed.
7. Empennage.
   a. Right horizontal stabilizer — check.
   b. Right elevator and trim tab — check.
   c. Vertical fin — check.
   d. Rudder — check; trim tab for anti-servo action.
   e. Navigation light — check.
   f. Left elevator and trim tab — check.
   g. Left horizontal stabilizer — check.
8. Fuselage left side.
   a. Tail skid — check.
   b. Under side — check.
   c. Static air vent — unobstructed.
   d. Baggage compartment — check, door secured.
   e. Fuel tank vent — check, 12 degrees forward pitch.

INTERIOR INSPECTION.
1. Seat — adjust and lock.
2. Seat belt and shoulder harness — fastened.
3. Inertia reel lock — check.
4. Parking brakes — set.
5. Flight controls — check freedom of movement and response.
6. Wing flap lever — NEUTRAL.
7. Landing light switches — OFF.
8. Fuel selector valve handle — LEFT TANK.
9. Fuel booster pump switch — LEFT.
10. Trim tabs — set for take-off.
    a. Aileron trim tab wheel — 0 degrees.
    b. Rudder trim tab knob — 3 degrees right.
    c. Elevator trim tab wheel — 3 degrees UP.

T.O. 1T-34A-1
10 February 1958

3

11. Engine control quadrant friction lock knob — adjusted.
12. Mixture lever — IDLE CUT-OFF.
13. Propeller lever — FULL INCREASE.
14. Throttle — cracked ¼ inch.
15. Ignition switch — OFF.
16. Landing gear handle — DOWN.
17. Landing gear emergency retract switch — guard safetied.
18. Carburetor heat handle — IN and LOCKED.
19. Clock and altimeter — set.
20. Attitude indicator and directional indicator — uncaged.

21. Primer switch — OFF.
22. Starter switch — OFF.
23. Battery switch — OFF.
24. Generator switch — ON.
25. Cockpit air handles — as desired.
26. Landing gear emergency handcrank — disengaged (clutch knob up and LOCKED).

27. Inverter switch — OFF.
28. Light switches and rheostats — OFF.
29. Radio switch — OFF.
30. Pitot heater switch — OFF (guard down).
31. Circuit breakers — IN.
32. Battery switch — ON.
33. Landing gear position indicators — check.
34. Landing gear warning light — test.
35. Fuel quantity gages — check.
36. Fuel pressure (booster pump) — check.
37. Generator and inverter warning lights — check illuminated.

38. Navigation lights — check, STEADY and FLASH positions.
39. External gear down indicator lights — check illuminated.

T.O. 1T-34A-1
10 February 1958

4

40. Passing light — check.
41. Pitot heat — check.
42. Instrument and console lights — check.
43. Landing lights — check.
44. Flashlight on board and ready for use — check.

STARTING ENGINE.
1. Starter — engage.
2. Ignition switch — BOTH (after two engine revolutions).
3. Mixture lever — FULL RICH.
4. Starter switch — OFF (after engine starts).
5. Throttle — 1000 rpm.
6. Oil pressure gage — check.

ENGINE GROUND OPERATION.
1. Throttle — 1200 to 1600 rpm (for engine warm-up).

BEFORE TAXIING.
1. Engine instruments — check.
2. Manifold pressure purge valve button — DEPRESS (hold for 3 to 5 seconds).
3. Radio switch — ON.
   a. "SENS" knob — rotate clockwise.
4. Electrical system.
   a. Generator voltage — 28 to 28.5 volts.
   b. Loadmeter — check.
   c. Generator warning light — out at 900 rpm.
   d. Inverter switch — check STANDBY and MAIN.
5. Wing flaps — check operation, wing flap lever — NEUTRAL.
6. Fuel booster pump switch — OFF.
7. Fuel selector valve handle — RIGHT TANK.
8. Idle speed — check.

9. Ignition switch — check (grounded).
10. Radio — check operation.

TAXIING.

1. Area — check clear for taxi.
2. Wheel chocks — removed.
3. Brakes — check.

ENGINE RUN-UP.

1. Fuel selector valve handle — fullest tank.
2. Propeller lever — FULL INCREASE.
3. Mixture lever — FULL RICH.
4. Engine instruments — check.
5. Propeller governor — check at 1800 rpm. Note 150-200 rpm drop.
6. Ignition system — check at 2000 rpm, 75 rpm maximum drop.
7. Carburetor heat system — check at 2000 rpm.
8. Engine power check (2475 ±75 rpm).

BEFORE TAKE-OFF.

1. Wing flaps — up (lever — NEUTRAL).
2. Trim tabs — repeat 10, interior inspection.
3. Friction lock knob — adjusted.
4. Mixture lever — FULL RICH.
5. Propeller lever — FULL INCREASE.
6. Engine instruments — check.
7. Flight controls — freedom of movement and proper response.
8. Canopy — position optional.
9. Safety belt and shoulder harness — adjusted.
10. Inertia reel — LOCKED.

T.O. 1T-34A-1
10 February 1958

6

CUT ON LINE

T-34A
Take-Off Data Card

Conditions

Gross Weight .... _____ Lb.

Runway Length .... _____ Ft.

Field Pressure Altitude .... _____ Ft.

Outside Air Temperature .... _____ °C

Wind .... _____ Knots

Take-Off

Take-Off Distance .... _____ Ft.

Take-Off Over 50 Ft. .... _____ Ft.

Indicated Take-Off Speed .... _____ Knots

Indicated Best Climb Speed .... _____ Knots

T.O. 1T-34A-1
10 February 1958

7

CUT ON LINE

8

T.O. 1T-34A-1
10 February 1958

NOTES:

CUT ON LINE

AFTER TAKE-OFF — CLIMB.
1. Landing gear handle — UP.
2. Landing gear position indicators — check.
3. Propeller lever — 2400 rpm (at 100 knots IAS).
4. Carburetor heat handle — climatic.

DESCENT.
1. Carburetor heat handle — climatic.
2. Mixture lever — FULL RICH.
3. Throttle — 15 inches Hg.

BEFORE LANDING.
1. Radio — check proper frequency.
2. Parking brake handle — IN.
3. Carburetor heat handle — IN and LOCKED.
4. Mixture lever — FULL RICH.
5. Fuel selector valve handle — fullest tank.

Entry to Pattern.
6. Propeller lever — 2400 rpm.
7. Landing gear warning horn and light — checked.
8. Landing gear handle — DOWN.
9. Landing gear position indicator — check.

Downwind.
10. Airspeed — 100 knots.
11. Canopy position — optional.
12. Shoulder harness — LOCKED.

Base Leg.
13. Landing gear warning horn — silent.
14. Landing gear warning light — out.
15. Propeller lever — FULL INCREASE.
16. Wing flap lever — as required.

T.O. 1T-34A-1
10 February 1958

9

CUT ON LINE

10

T.O. 1T-34A-1
10 February 1958

BLANK

CUT ON LINE

T-34A
Landing Data Card

Conditions

Runway Length .... ____ Ft.

Gross Weight .... ____ Lb.

Pressure Altitude .... ____ Ft.

Outside Air Temperature .... ____ °C

Wind .... ____ Knots

Landing

Landing Distance Over 50 Ft. .... ____ Ft.

Landing Ground Roll .... ____ Ft.

Indicated Approach Speed @ 50 Ft. ...... ____ Knots

T.O. 1T-34A-1
10 February 1958

11

CUT ON LINE

NOTES:

T.O. 1T-34A-1
10 February 1958

12

AFTER LANDING.
1. Wing flaps — up (lever — NEUTRAL).
2. Trim tabs — set.
    a. Aileron trim tab wheel — 0 degrees.
    b. Rudder trim tab knob — 0 degrees.
    c. Elevator trim tab wheel — 0 degrees.

POST FLIGHT ENGINE CHECK.
1. Instruments — check.
2. Engine idle speed — check.
3. Ignition switch — check (grounded).
4. Ignition system — check at 2000 rpm, 75 rpm maximum drop.
5. Engine power — check (2475 ±75 rpm).

ENGINE SHUT-DOWN.
1. Parking Brake — set.
2. Ignition switch — check (if not done during post flight).
3. Throttle — 1000 rpm (for one minute).
4. Mixture lever — IDLE CUT-OFF.
5. Fuel selector valve handle — OFF.
6. Throttle — CLOSED.
7. Ignition switch — OFF.
8. Electrical switches — OFF.

BEFORE LEAVING AIRCRAFT.
1. Flight controls — LOCKED.
2. DD form 781 — completed.
3. Wheel chocks — in place.
4. Parking brake handle — IN.
5. Pitot cover — in place.

T.O. 1T-34A-1
10 February 1958

Blank

Section 3

Emergency Procedures

TABLE OF CONTENTS

Engine Failure	3-1
Fuel Pressure Drop — Engine Operating Normally	3-3
Maximum Glide	3-4
Simulated Forced Landing	3-4
Propeller Failure	3-5
Fire	3-5
Smoke and Fume Elimination	3-7
Bail-Out	3-7
Landing Emergencies (Except Ditching)	3-8
Emergency Entrance	3-9
Ditching	3-9
Fuel System Emergency Operation	3-10
Electrical Power Supply System Emergency Operation	3-10
Wing Flap Emergency Operation	3-10
Landing Gear Emergency Operation	3-11
Condensed Check List	3-13

ENGINE FAILURE.

Engine failure is usually preceded by symptoms which will enable you to take preventive action if you are alert to operating conditions at all times. Instant and complete engine failure most often occurs due to fuel flow or ignition failure. This type of failure due to mechanical causes is seldom encountered. Failure due to carelessness or improper operating techniques is not at all rare and should be guarded against by constant attention to such things as cylinder head temperature, oil pressure, sound of the engine, manifold pressure and rpm and by observing the operating limitations discussed in Section V. Land as soon as possible if engine failure is indicated.

ENGINE FAILURE DURING TAKE-OFF (prior to becoming airborne).

1. Throttle — CLOSED.
2. Brakes — apply.
3. Canopy position — open.
4. Mixture lever — IDLE CUT-OFF.
5. Fuel selector valve handle — OFF.
6. Ignition switch — OFF.
7. Battery switch — OFF.
8. Generator switch — OFF.

As soon as the aircraft stops, get clear at once.

ENGINE FAILURE DURING TAKE-OFF (after becoming airborne).

1. Glide — establish.
2. Canopy position — open.
3. Mixture lever — IDLE CUT-OFF.
4. Fuel selector valve handle — OFF.
5. Ignition switch — OFF.
6. Battery switch — OFF.
7. Generator switch — OFF.

Complete landing and as soon as the aircraft stops, get clear at once.

NOTE

When engine failure from an unknown cause occurs, there is always the possibility of a resultant engine fire. For this reason, any items of the engine shutdown which cannot be completed before landing, should be completed as soon as practicable on the ground.

If the engine fails after the aircraft has left the ground and there is not sufficient prepared landing area remaining in front of the aircraft, lower the nose to avoid a stall and prepare to land straight ahead.

WARNING

Under no circumstances should a turn be attempted at low altitude with a dead engine, except slight deviations to avoid hitting an obstacle. A controlled crash landing straight ahead is preferable to the likelihood of a stall causing an uncontrolled roll, and crash, out of a turn.

1. Landing gear handle — UP.

WARNING

Make no attempt to land on unprepared or unfamiliar terrain with the landing gear extended.

NOTE

Approximately 7 to 8 seconds are required to extend the gear and approximately 10 seconds are required for retraction.

2. Canopy — open.
3. Mixture lever — IDLE CUT-OFF.
4. Fuel selector valve handle — OFF.
5. Ignition switch — OFF.
6. Battery switch — OFF.
7. Generator switch — OFF.

Accomplish a gear-up landing.

ENGINE FAILURE DURING FLIGHT.

In the event of engine failure during flight, maintain 90 knots IAS for best glide distance and prepare for a forced landing. Attempt to start engine if deemed reasonably safe and if altitude permits. If engine fails to re-start, shut down engine and make a forced landing; at night or if a forced landing is not possible, bail out.

Immediately upon encountering partial power failure or noting any condition which would point to imminent engine failure, such as loss of power, loss of fuel pressure, rough running engine, etc., proceed as follows:

1. Airspeed — maintain 90 knots.

CAUTION

Many engine failures are the result of fuel starvation due to poor fuel planning, therefore, if not certain from which tank fuel is being used, LOOK at the fuel selector valve handle when switching tanks. It is otherwise possible to switch into the OFF position inadvertently.

NOTE

Do not lock shoulder harness until after cutting all switches that cannot be reached with the harness locked. If you don't have time to get the harness locked, the automatic lock will function on impact.

2. Fuel selector valve handle — switch tanks.
3. Fuel booster pump switch — ON (appropriate tank).
4. Throttle — advance ½ inch beyond present setting.
5. Mixture lever — FULL RICH.
6. Propeller lever — FULL INCREASE.
7. Ignition switch — check BOTH.
8. Battery switch — check ON.
9. Generator switch — check ON.
10. Carburetor heat handle — climatic.

If Complete Engine Failure Is Encountered, Proceed as Follows:

11. Airspeed — maintain 90 knots.

Attempt to Restart Engine if Altitude Permits:

12. Mixture lever — IDLE CUT-OFF.
13. Fuel selector valve handle — OFF.

Turning the fuel selector valve OFF for a few seconds will clear the engine in the event of excessive fuel flow.

NOTE

If the failure was due to the fuel metering valve sticking in full open position, the carburetor will deliver an excess of fuel, with constant flooding. Shutting off fuel momentarily will clear the engine and possibly restore operation.

14. Throttle — FULL OPEN.
15. Fuel selector valve handle — ON (fullest tank).
16. Fuel booster pump switch — ON.
17. Throttle — ¼ inch OPEN.
18. Mixture lever — FULL RICH.
19. Primer switch — ON (intermittently as required to start engine).
    a. If engine fires, primer switch — ON (as required to reach field).

If Engine Fails to Restart:

20. Mixture lever — IDLE CUT-OFF.
21. Throttle — CLOSED.
22. Ignition switch — OFF.
23. Fuel selector valve handle — OFF.
24. All switches — OFF.
25. Shoulder harness — locked.

FUEL PRESSURE DROP-ENGINE OPERATING NORMALLY.

ON THE GROUND.

If fuel pressure should drop below operating minimum while the engine is operating normally on the ground, shut down the engine and have a fire guard stand by. Do not take off until the cause has been determined and corrected.

IN FLIGHT.

A drop in fuel pressure reading with continued normal engine operation in flight may be the result of one or more of the following:

1. Primer solenoid leakage.
2. Clogged pressure line.
3. Instrument failure.
4. Line leakage.
5. Failure of engine-driven pump.

If the low pressure gage reading is the result of a clogged pressure line or faulty instrument, normal engine operation can be continued. If a leak is found, land at once. If the cause cannot be determined, you may elect either to attempt to continue operation long enough to reach your home field, or make an emergency landing, depending on such factors as power requirements, urgency of the mission, availability of emergency landing area, known condition of engine, etc. In any case, you should plan to land as soon as possible. If the decision is to continue flight to destination, a constant watch should be kept for fire. In addition, power should not be reduced

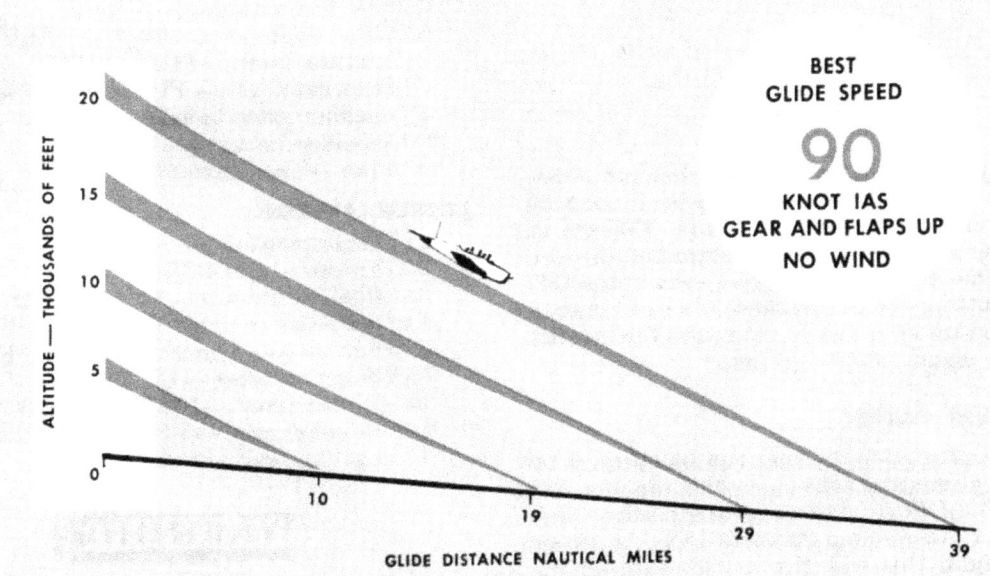

Figure 3-1

Emergency Equipment

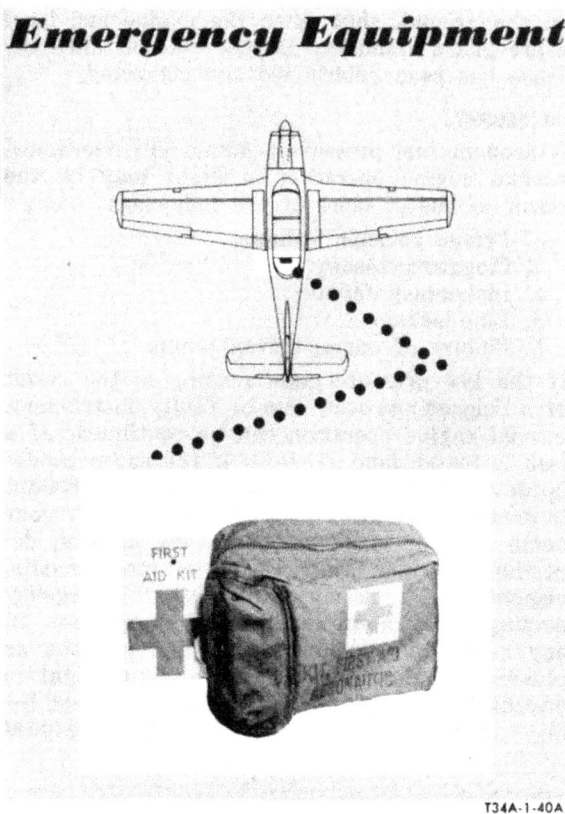

Figure 3-2

and airspeed should be maintained at or above cruising; if an unknown leak exists, it may be that the airflow is preventing a fire. Because of the danger of backfire, never retard the throttle at any time that a fuel leak is even suspected. When shutting the engine down, do so by means of the mixture lever and do not retard the throttle until the engine stops turning.

MAXIMUM GLIDE.

The greatest gliding distance can be attained by leaving the gear and flaps up, pulling the propeller lever to full DECREASE (selecting positive high pitch) and maintaining 90 knots IAS. At design gross weight, this will give a glide ratio of approximately 10.5 to 1 (figure 3-1) with a no-wind condition.

NOTE

Opening the canopy will slightly decrease the glide ratio.

To obtain positive high pitch on aircraft equipped with a detent in the engine control quadrant, bypass the detent and pull the propeller lever to the full extent of quadrant travel. With the propeller lever in the full DECREASE position, the glide distances shown in figure 3-1 can be increased approximately 25 percent.

CAUTION

The engine is not to be operated at speeds below 1600 rpm, with power on, because of the development of excessively high B.M.E.P.

Once over a chosen landing area, the glide ratio can be decreased by positioning the propeller lever to full INCREASE. Additional drag, if required, may be gained by lowering the flaps and gear.

NOTE

The landing gear should be down only if landing is to be made on a prepared runway or smooth surface.

SIMULATED FORCED LANDING.

1. Throttle — CLOSED.
2. Glide — establish 90 knots IAS.
3. Fuel selector valve handle — switch tanks.
4. Fuel pressure gage — check.
5. Wing flaps — up, (lever — NEUTRAL).
6. Mixture lever — FULL RICH.
7. Propeller lever — FULL INCREASE.
8. Landing gear handle — UP.
9. Shoulder harness — locked.
10. Trim — as necessary.

FORCED LANDING.

1. Canopy position — open.
2. Throttle — CLOSED.
3. Glide — establish — 90 knots IAS.
4. Fuel selector valve handle — OFF.
5. Fuel booster pump switch — OFF.
6. Wing flap lever — UP.
7. Mixture lever — IDLE CUT-OFF.
8. Propeller lever — FULL DECREASE.
9. Landing gear switch — UP.

WARNING

Lower the landing gear only when you are certain terrain is suitable.

10. Ignition switch — OFF.
11. Battery switch — OFF.
12. Generator switch — OFF.
13. Shoulder harness — locked.
14. Trim — as necessary.

PROPELLER FAILURE.

1. Throttle — CLOSED.
2. Pitch attitude — increase.
3. Propeller lever — FULL DECREASE.

If Propeller Is Uncontrollable:

4. Wing flap lever — DOWN.
5. Airspeed — approximately 60 knots.

Failure of either the governing system or the linkage from the propeller lever will result in the propeller going to full low pitch (high rpm). The governor control arm connecting with the propeller lever linkage is spring-loaded to the full high rpm position and any other failure resulting in loss of oil flow or oil pressure to the propeller hub will also result in full low pitch due to the centrifugal twisting moment on the blades. Under power-on conditions, full low pitch will result in engine over-speeding. Should a runaway propeller condition occur, close the throttle immediately and pull the aircraft up into a climb to introduce a load on the engine and slow it down, then attempt to bring the rpm within normal range with the propeller lever. If the propeller cannot be controlled, continue flight under reduced power. Slow the aircraft until airspeed is below gear and flaps-down limit airspeed then lower the flaps and maintain approximately 15 knots above stalling speed, keeping rpm from exceeding maximum, if possible, and land immediately.

PROPELLER OPERATION WITH NO POWER.

In the event of engine failure, provided there is oil pressure, sufficient propeller control is available to establish and maintain positive high pitch operation and consequently maximum glide.

FIRE.

NOTE

No engine fire extinguishing system is installed on this aircraft.

FIRE DURING ENGINE START.

If Fire Is Other Than Exhaust or Induction — Discontinue Starting Attempt:

1. Mixture lever — IDLE CUT-OFF.
2. Battery switch — OFF.
3. Ignition switch — OFF.
4. Generator switch — OFF.

Combat fire with all available fire extinguishers.

If Fire Is Exhaust or Induction — Continue Starting Attempt; if Fire Persists:

1. Mixture lever — IDLE CUT-OFF.
2. Throttle — FULL OPEN, continue cranking.

CAUTION

Do not use primer to start engine, priming will not facilitate most starts and may aggravate the fire.

3. Fuel control valve handle — OFF.
4. Ignition switch — OFF.
5. Starter switch — OFF.
6. Battery switch — OFF.
7. Generator switch — OFF.

Get clear of aircraft and signal ground crew to use fire extinguishers. The engine compartment is accessible for fire fighting through a push-in access door (figure 3-3) on the right side of the engine compartment.

Do not attempt to restart the engine if the fire extinguisher is used. If engine starts and fire persists, shut engine down and signal for fire extinguishing equipment. Clear the aircraft at once.

Fire during starting may occur in either the induction or exhaust systems. However, pilot technique is the same in combating both types. When the fire occurs, keep the engine turning in an attempt to clear or start the engine, as the fire may be blown out the exhaust or drawn through the engine and extinguished. Engine fire is not readily apparent from the cockpit, since the exhaust augmentor tubes are at the underside of the fuselage. Should a fire occur during starting, continue cranking with starter in an attempt to get engine started.

ENGINE FIRE AFTER STARTING.

If engine fire occurs after starting, follow the procedure used for FIRE DURING ENGINE START, this section.

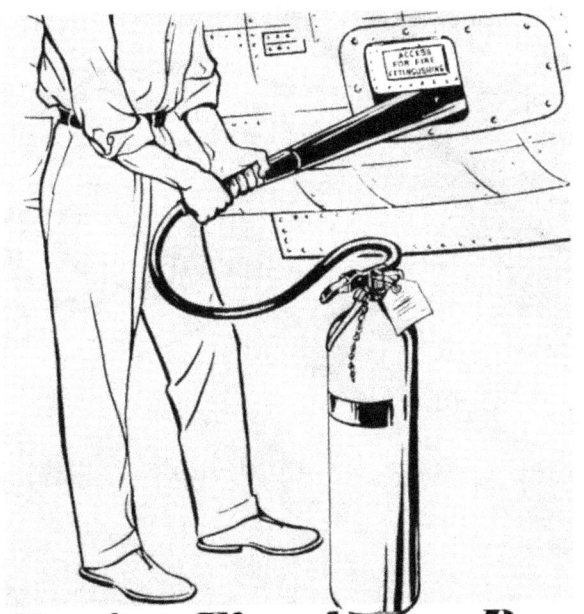

Engine Fire Access Door

Figure 3-3

Section III — T.O. 1T-34A-1

Typical Forced Landing

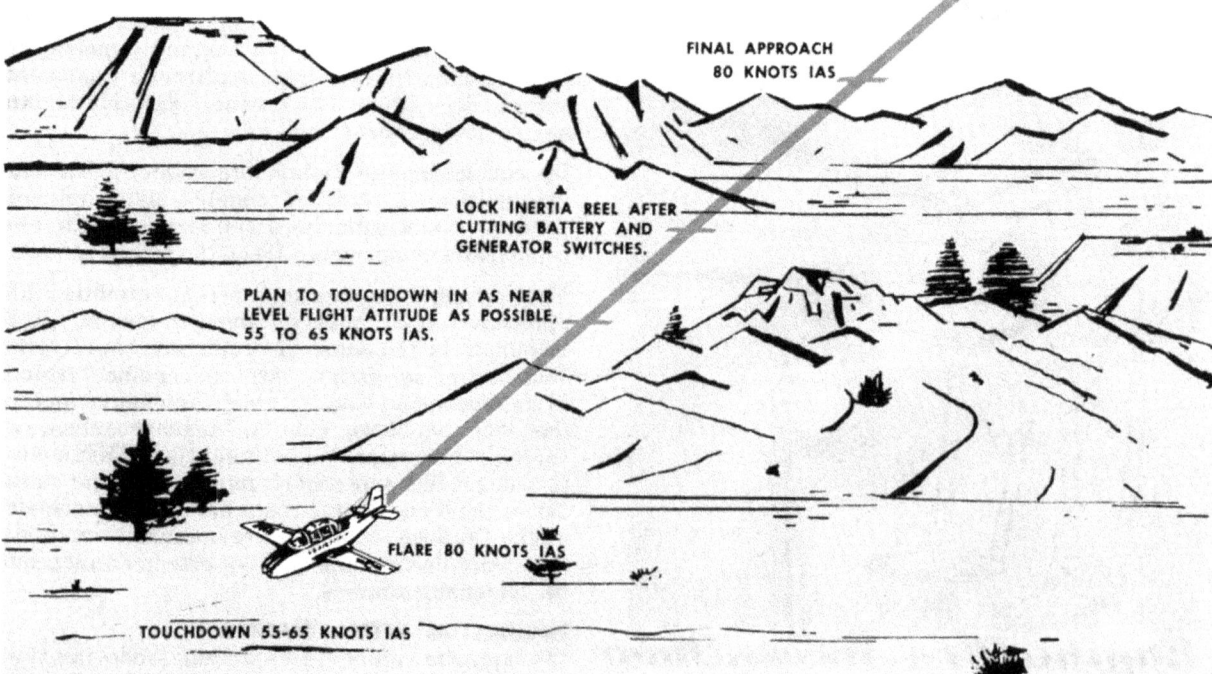

Figure 3-4

3-6

ENGINE FIRE DURING FLIGHT.

1. Mixture lever — IDLE CUT-OFF.
2. Fuel selector valve handle — OFF.
3. Ignition switch — OFF.
4. Battery switch — OFF.
5. Throttle — CLOSED.

Use the foregoing procedure if it is deemed impractical to attempt to extinguish an engine fire in flight. Never attempt to land the aircraft with a serious fire that cannot be extinguished if there is sufficient altitude to bail out. The decision to bail out will depend on judgment and the seriousness of the fire.

NOTE

If a forced landing is possible on a runway, turn battery switch on long enough to extend the gear, if it appears reasonably safe, otherwise, extend the gear manually or land with gear up.

FUSELAGE FIRE IN FLIGHT.

1. Canopy position — closed.

Closing the canopy and reducing airspeed will minimize draft through the cockpit.

2. Cockpit air handles — FULL OUT.
3. Battery switch — OFF.
4. Generator switch — OFF.

Turn on the switches, one at a time, in an attempt to determine the nature of the fire. If the fire is not stopped by turning off electrical power supply and no other means of extinguishing it appears feasible, either bail out or land the aircraft, depending on altitude and seriousness of fire. A landing should not be attempted with a serious fire if there is sufficient altitude to bail out.

WING FIRE.

There is little that can be done to control a wing fire, except to try to blow fire out by slipping the aircraft away from the fire. If the fire cannot be extinguished immediately in this manner, bail out.

ELECTRICAL FIRE.

1. Battery switch — OFF.
2. Generator switch — OFF.
3. All electrical equipment — OFF.
4. All circuit breakers — OUT.

All circuits except starter relays are protected by circuit breakers, which isolate a short-circuit and tend to prevent a fire. Should an electrical fire start, however, try to locate the faulty circuit by using the foregoing procedure. Turn on the generator and battery switches, one at a time, to determine if either circuit is faulty. If the generator and battery circuits are all right, monitor the remaining switches and circuit breakers one at a time to locate and isolate the shorted circuit. If the shorted circuit is not located, use only that equipment which it may become necessary to use. Refer to ELECTRICAL SYSTEM EMERGENCY OPERATION, this section.

SMOKE AND FUME ELIMINATION.

1. Cockpit cold air handle — IN.
2. Cockpit hot air handle — OUT.

NOTE

The cockpit hot air valves should be left closed since the possibility of the duct system being damaged by the fire may direct additional smoke to the cockpit.

3. Canopy position — open.

Reduce airspeed and use the foregoing procedure to relieve the cockpit of smoke and fumes. If conditions get worse, stand by to bail out.

BAIL OUT.

1. Wing flap lever — DOWN.

Reduce speed as much as possible, with full flaps, to provide a more tail high attitude.

2. Canopy — OPEN or jettison.
3. Seats — full up.
4. Safety belt and shoulder harness — unfasten.

Figure 3-5

Make sure safety belts and shoulder harness will not foul on clothing or parachute on exit.

5. Headset — remove.

WARNING

- In a spin, both pilots should bail out toward the outside of the spin to minimize the possibility of being struck by the aircraft.
- Seat cannot be raised to full up position for spin bailout, due to centrifugal force.

Make the decision to abandon the aircraft while there is still plenty of altitude and (when possible) power and directional control. Head the aircraft toward an uninhabited area and jettison the canopy if desired (figure 3-7). To leave the front cockpit, crawl out on the wing and dive off the trailing edge head first (at high airspeed, pull yourself out in a vaulting dive onto the wing, as it is possible to be swept off the wing while climbing out), figure 3-5. To leave the rear cockpit, dive overboard toward the trailing edge.

LANDING EMERGENCIES
(Except ditching).

GEAR UP LANDING.
1. Canopy position — open.
2. Wing flap lever — DOWN.

When Committed to Landing:
3. Throttle — CLOSED.
4. Mixture lever — IDLE CUT-OFF.
5. Fuel selector valve handle — OFF.

Just Before Touchdown:
6. Ignition switch — OFF.
7. Battery switch — OFF.
8. Generator switch — OFF.
9. Inertia reel — LOCKED.

NOTE
Lock inertia reel only after turning off all switches which would be out of reach after the inertia reel is locked. If aircraft hits before the inertia reel is locked, the automatic lock will function on impact.

If the gear cannot be extended, use the foregoing procedure and land wheels-up. Make a normal approach using power and flaps as required to provide a slightly nose high attitude, but not fully stalled. Touch down in this attitude and as soon as the aircraft has stopped, get clear at once.

Gear-up landings should be accomplished preferably on hard surface, since soft ground or sod tends to roll up into chunks, damaging the underside of the fuselage.

LANDING WITH NOSE GEAR RETRACTED.
1. Canopy position — open.
2. Throttle — CLOSED.
3. Mixture lever — IDLE CUT-OFF.
4. Elevator trim tab wheel — full nose down.
5. Ignition switch — OFF.
6. Battery switch — OFF.
7. Generator switch — OFF.
8. Fuel selector valve handle — OFF.

Should the nose gear fail to extend, make a normal approach and landing. After touching main wheels down, hold the nose up as long as possible with full back stick and initiate the foregoing procedure before the nose settles onto the ground. Get clear of the aircraft as soon as it stops.

LANDING ON UNPREPARED RUNWAY.
Landing procedure for unprepared strips is similar to normal landing on paved runways, except that if the surface is very rough, touch down as smoothly as possible to minimize shock loads on the landing gear. If feasible, avoid using full flaps on loose gravel, as particles thrown up by the wheels would damage flaps. Use brakes with caution on soft or uncertain ground, to prevent digging the nose wheel into the ground. Observe the additional precautions noted in AFTER LANDING, Section II.

LANDING WITH FLAT TIRE.
A flat tire on a main wheel will act as a brake when on the ground, tending to turn the aircraft into the flat. Touch down well over to the opposite side of the runway to allow room for a swerve and hold directional control with opposite brake. A flat nose wheel tire will reduce nose wheel stability and hard applications of brake should be avoided. After landing with a flat tire, park the aircraft clear of the runway and shut down the engine; do not taxi in with a flat tire.

LANDING WITH BRAKE FAILURE.
If brake failure is suspected, land the aircraft as short as possible using full flaps and holding up the nose wheel to shorten the landing roll. Lose as much speed as possible on the landing roll, then clear the runway, shut down the engine and stop; turning onto rough ground if necessary.

CAUTION

Do not taxi without brakes. Call the tower operator and request a tow to move the aircraft into maintenance.

LANDING WITH ONE MAIN GEAR RETRACTED.

Due to the design of the gear actuation system, all gear being extended and retracted through push rods from a single actuator, failure of one gear to extend is very unlikely. Should a break in the linkage occur, the affected gear will usually drop to the extended position. If at any time one gear position indicator fails to indicate gear fully extended, have the gear position checked visually by another pilot or by the control tower on a fly-by. If it is verified that one gear is not fully extended, attempt to retract all gear and make a gear up landing.

If all gear cannot be retracted, make a normal approach with full flaps and power on, to reduce landing speed to a minimum, carrying the wing slightly lower on the down and locked side. Touch down smoothly on the down and locked main gear, holding the opposite wing up with aileron as long as possible after nose wheel touches down. As soon as the down and locked gear touches down, proceed as follows:

1. Canopy position — open.

2. Throttle — CLOSED.
3. Mixture lever — IDLE CUT-OFF.
4. Fuel selector valve handle — OFF.
5. Ignition switch — OFF.
6. Battery switch — OFF.
7. Generator switch — OFF.

As wing tip strikes the ground, apply opposite brake hard. Get clear of the aircraft as soon as it stops.

EMERGENCY ENTRANCE.

Both canopies can be removed from the outside in an emergency, (figure 3-6), by means of an external canopy emergency release handle on the right side of the fuselage, just below the forward end of the front canopy rail. Pulling the handle out releases both sets of canopy rails from the fuselage and both assemblies can then be removed.

DITCHING.

Since all survival equipment carried will be personal equipment, there is usually no reason to

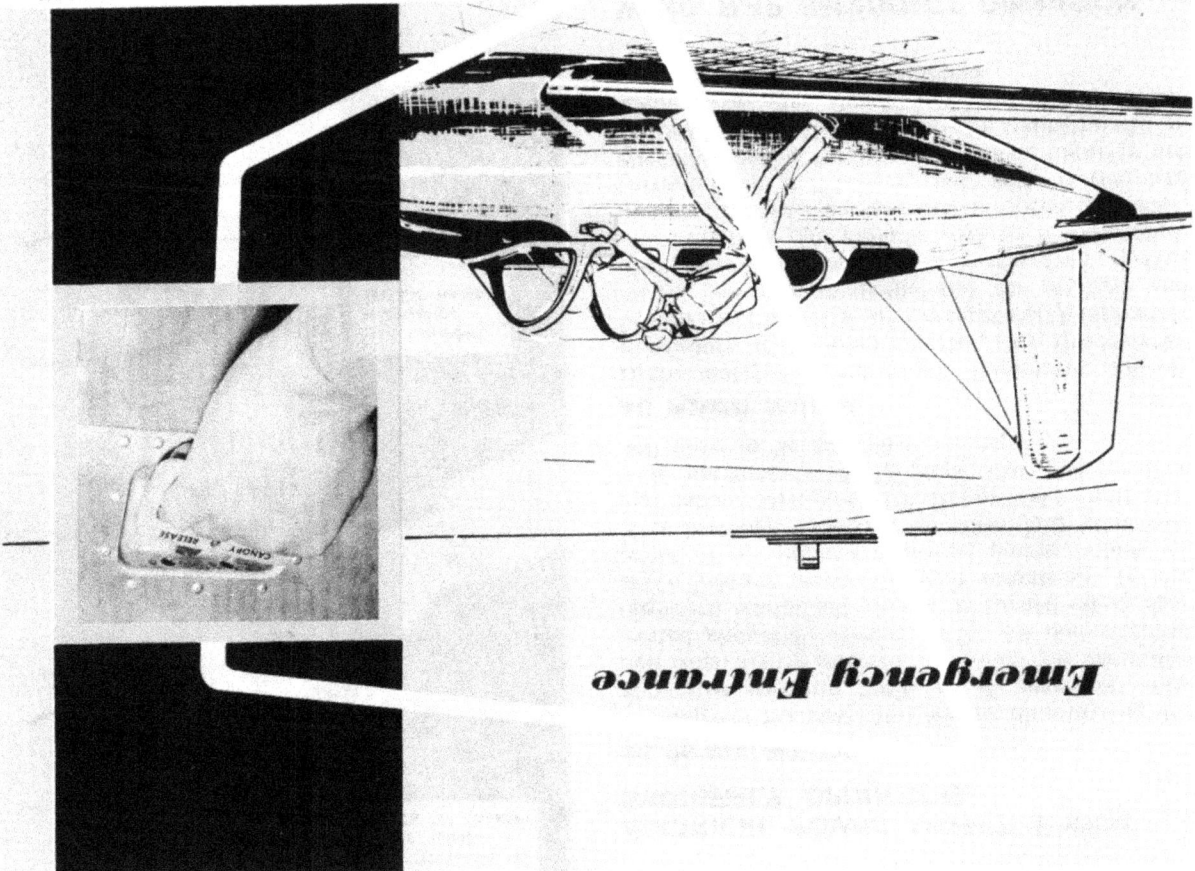

Figure 3-6

Canopy Jettison Procedure

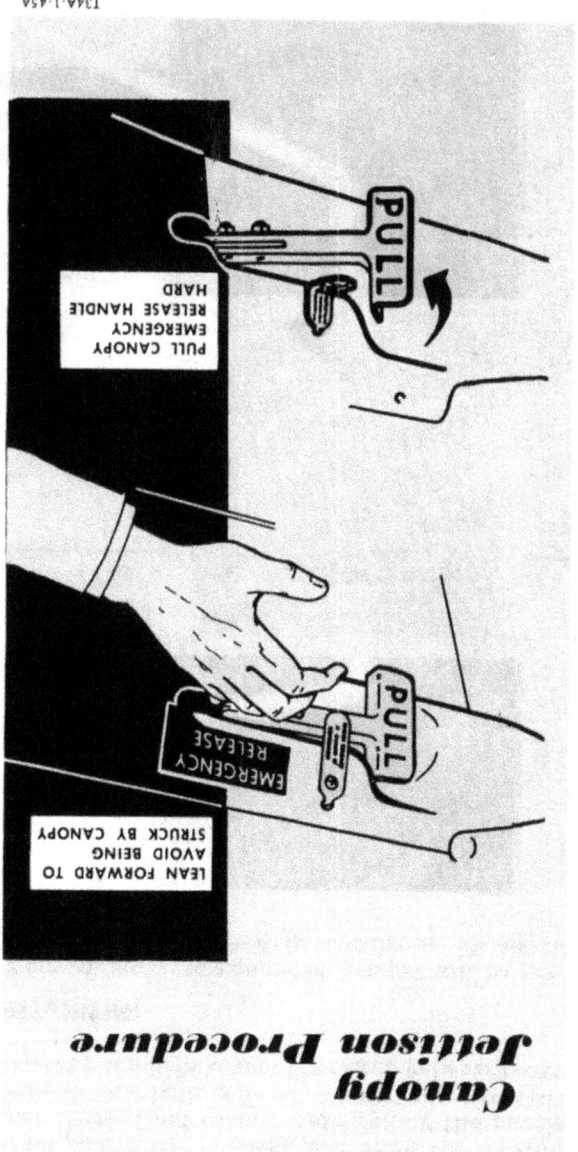

Figure 3-7

ditch the aircraft; a bail-out is preferable. If, for some reason, ditching is necessary, use the radio distress procedure and plan to touch down before all fuel is exhausted, to have power for a controlled approach.

1. Landing gear handle — check UP.
2. Canopy position — open.
3. Battery switch — OFF.
4. Safety belt — fastened.
5. Life raft or life preserver — check.
6. Wing flap lever — DOWN.

Make normal approach with power, if possible, and flare out to normal landing attitude. Approach stall attitude at a speed at which full control of aircraft can be maintained. Unless wind is high or sea is rough, plan approach heading parallel to any uniform swell pattern and try to touch down along wave crest just after crest passes. If wind is as high as 25 knots or surface is irregular, the best procedure is to approach into the wind and touch down on falling side of wave. Just before touchdown:

7. Ignition switch — OFF.
8. Inertia reel — LOCKED.

Get clear of the aircraft as soon as it comes to rest, since it may stay afloat only a few seconds. Stay near the site of the ditching if possible, to aid search personnel in rescue efforts.

FUEL SYSTEM EMERGENCY OPERATION.

FUEL PUMP FAILURE.

If the engine-driven fuel pump fails, fuel can be supplied to the engine by turning on the electrically-driven booster pump in the tank being used. The booster pump provides sufficient pressure for all normal engine operation in flight.

ELECTRICAL POWER SUPPLY SYSTEM EMERGENCY OPERATION.

DC POWER FAILURE.

If failure of the generator occurs, illuminating the generator warning light, or if generator voltage consistently exceeds 30 volts, the generator switch should be turned OFF. All non-essential electrical equipment should be turned off to conserve battery power for gear extension. In the event of a complete electrical power failure, or if it becomes necessary to turn both generator and battery switches OFF, the primary flight attitude instruments will be inoperative and the gear will have to be extended manually.

AC POWER FAILURE.

If the inverter warning light illuminates, indicating failure of the main inverter, turn the inverter switch to STANDBY. If the light still illuminates, no ac power is available and the attitude and directional indicators will be inoperative. Instrument flight is still possible with ac power failure by using the rate instruments (airspeed, altimeter, turn-and-slip indicators), but with a complete electrical power failure, instrument flight is not advisable, since the turn-and-slip indicator will be inoperative. See figure 1-15 for a list of the electrically operated equipment.

WING FLAP EMERGENCY OPERATION.

No emergency operation of the wing flaps is provided.

Landing Gear Emergency Operation.

Landing Gear Emergency Retraction.

To retract the landing gear on the ground in an emergency, move the landing gear emergency retract switch UP.

NOTE

The landing gear emergency retract switch is guarded in the DOWN position with a safety wired guard. To operate the switch, break the safety wire by forcing the guard up.

Landing Gear Emergency Extension.

Procedure to follow in lowering the gear manually is shown in figure 3-8. Exercise care to fully engage the clutch knob before attempting to crank the gear down.

NOTE

If electrical power is available, continue extension until gear position indicators show all gear fully extended; if all electrical power is off, the gear position indicators will be inoperative and the crank should be operated until it cannot be moved further.

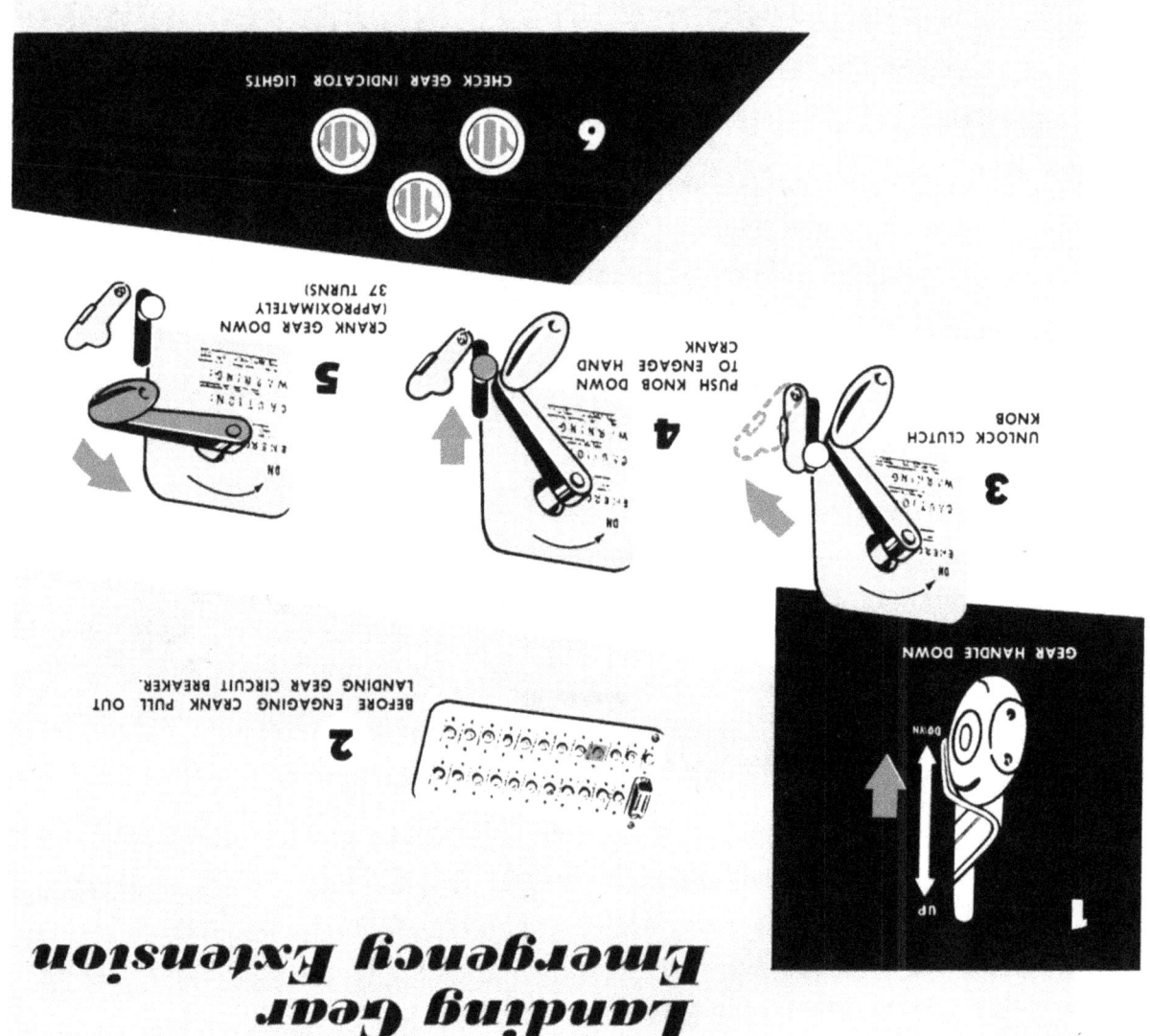

Landing Gear Emergency Extension

1. GEAR HANDLE DOWN

2. BEFORE ENGAGING CRANK PULL OUT LANDING GEAR CIRCUIT BREAKER.

3. UNLOCK CLUTCH KNOB

4. PUSH KNOB DOWN TO ENGAGE HAND CRANK

5. CRANK GEAR DOWN (APPROXIMATELY 37 TURNS)

6. CHECK GEAR INDICATOR LIGHTS

Figure 3-8

T34A-1-46A

Blank

T-34A – CONDENSED CHECK LIST EMERGENCY PROCEDURES

ENGINE FAILURE.
ENGINE FAILURE DURING TAKE-OFF
(Prior to becoming airborne).
1. Throttle — CLOSED.
2. Brakes — apply.
3. Canopy position — open.
4. Mixture lever — IDLE CUT-OFF.
5. Fuel selector valve handle — OFF.
6. Ignition switch — OFF.
7. Battery switch — OFF.
8. Generator switch — OFF.

ENGINE FAILURE DURING TAKE-OFF
(after becoming airborne).
1. Glide — establish.
2. Canopy position — open.
3. Mixture lever — IDLE CUT-OFF.
4. Fuel selector valve handle — OFF.
5. Ignition switch — OFF.
6. Battery switch — OFF.
7. Generator switch — OFF.

ENGINE FAILURE DURING FLIGHT.
Partial Power Failure:
1. Airspeed — maintain 90 knots.
2. Fuel selector valve handle — switch tanks.
3. Fuel booster pump switch — ON (appropriate tank).

T.O. 1T-34A-1
10 February 1958

1

4. Throttle — advance ½ inch beyond present setting.
5. Mixture lever — FULL RICH.
6. Propeller lever — FULL INCREASE.
7. Ignition switch — check BOTH.
8. Battery switch — check ON.
9. Generator switch — check ON.
10. Carburetor heat handle — climatic.

If Complete Engine Failure Is Encountered, Proceed as Follows:

11. Airspeed — Maintain 90 knots.

Attempt to Restart Engine if Altitude Permits:

12. Mixture lever — IDLE CUT-OFF.
13. Fuel selector valve handle — OFF.
14. Throttle — FULL OPEN.
15. Fuel selector valve handle — ON (fullest tank).
16. Fuel booster pump switch — ON.
17. Throttle — ¼ inch OPEN.
18. Mixture lever — FULL RICH.
19. Primer switch — ON (intermittently as required to start engine).
    a. If engine fires, primer switch — ON (as required to reach field).

If Engine Fails to Restart:

20. Mixture lever — IDLE CUT-OFF.
21. Throttle — CLOSED.
22. Ignition switch — OFF.
23. Fuel selector valve handle — OFF.
24. All switches — OFF.
25. Shoulder harness — locked.

T.O. 1T-34A-1
10 February 1958

2

SIMULATED FORCED LANDING.
1. Throttle — CLOSED.
2. Glide — establish 90 knots IAS.
3. Fuel selector valve handle — switch tanks.
4. Fuel pressure gage — check.
5. Wing flaps — up (lever — NEUTRAL).
6. Mixture lever — FULL RICH.
7. Propeller lever — FULL INCREASE.
8. Landing gear handle — UP.
9. Shoulder harness — locked.
10. Trim — as necessary.

FORCED LANDING.
1. Canopy position — open.
2. Throttle — CLOSED.
3. Glide — establish — 90 knots IAS.
4. Fuel selector valve handle — OFF.
5. Fuel booster pump switch — OFF.
6. Wing flap lever — UP.
7. Mixture lever — IDLE CUT-OFF.
8. Propeller lever — FULL DECREASE.
9. Landing gear switch — UP.
10. Ignition switch — OFF.
11. Battery switch — OFF.
12. Generator switch — OFF.
13. Shoulder harness — locked.
14. Trim — as necessary.

PROPELLER FAILURE.
1. Throttle — CLOSED.
2. Pitch attitude — increase.
3. Propeller lever — FULL DECREASE.

T.O. 1T-34A-1
10 February 1958

3

If Propeller Is Uncontrollable:
    4. Wing flap lever — DOWN.
    5. Airspeed — approximately 60 knots.

FIRE.

FIRE DURING ENGINE START.

If Fire Is Other Than Exhaust or Induction — Discontinue Starting Attempt.
    1. Mixture lever — IDLE CUT-OFF.
    2. Battery switch — OFF.
    3. Ignition switch — OFF.
    4. Generator switch — OFF.

If Fire Is Exhaust or Induction — Continue Starting Attempt; if Fire Persists:
    1. Mixture lever — IDLE CUT-OFF.
    2. Throttle — FULL OPEN, continue cranking.
    3. Fuel control valve handle — OFF.
    4. Ignition switch — OFF.
    5. Starter switch — OFF.
    6. Battery switch — OFF.
    7. Generator switch — OFF.

ENGINE FIRE DURING FLIGHT.
    1. Mixture lever — IDLE CUT-OFF.
    2. Fuel selector valve handle — OFF.
    3. Ignition switch — OFF.
    4. Battery switch — OFF.
    5. Throttle — CLOSED.

FUSELAGE FIRE IN FLIGHT.
    1. Canopy position — closed.
    2. Cockpit air handles — FULL OUT.
    3. Battery switch — OFF.
    4. Generator switch — OFF.

T.O. 1T-34A-1
10 February 1958

4

ELECTRICAL FIRE.
1. Battery switch — OFF.
2. Generator switch — OFF.
3. All electrical equipment — OFF.
4. All circuit breakers — OUT.

SMOKE AND FUME ELIMINATION.
1. Cockpit cold air handle — IN.
2. Cockpit hot air handle — OUT.
3. Canopy position — open.

BAIL OUT.
1. Wing flap lever — DOWN.
2. Canopy — open or jettison.
3. Seats — full up.
4. Safety belt and shoulder harness — unfastened.
5. Headset — remove.

LANDING EMERGENCIES (Except ditching).

GEAR UP LANDING.
1. Canopy position — open.
2. Wing flap lever — DOWN.
3. Throttle — CLOSED.
4. Mixture lever — IDLE CUT-OFF.
5. Fuel selector valve handle — OFF.
6. Ignition switch — OFF.
7. Battery switch — OFF.
8. Generator switch — OFF.
9. Inertia reel — LOCKED.

T.O. 1T-34A-1
10 February 1958

5

LANDING WITH ONE MAIN GEAR RETRACTED.
1. Canopy position — open.
2. Throttle — CLOSED.
3. Mixture lever — IDLE CUT-OFF.
4. Fuel selector valve handle — OFF.
5. Ignition switch — OFF.
6. Battery switch — OFF.
7. Generator switch — OFF.

LANDING WITH NOSE GEAR RETRACTED.
1. Canopy position — open.
2. Throttle — CLOSED.
3. Mixture lever — IDLE CUT-OFF.
4. Elevator trim tab wheel — full nose down.
5. Ignition switch — OFF.
6. Battery switch — OFF.
7. Generator switch — OFF.
8. Fuel selector valve handle — OFF.

DITCHING.
1. Landing gear handle — check UP.
2. Canopy position — open.
3. Battery switch — OFF.
4. Safety belt — fastened.
5. Life raft or life preserver — check.
6. Wing flap lever — DOWN.
7. Ignition switch — OFF.
8. Inertia reel — LOCKED.

T.O. 1T-34A-1
10 February 1958

6

Section 4

Description and Operation of Auxiliary Equipment

TABLE OF CONTENTS

Heating and Ventilation System	4-1
Pitot Heat	4-3
Communications and Associated Electronic Equipment	4-4
Exterior Lighting	4-5
Interior Lighting	4-6
Instrument Flying Hood	4-7
Baggage Compartment	4-7
Miscellaneous Equipment	4-7

HEATING AND VENTILATION SYSTEM.

Air for cockpit heating and ventilation and for windshield defogging (figure 4-1) is supplied by a system of ducts, obtaining heated air from shrouds around each of two exhaust collectors and ventilating air from an intake in each wing leading edge. Air heated in passing through the exhaust shrouds is directed through two manually controlled three-way valves, which regulate the flow of heated air reaching the cockpit by dividing the airflow and dumping excess air overboard. Ventilating air from the wing intakes enters the duct system at mixing valves designed to prevent the ram effect from forcing unheated air back through the hot air ducts. The hot air valves and mixing valves are separately controlled from the front cockpit. Air enters the cockpits through two adjustable air outlets (figure 4-1) on each cockpit sidewall and a foot warmer outlet located in the lower left hand section of the front cockpit and in the lower right hand section of the rear cockpit, adjacent to the rudder pedals. A part of the airflow to the cockpits is directed to an outlet below the windshield, for defogging

HEATING AND VENTILATION SYSTEM CONTROLS.

Cockpit Cold Air Handle.

The cockpit cold air handle is located on the right subpanel (10, figure 1-7) in the front cockpit only. With the handle pulled full OUT, all air flow is cut off. Pushing the handle full IN opens the mixing valve and allows fresh air to enter the cockpits. The proper amount of air can be controlled by placing the handle in any intermediate position between full IN and full OUT. Rotating the handle clockwise, locks it in position.

Cockpit Hot Air Handle.

The cockpit hot air handle is located on the right subpanel, adjacent to the cold air handle (9, figure 1-7), in the front cockpit only. With the hot air handle full OUT, all hot air flow from the engine compartment is shut off. Pushing the handle full IN opens the mixture valves and allows warm air

Section IV T.O. 1T-34A-1

Heating and Ventilation System

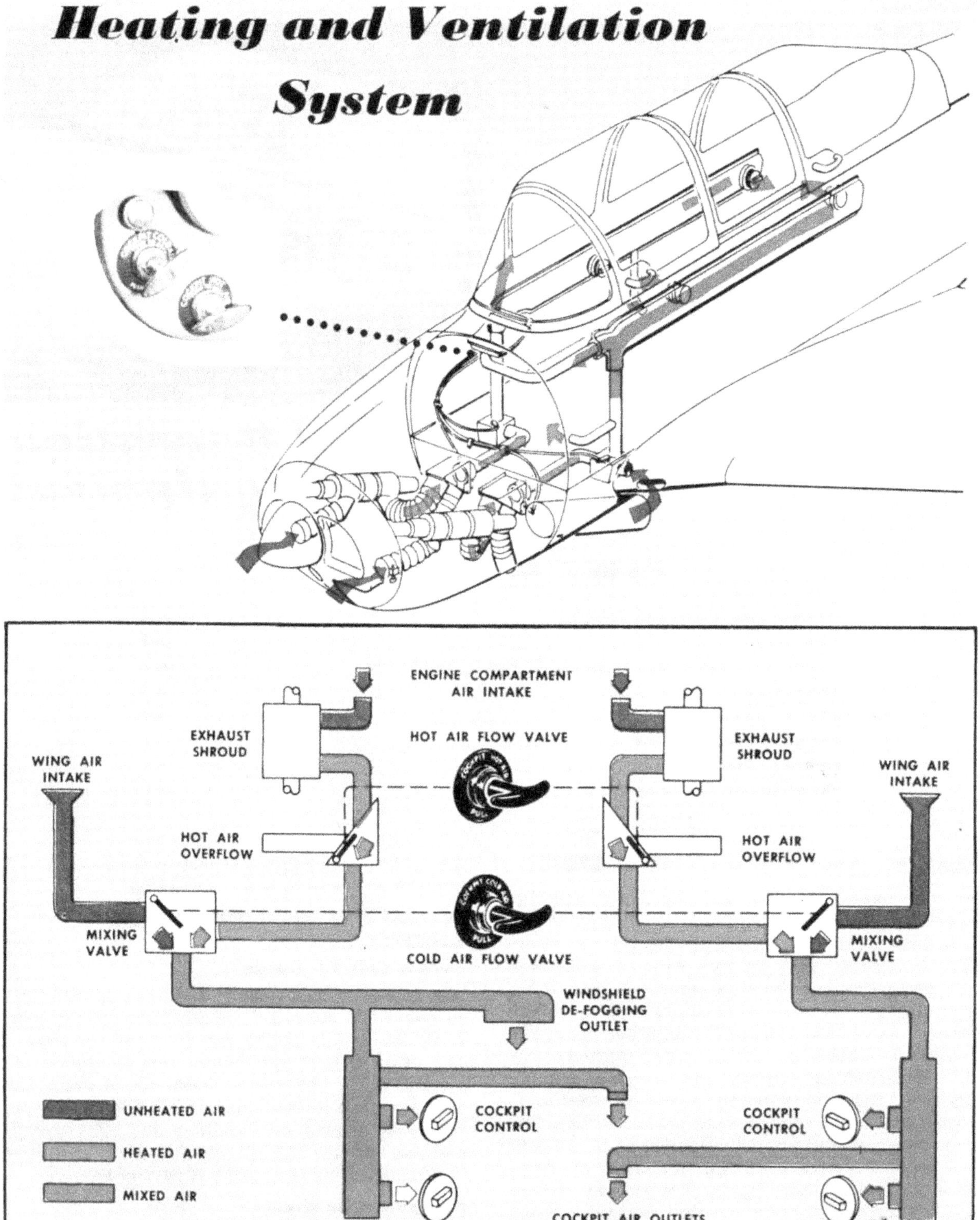

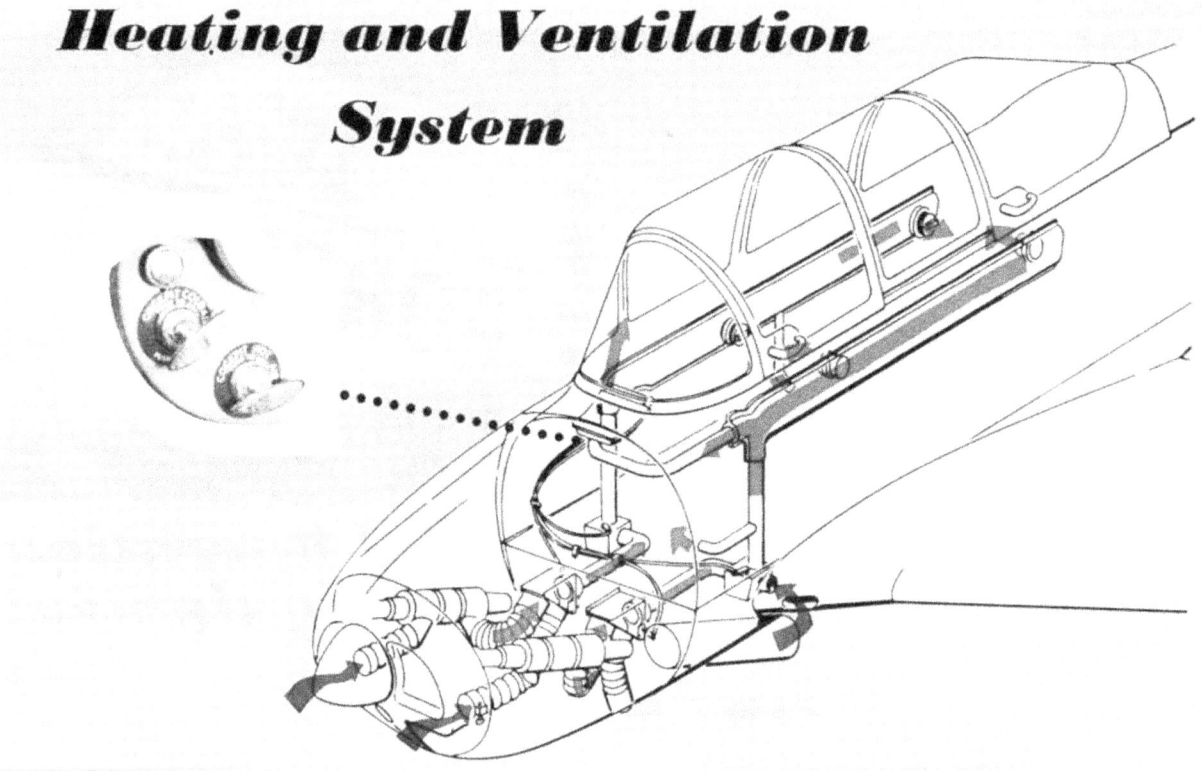

Figure 4-1

Communication and Associated Electronic Equipment

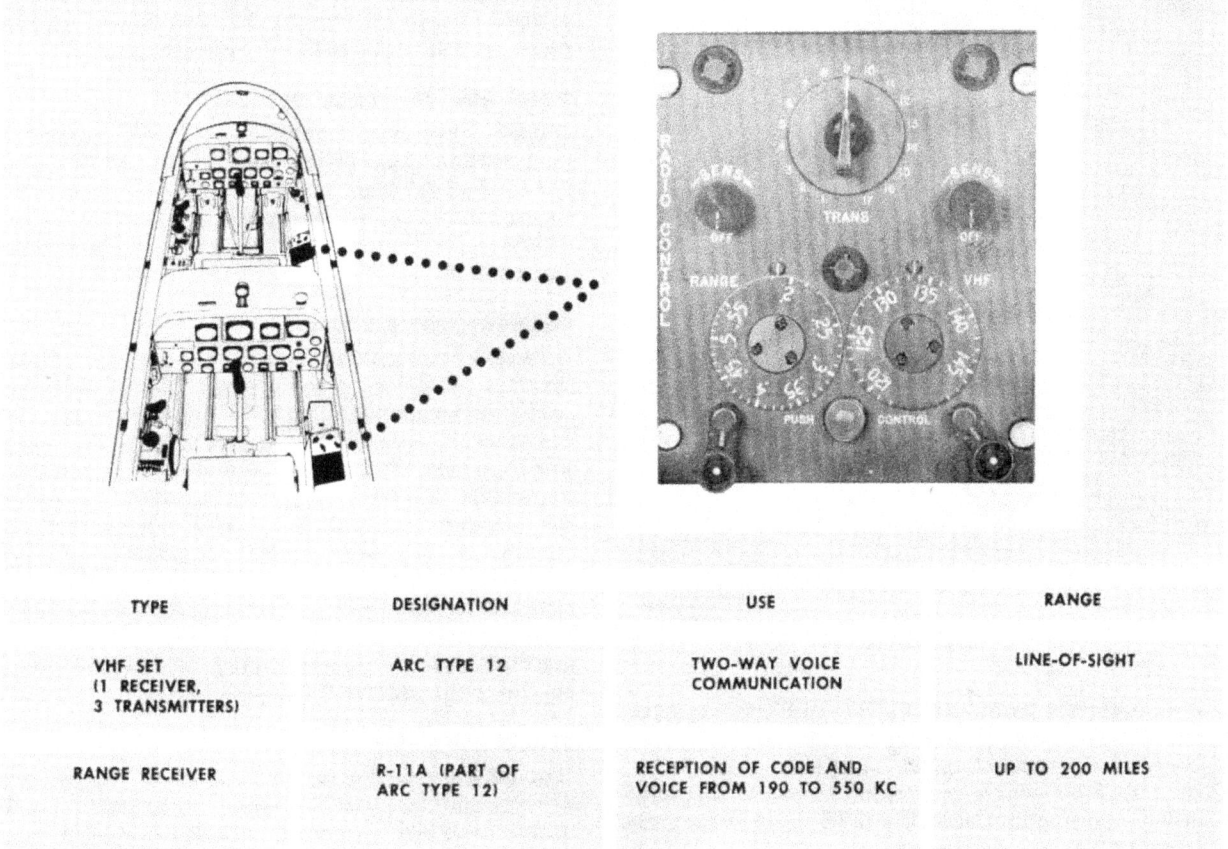

TYPE	DESIGNATION	USE	RANGE
VHF SET (1 RECEIVER, 3 TRANSMITTERS)	ARC TYPE 12	TWO-WAY VOICE COMMUNICATION	LINE-OF-SIGHT
RANGE RECEIVER	R-11A (PART OF ARC TYPE 12)	RECEPTION OF CODE AND VOICE FROM 190 TO 550 KC	UP TO 200 MILES

Figure 4-2

to enter the cockpit. Any desired amount of warm air may be obtained by placing the hot air handle in any intermediate position between full IN and full OUT.

Rotating the handle clockwise, locks it in position. A combination of warm and cold air may be obtained by pushing both hot and cold air handles in until a satisfactory airflow and temperature is obtained.

No separate control is provided for windshield defogging. The windshield outlet receives its air from the left-hand heating system and is dependent on positioning of the cockpit air handles as to temperature and quantity of air. The air outlet diffusers may be turned to direct the airflow into the cockpits as desired, but there is no ON or OFF position.

No separate control or diffuser exists for the foot warmers.

PITOT HEAT.

Heat for the pitot tube is furnished by an electrically operated heating element located inside the pitot tube head. Electrical power for the operation is supplied directly from the main dc bus.

CAUTION

The pitot heater should not be operated on the ground since the absence of airstream may cause the unit to overheat.

PITOT HEATER SWITCH.

The electric heater in the pitot tube is controlled

Interphone and Transmitter Buttons

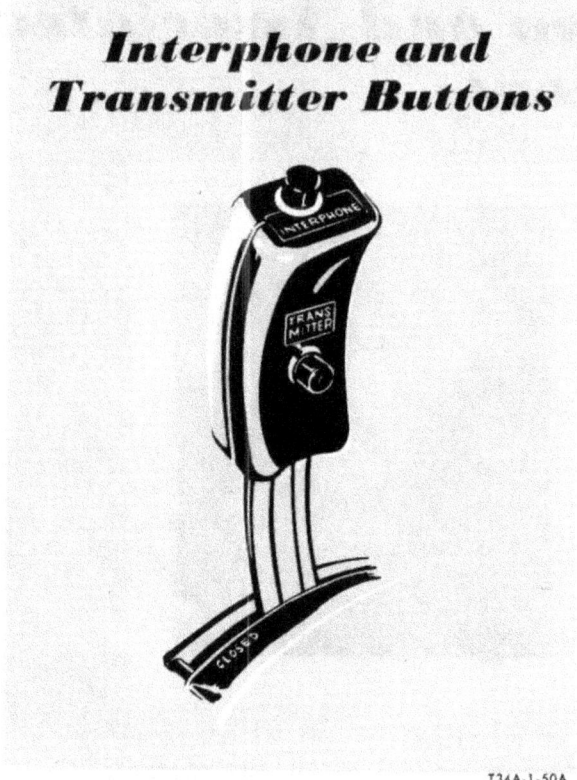

Figure 4-3

by a 5-ampere two-position, ON-OFF, switch-type circuit breaker on the main circuit breaker panel (figure 1-16) located on the right side of the front cockpit. This switch receives power from the main dc bus and is guarded in the OFF position to prevent inadvertent operation.

COMMUNICATIONS AND ASSOCIATED ELECTRONIC EQUIPMENT.

Communications equipment installed in this aircraft includes three VHF transmitters, a VHF receiver, a low-frequency range receiver and interphone. The equipment is part of Radio Set ARC type 12. The VHF signal is received by a rod type antenna located on the belly, aft of the rear cockpit (9, figure 1-2) while the range receiver utilizes a fixed wire antenna which extends from the vertical stabilizer to the fuselage (1, figure 1-2). Electrical power for the operation of all radio equipment, either dc type current or the ac type furnished by dynamotors, is supplied directly from the main dc bus.

TABLE OF COMMUNICATIONS AND ASSOCIATED ELECTRONIC EQUIPMENT.

All equipment installed is tabulated in figure 4-2.

RADIO SWITCH.

The radio switch, labeled RADIO (12, figure 1-9) and located on the right console in the front cockpit, must be turned ON before it is possible to operate any radio equipment. With the switch in the ON position, it is possible to operate the radio equipment with either of two identical radio control panels (11, figure 1-9 and figure 4-2) located on the right side of each cockpit.

PUSH FOR CONTROL BUTTON.

A push for control button (figure 4-2), located on each radio control panel, may be pressed to transfer control to that panel. A red indicator light, located adjacent to the push for control button (figure 4-2) illuminates when that particular panel has control.

TRANSMITTER BUTTON.

A transmitter button is located in the side of each throttle handgrip (figure 4-3). The transmitter switches inside both throttle handgrips are tied together electrically by a bus bar in the radio junction box. This allows either pilot to transmit regardless of which cockpit is in control, however, the cockpit which is in control selects the frequency of the transmitter. Headsets with attached lip microphones are installed in both cockpits and are plugged in a jack on the front of each seat bottom. Jacks for plugging in hand-held microphones are also installed in the jack-boxes on the right side of both cockpits.

INTERPHONE BUTTON.

The interphone button is located on top of each throttle handgrip (figure 4-3). Interphone operation is provided by simply pressing the interphone button at any time when the radio switch and VHF transmitter is turned on. Interphone operation utilizes the VHF circuits and no separate interphone amplifier is required.

VHF COMMUNICATIONS EQUIPMENT.

Two way VHF voice communication is provided by three transmitters providing for fifteen preset channels in the frequency range from 116 to 148 megacycles and a receiver continuously tunable from 115 to 148 megacycles. The channel selector switch and receiver tuning dial are on the control panel (figure 4-2) with a receiver sens knob adjacent to the tuning dial. The sens knob provides a means for volume control or turning the unit ON or OFF.

Operation of the VHF Communications Equipment.

NOTE

No transmission will be made on emergency (distress) frequency channels except for emergency purposes. For test, demonstration, or drill purposes, the radio equipment will be operated in a shielded room to prevent transmission of messages that could be construed as actual emergency messages.

1. Turn the radio switch ON and rotate the sens knob, for the VHF receiver, clockwise from OFF. Select transmitting frequency by rotating the channel selector knob to the desired channel, allowing one minute for warm-up.

2. If the red light adjacent to the push for control button does not illuminate, press the push for control button. The light should then illuminate.

3. If simultaneous reception is not desired, rotate the range receiver sens knob counterclockwise to OFF.

4. Rotate the receiver tuning dial to the desired frequency and adjust the sens knob for the desired volume.

5. To transmit, press the transmitter button on the side of the throttle. Release the button after transmission is completed to restore receiver operation.

NOTE

If a hand-held microphone is used, press the button on the microphone instead of the throttle transmitter button.

6. To turn the equipment off, move the radio switch to OFF position.

RADIO RANGE RECEIVER (R-11A).

The range receiver is continuously tunable between 190 and 550 kilocycles (0.19 and 0.55 megacycles), providing reception of all low-frequency radio range stations and control towers. Receiver tuning dial and sens knob are on the control panel.

Operation of Range Receiver.

1. Turn the radio switch ON and rotate the sens knob for the range receiver clockwise from OFF, allowing one minute for warm-up.

2. If the red light adjacent to the push for control button does not illuminate, push the push for control button. The light should then illuminate.

3. Select receiver frequency with tuning dial.

4. Adjust volume with the range receiver sens knob.

EXTERIOR LIGHTING.

Exterior lighting includes a recessed landing light in the leading edge of each wing panel, a red passing light in the nose, navigation lights on the wing tips and tail cone and exterior gear down indicator lights located next to each main gear wheel well for ground observation of the landing gear position. Exterior lighting is controlled from the front cockpit only. Electrical power for operation of the exterior lighting is furnished directly from the main dc bus.

LANDING LIGHT SWITCHES.

The left and right landing lights operate off of the aircraft's dc electrical system and are turned off and on by two switches (14 and 15, figure 1-8 and figure 4-4) located on the left console in the front cockpit only. Each switch is guarded to preclude the possibility of inadvertent operation and has three placarded positions; ON, OFF and MC ON (momentary contact). When in the MC ON position, the switch is spring loaded to OFF. The landing light circuit is protected by a 20 ampere circuit breaker located on the main circuit breaker panel (figure 1-16) on the right side of the front cockpit.

PASSING LIGHT SWITCH.

The passing light operates directly from the aircraft's dc electrical system and is controlled by a two position ON-OFF toggle switch (13, figure 1-9 and figure 4-4) on the right side of the front cockpit only. The passing light circuit is protected by a 5-ampere circuit breaker located on the main circuit breaker panel (figure 1-16) on the right side of the front cockpit.

NAVIGATION LIGHTS SWITCH.

The navigation lights are operated by power from the dc electrical system and are controlled by a three position switch (15, figure 1-9 and figure 4-4) located on the right side of the front cockpit just below the landing gear emergency handcrank. This switch is placarded FLASH-OFF-STEADY and provides for operation corresponding to its position. Should the flasher unit fail, the lights will automatically revert to steady operation. The navigation lights circuit is protected by a 10-ampere circuit breaker located on the main circuit breaker panel (figure 1-16) on the right side of the front cockpit.

NAVIGATION LIGHTS INTENSITY SWITCH.

The navigation lights intensity switch (14, figure 1-9 and figure 4-4) is located on the right side of the front cockpit, adjacent to the passing light switch. This switch is placarded DIM-BRIGHT and is used to control the brilliancy of the navigation lights.

EXTERNAL GEAR-DOWN INDICATOR LIGHTS SWITCH.

The external gear-down indicator lights switch is an integral part of the landing gear limit and dynamic brake switch located beneath the floor

Section IV

T.O. 1T-34A-1

Lighting Controls

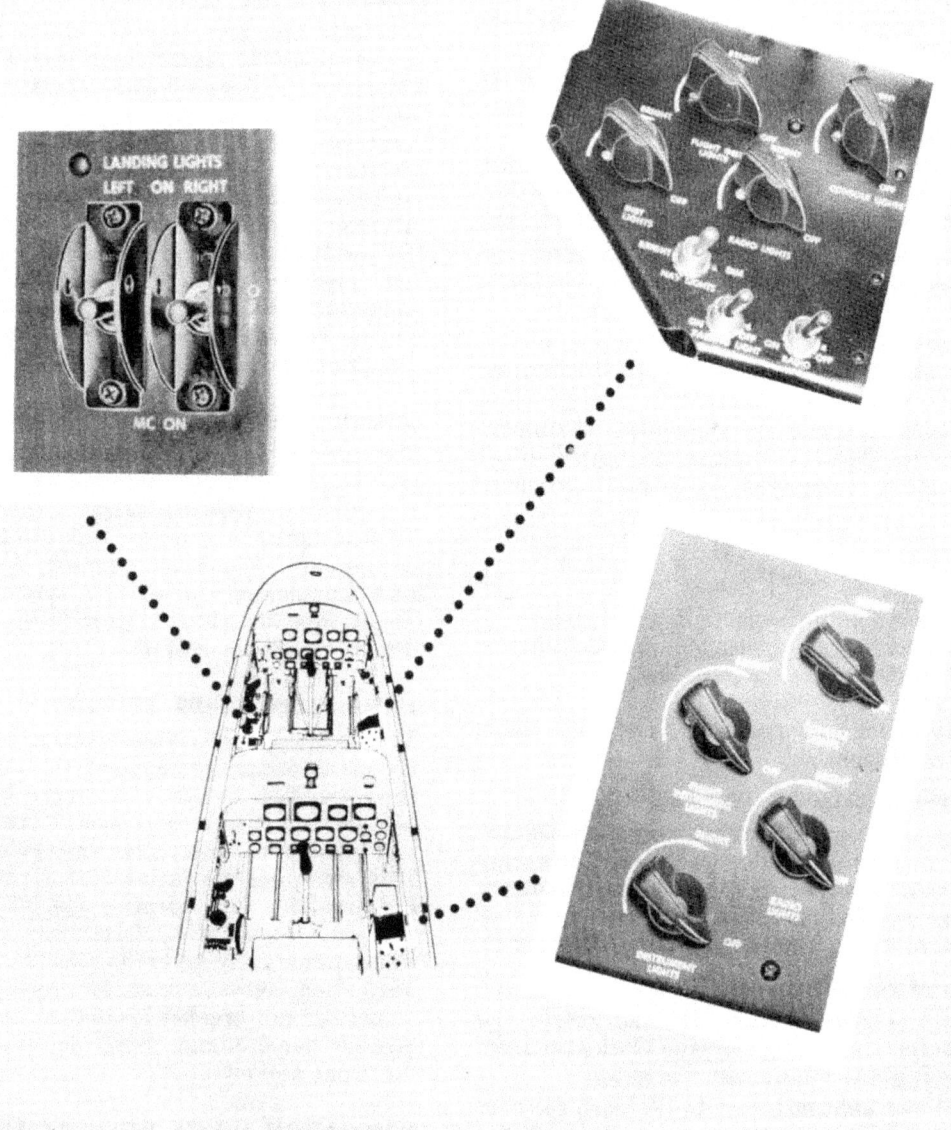

Figure 4-4

boards. The switch is normally open and with the gear in the down position the light circuit is closed. To prevent the lights from illuminating at all times when the main gears are down, the switch is electrically connected to the navigation lights switch, therefore, with the navigation lights switch in either the FLASH or STEADY position, the external gear-down indicator lights will illuminate when the main gears are fully extended.

INTERIOR LIGHTING.

Interior lighting in both cockpits is identical and each cockpit is equipped as follows: all instru-

4-6

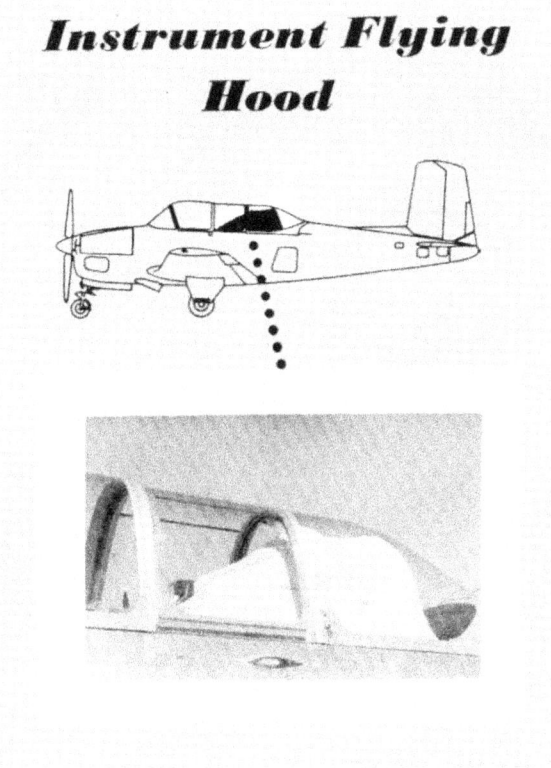

Figure 4-5

ments are individually lighted, a light is installed over each console, a utility light is installed on the right sidewall and the instrument panel check list and radio control panel are edge-lighted. Electrical power for the operation of the interior lighting is supplied by the main dc bus.

INTERIOR LIGHTING CONTROL RHEOSTATS.

Four rheostats (figure 4-4) are located on the right console in each cockpit. These rheostats control all lighting in the cockpit except the utility light, which has a switch integral with its case. Each rheostat is placarded to indicate which lighting circuit within the cockpit that it controls. Turning the rheostats clockwise from the OFF position first turns the lights on dim and then progressively increases them to full brilliance. The check list edge lighting is controlled by either the console lights rheostat or by the radio light rheostat. Radio panel lighting is independent of radio controls.

INSTRUMENT FLYING HOOD.

The rear cockpit incorporates an instrument flying hood for student instrument flight training (figure 4-5). The instrument flying hood can be hooked up and unhooked manually from the rear cockpit but can be unhooked mechanically from the front cockpit only. When released, the hood is spring loaded to position itself above and aft of the rear cockpit seat.

INSTRUMENT FLYING HOOD RELEASE.

The instrument flying hood release is located on the left hand side of the front cockpit (2, figure 1-8) just below the canopy track. Pushing the release forward, allows the hood to return to its position behind and above the rear cockpit seat.

BAGGAGE COMPARTMENT.

The baggage compartment (figure 4-6) is located behind the rear cockpit and is accessible through a door on the left side of the fuselage. For baggage compartment loading limitations, refer to Section V.

MISCELLANEOUS EQUIPMENT.

The following miscellaneous equipment is installed in the aircraft: a rear-view mirror in each cockpit, map case and flight report holder in the front cockpit integral with the left and right sidewalls, respectively, and a relief tube under each seat.

Figure 4-6

Blank

Section 5

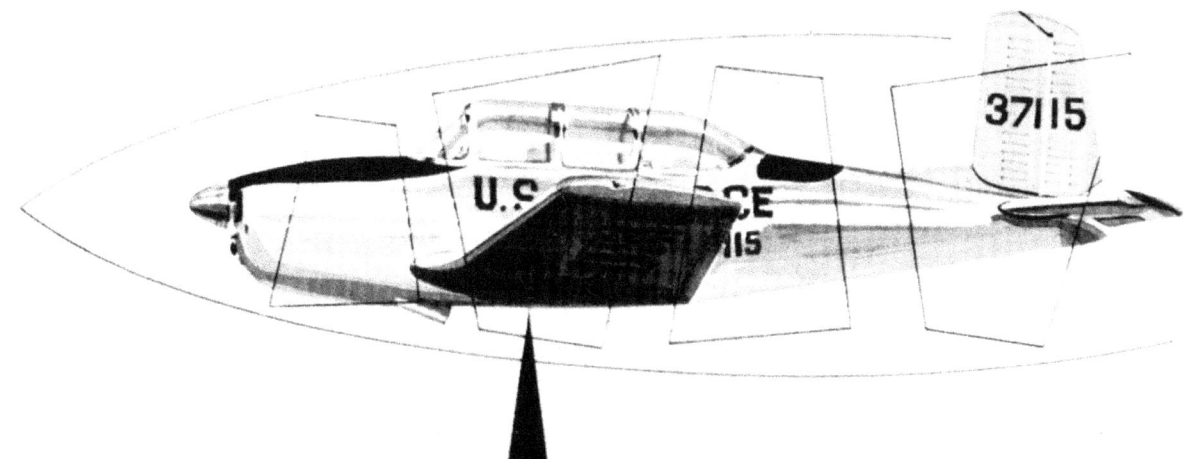

Operating Limitations

TABLE OF CONTENTS

General Limitations	5-1
Minimum Crew	5-1
Engine Limitations	5-1
Propeller Limitations	5-1
Airspeed Limitations	5-4
Prohibited Maneuvers	5-5
Acceleration Limits	5-5
Operating Flight Strength	5-5
Center-of-Gravity Limitations	5-5
Loading Limitations	5-5
Gross Weight Limitations	5-5

GENERAL LIMITATIONS.

Most operating limitations are covered by the instrument markings shown in figure 5-1. Other limitations and conditions contributing to their requirements are discussed in the following paragraphs:

MINIMUM CREW.

The aircraft can be safely and efficiently operated by one pilot, however, since all controls are not duplicated in the rear cockpit, solo flight must be made from the front cockpit only.

ENGINE LIMITATIONS.

Engine operating limitations are illustrated in figure 5-1, no additional engine dive overspeed limitation is allowed. If airspeed is maintained within limits, propeller control range is adequate to prevent overspeed. The engine is not to be operated at speeds below 1600 rpm, with power on, to preclude excessive B.M.E.P. The engine overspeed limitation is 2760 rpm. Operation between 2760 to 3120 rpm — engine shall be inspected. Operation above 3120 rpm — engine shall be removed. Enter any overspeed occurrence in DD Form 781.

PROPELLER LIMITATIONS.

Propeller limitations for the aircraft are confined to propeller overspeed, which is defined as not exceeding 3500 rpm at any time. This 3500 rpm limitation, although it exceeds the 2760 rpm overspeed limitation of the engine, is to be observed. Overspeed beyond engine limits and above 3500 rpm will result in the need for replacement of both the propeller and the engine.

5-1

Section V T.O. 1T-34A-1

Instrument Markings

OIL TEMPERATURE

▬ 40° C — MINIMUM FOR FLIGHT
▬ 40° C TO 107° C — NORMAL OPERATING RANGE
▬ 107° C — MAXIMUM

BASED ON FUEL GRADE 80

MANIFOLD PRESSURE

▬ 15-29.6 IN. HG — NORMAL RANGE
▬ 29.6 IN. HG — MAXIMUM (METO)
   (FULL THROTTLE)

TACHOMETER

▬ 1600 - 2600 RPM — NORMAL RANGE
▬ 2600 RPM — MAXIMUM (METO)

Figure 5-1 (Sheet 1 of 2 Sheets)

T.O. 1T-34A-1
Section V

CYLINDER HEAD TEMPERATURE
- 107° C TO 240° C — NORMAL OPERATING RANGE
- 240° C — MAXIMUM (TAKE-OFF)

FUEL PRESSURE
- 9 PSI — MINIMUM FOR FLIGHT
- 9 - 15 PSI — NORMAL RANGE
- 15 PSI — MAXIMUM

OIL PRESSURE
- 30 PSI — MINIMUM FOR FLIGHT
- 30 - 60 PSI — NORMAL OPERATING RANGE
- 80 PSI — MAXIMUM

BASED ON FUEL GRADE 80

CARBURETOR AIR TEMPERATURE
- −10° C TO 15° C — DANGER OF ICING
- 15° C TO 50° C — NORMAL OPERATING RANGE
- 50° C — MAXIMUM — DANGER OF DETONATION

AIRSPEED
- 109 KNOTS IAS — GEAR AND FLAPS EXTENDED
- 243 KNOTS IAS — MAXIMUM PERMISSIBLE

Figure 5-1 (Sheet 2 of 2 Sheets)

Section V T.O. 1T-34A-1

Operating Flight Strength

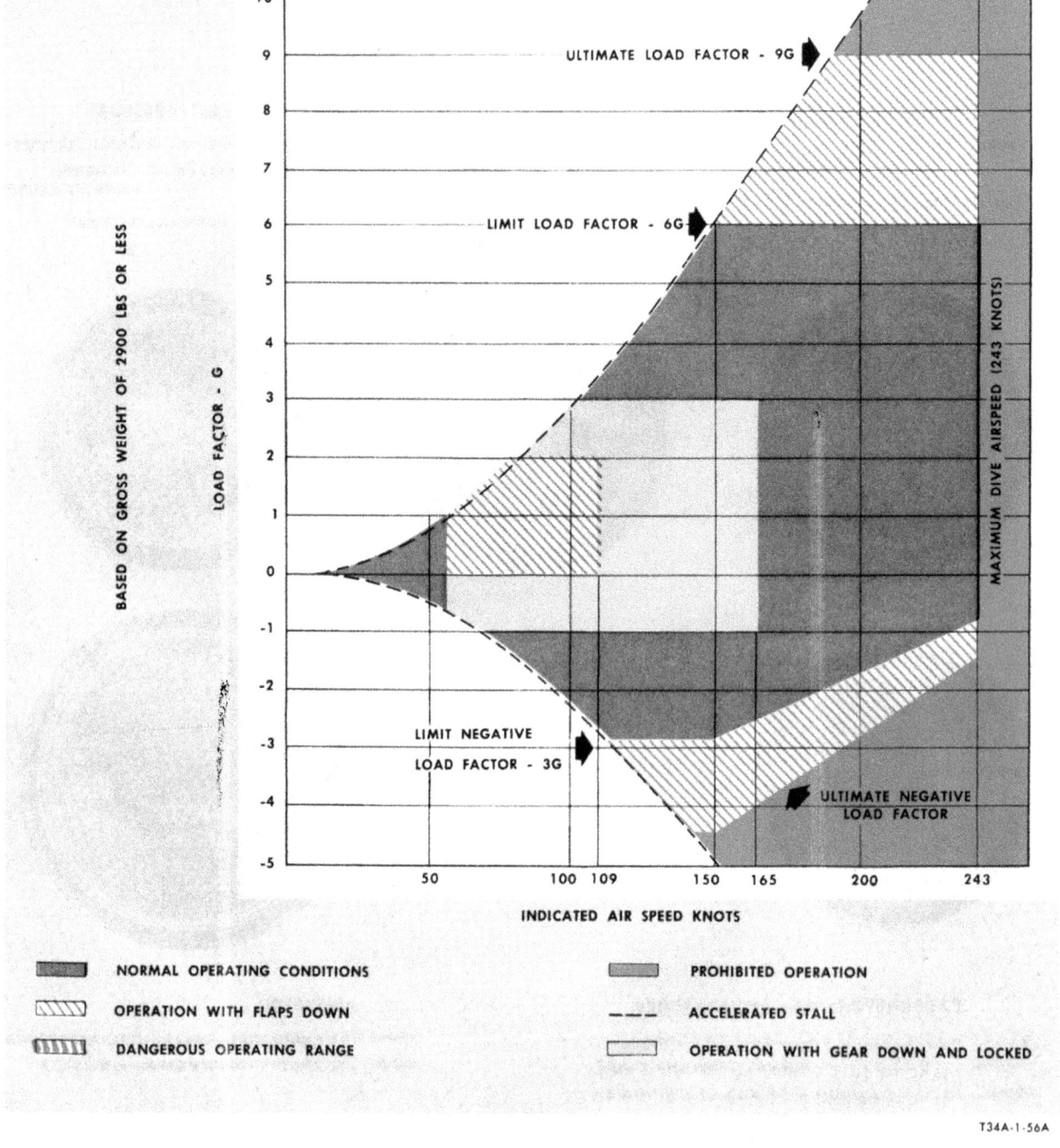

Figure 5-2

AIRSPEED LIMITATIONS.

The red line airspeed of 243 knots is the maximum permissible indicated airspeed for diving in this aircraft.

NOTE

The yellow line airspeed is the maximum allowable speed for actuating the gear. The gear is stressed, however, to withstand speeds up to 165 knots after it is fully extended and locked. A warning placard, which shows the above airspeed information, is located below the airspeed indicator on each instrument panel.

PROHIBITED MANEUVERS.

Acrobatic maneuvers, with the exception of inverted spins, are permitted in this aircraft, however, the aircraft should not be subjected to negative G forces for periods in excess of 15 seconds. Prolonged inverted flight in excess of this period causes fuel starvation as there is no means of insuring a continuous flow of fuel in this attitude.

WARNING

Prior to a flight during which acrobatic maneuvers are to be performed, check the baggage compartment and remove any items contained therein.

CAUTION

Extended acrobatics or numerous inversions will deplete the oil supply, due to a small amount of oil loss through the vent line, until eventually propeller control may be momentarily lost during the maneuvers.

CAUTION

All acrobatic maneuvers should be practiced at an altitude sufficient to permit a complete recovery at 3000 feet above the terrain.

ACCELERATION LIMITS.

Limitations on the acceleration to which the aircraft may be subjected in maneuvering is determined by the structural load limitations on the wings, expressed as a factor of the force exerted by gravity (G). This aircraft is limited to a maximum positive factor of 6G's, clean, and 2G's with flaps down. The limit negative load factor is 3G's. These limitations are based on the design gross weight of 2950 pounds and apply only to straight pull-outs. Rolling pull-outs impose considerably more stress on the aircraft, therefore, they should be less severe. Remember, the maximum allowable G-limit for a rolling pull-out is two-thirds the maximum G-limit for straight pull-outs.

OPERATING FLIGHT STRENGTH.

The accelerating load limits on the aircraft, based on structural limitations are shown in figure 5-2.

The normal operating conditions are represented by two green areas and prohibited operation is represented by red areas. The curved dashed lines represent the airspeeds at which the aircraft will stall at various G-loads. Note that the intersection of the dashed line with the 1G line indicates the stalling speed in straight and level flight.

The red cross hatched area, between normal operating limit load factor and ultimate load factor, represents operation that the aircraft will withstand but that which will result in permanent structural damage. The solid red area represents operation beyond the structural capabilities of the aircraft. Such operation will result in complete structural failure of one or more airframe components.

CENTER-OF-GRAVITY LIMITATIONS.

Location of the center of gravity (CG) of the aircraft is expressed in terms of inches aft of the datum line. The forward CG limit is 84.1 inches aft of the datum at a gross flying weight of 2750 pounds, progressing uniformly to 87.6 inches aft at design gross weight of 2950 pounds. The aft CG limit is 90.3 inches aft of the datum at 2600 pounds, progressing to 89.0 inches aft at 2950 pounds. The CG limits will not normally be exceeded in any loading condition within the design gross weight, but under overload conditions, a marginal aft CG location may exist.

LOADING LIMITATIONS.

Loading limitations are dictated by center-of-gravity location. All load carried in addition to fuel, oil and crew is carried in the baggage compartment, which is limited to a maximum allowable load of 100 pounds with one cockpit occupied. No baggage is permitted with the rear seat occupied, due to marginal aft CG conditions. As fuel is expended, the center-of-gravity moves aft slightly, but with the corresponding reduction in gross weight, the CG limits also move aft and CG remains within limits. These limitations are based on a crew weight of 200 pounds per cockpit.

GROSS WEIGHT LIMITATIONS.

The design gross weight and recommended maximum weight for take-off and landing is 2950 pounds. This is based on a full fuel and oil capacity and maximum crew weight of 400 pounds.

NOTE

Gross weight limitations may be exceeded by approval of the commander if urgency of the situation dictates.

Blank

Section 6

Flight Characteristics

TABLE OF CONTENTS

General Flight Characteristics	6-1
Stalls	6-1
Spins	6-3
Flight Control	6-5

GENERAL FLIGHT CHARACTERISTICS.

The aircraft is characterized by excellent stability and handling characteristics and high maneuverability. When properly trimmed, the aircraft tends to maintain straight and level flight and controls are effective throughout the speed range from stall to maximum diving speed.

STALLS.

Stalls in this aircraft (figure 6-1) are characterized by an exceptionally clean break and extremely rapid recovery. It is difficult to stall the aircraft accidentally, except as the result of acceleration, since the stall attitude is very steep. Very little aerodynamic warning precedes the stall and the best indications of an approaching stall condition are attitude, airspeed and rapid increase in control sloppiness. However, because of the rapid recovery that is possible, with minimum loss of altitude, this condition is not considered dangerous. The stall itself is characterized by an immediate pitch-down. If the aircraft is allowed to yaw, a roll will develop which may continue up to 30 to 45 degrees, then stop. This roll is easily corrected with coordinated control during recovery. Position of the landing gear has little or no effect on stall characteristics.

POWER-ON STALLS.

As the aircraft decelerates, the trim counteracting the precession effect due to torque becomes less effective and right rudder must be added proportionately to maintain straight flight and prevent a yaw. A yaw present at the initial break of the stall will cause the aircraft to roll. After the stall breaks and the nose drops through the horizon, rudder and aileron are both effective in returning the wings to level. The roll is most pronounced with flaps down.

POWER-OFF STALLS.

With power off, the stall occurs at slightly higher airspeed than with power on. Stall characteristics are not materially affected except there is less tendency for a roll to develop should the aircraft be allowed to yaw. With gear and flaps down, some aircraft buffet occurs at 2 or 3 knots above stalling speed. This configuration represents the most common landing condition.

STALL RECOVERY.

Stall recovery, where there is sufficient room for a normal recovery, will be made as follows:

1. Release back pressure on the stick immediately and smoothly advance the throttle. Do not exceed the maximum allowable manifold pressure for the existing rpm.

2. Use coordinated aileron and rudder to roll the wings level and smoothly apply back pressure

Stalling Speeds – Knots IAS

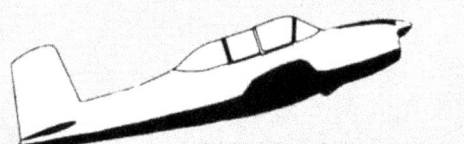

GEAR & FLAPS UP

GROSS WEIGHT LB.	POWER ON (METO POWER)				POWER OFF (WINDMILLING PROP)			
	LEVEL	DEGREE OF BANK			LEVEL	DEGREE OF BANK		
		15°	30°	45°		15°	30°	45°
2775	54	55	58	64	58	59	62	69
2950	55	56	59	65	59	60	63	70

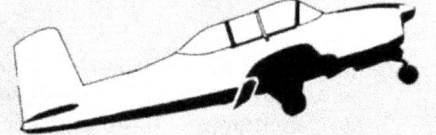

GEAR & FLAPS DOWN
100% FLAPS

GROSS WEIGHT LB.	POWER ON (APPROACH POWER)				POWER OFF (WINDMILLING PROP)			
	LEVEL	DEGREE OF BANK			LEVEL	DEGREE OF BANK		
		15°	30°	45°		15°	30°	45°
2775	44	45	47	53	47	48	51	56
2950	45	46	48	54	48	49	52	57

Figure 6-1

on the stick to return to level flight. Avoid pulling back too severely; a secondary stall or excessive loads may result.

3. When level flight is resumed, retard throttle to cruising power.

Traffic pattern or low altitude stall recovery will differ from normal recovery as follows:

1. Recovery will be attempted by use of power and holding the altitude loss to a minimum. The nose of the aircraft will be allowed to drop only slightly below the horizon.

2. Use coordinated aileron and rudder to roll the wings level and smoothly apply back pressure on the stick to return to level flight as rapidly as possible.

3. As soon as control is attained, climb may be established.

PRACTICE STALLS.

For power-on stalls, gear and flaps up, use 2400 rpm; with gear and flaps down, use 2400 rpm. Reduce throttle to 23 in. Hg for power-on stalls and close smoothly to idle for power-off stalls.

Power-on Stall — Gear and Flaps Up.

Pull the nose of the aircraft above the horizon and, as speed decreases, it will be necessary to use right rudder to maintain straight flight. Hold the nose high attitude until the aircraft is stalled. Note that warning of the approaching stall is very little, if any; there is very little tendency to roll. Tail buffet is quite noticeable once the aircraft has stalled. Recovery is made by releasing stick back pressure and using coordinated control to level the wings. During recovery, the nose of the aircraft will drop slightly below the horizon before the aircraft regains flying airspeed. Return to level flight.

Power-on Stall in a Turn — Gear and Flaps Up.

Establish and maintain a 30-degree bank in a climbing turn until the aircraft is stalled. The aircraft may roll in either direction, depending on the accuracy of rudder coordination. Use the same recovery as for stalls in straight flight.

Power-on Stall — Gear and Flaps Down.

Practice these both in straight flight and in a 30-degree bank. Use the same procedure as above and note that with the flaps down, the tendency to roll is a little more noticeable. Practice until a minimum of altitude loss is attainable by using more power and less nose down attitude.

Power-off Stall — Gear and Flaps Up.

Power-off stalls should be practiced by holding the nose of the aircraft near the horizon and allowing the aircraft to lose airspeed until stalled. Recover by smooth application of power and at the same time allowing the nose to lower to approximately gliding attitude, until flying airspeed is attained. Use coordinated aileron and rudder control to bring the nose back up to straight and level flight. Avoid a secondary stall by allowing the aircraft to gain sufficient flying speed before attempting to bring the nose back up to level flight. If encountered, release sufficient back elevator pressure to reduce the angle of attack.

Power-off Stall in a Turn — Gear and Flaps Up.

With power off and in level flight, establish a 30-degree bank and hold until the aircraft is stalled. The aircraft may roll in either direction, depending on the accuracy of rudder correction for yaw. Use the same procedures as above for recovery.

Power-off Stall — Gear and Flaps Down.

Practice these both in straight flight and in a 30-degree bank. Use the same procedures as in power-off stalls and again note the tendency to roll when the flaps are down. Practicing these is important as this represents the conditions that could possibly be experienced in the traffic pattern and on the final approach. Again place special emphasis on minimum loss and rapid recovery of altitude.

ACCELERATED STALL.

An accelerated stall is, in general, any stall out of a condition imposing an acceleration load or a load greater than one G. An example of this condition is a level turn, during which the load imposed on the wings is greater than during straight-and-level flight; as the angle of bank increases, the load increases and the stalling speed becomes higher. Refer to figure 6-1 for an example of the effect of bank angle on stalling speed and to figure 5-2 for the G-load imposed. Another type of accelerated stall can be produced at much higher airspeeds by excessive back pressure on the stick, as in a steep turn or dive pull-out.

SPINS.

The spin characteristics of this aircraft are variable, the aircraft's behavior during the spin depending largely on the abruptness of entry and attitude, speed and power at the moment of entry. In general, normal spins are characterized by a very definite forward force on the stick with some stick buffet and moderate rudder buffet after three turns. The aircraft completes one full turn in approximately three seconds and loses approximately 440 feet per turn. During one half of the

Section VI T.O. 1T-34A-1

Altitude Loss in Dive Recovery

CONSTANT 4 G PULL-OUT

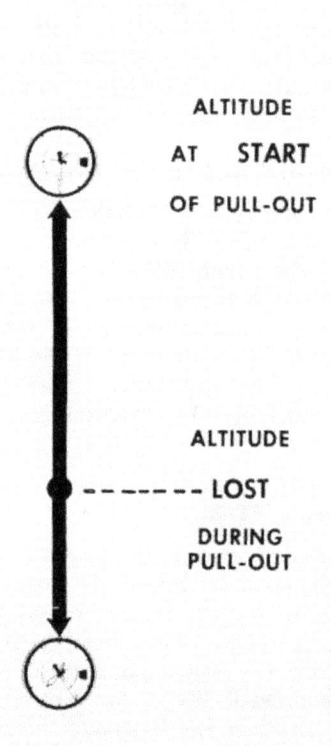

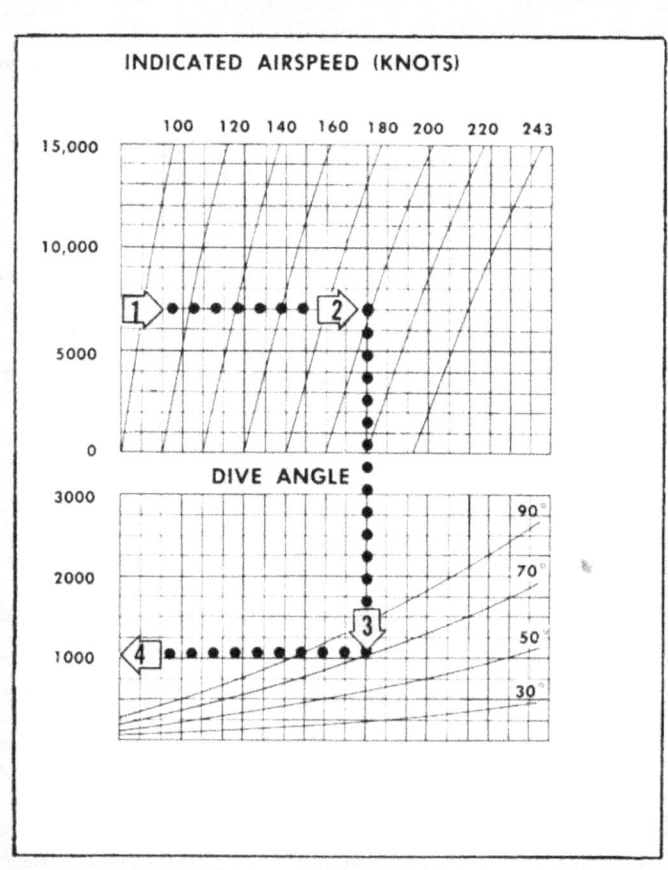

EXAMPLE USE OF CHART

 1. ENTER CHART AT ALTITUDE AT START OF PULL-OUT (7500 FT.).

 2. SIGHT HORIZONTALLY TO AIRSPEED AT START OF PULL-OUT (200 KNOTS).

3. SIGHT VERTICALLY TO DIVE ANGLE (70).

 4. SIGHT ACROSS TO READ ALTITUDE LOSS. SUBTRACT FROM INITIAL ALTITUDE TO FIND RECOVERY ALTITUDE.

Figure 6-2

turn, the nose-down attitude steepens and the turn rate speeds up to one-and-one-half the average rate of turn. During the next half of the turn, the nose rises to approximately 25 degrees below the horizon and the turn rate slows down to half the average rate. This cycle increases in intensity during the first three or four turns and continues throughout the spin. Recovery can be effected at any point in the cycle. Spins with gear and flaps down are considerably milder and the rotation rate is slower. Altitude loss is approximately 560 feet per turn and recovery characteristics are uniform.

Spins can be initiated out of any stall by leading with rudder in the direction of the spin and holding full back stick during the spin and full inside rudder. If the spin is entered from a power-on stall condition, close the throttle immediately on entering the spin. Spin characteristics are not greatly aggravated by power, but airspeed during the spin and recovery will be considerably higher with excessive loss of altitude. Spin characteristics are not greatly affected by aileron or canopy position, however, spins should be practiced with the canopy closed due to the probability of exceeding the canopy open limit airspeed of 152 knots IAS during recovery. All practice spins should be started at altitudes which will permit recovery 3000 feet above the ground. During a two-turn spin and recovery, using a constant 4G pull-out, altitude loss will be approximately 2000 to 2500 feet. Allow 500 feet more altitude for each additional turn.

SPIN RECOVERY.

Recovery from normal spins is effected most rapidly if started at the beginning of the steep half of the turn. Recovery is equally positive in the shallow portion, but is somewhat slower. Spin recovery is excellent. All that is necessary in a spin recovery is to release the flight controls and the aircraft immediately recovers in a nose-down attitude at normal CG loadings. Normal spin recovery should be practiced as follows:

1. Apply full rudder in the opposite direction, followed immediately by a brisk forward movement of the stick to slightly forward of neutral.

2. As the nose drops and the turn starts to slow down, neutralize the controls. The aircraft will be in a dive of 60 to 80 degrees, depending on recovery technique.

3. Start coordinated pull-out immediately to keep altitude loss to a minimum, but avoid entering an accelerated stall. With gear and flaps down, make pull-out tight enough to keep from exceeding the gear and flaps-down limit airspeed.

INVERTED SPINS.

No adverse characteristics are encountered in inverted spins. The aircraft must be held in the spin with full forward stick and full rudder into the spin. Acceleration during the spin varies between 2.1G negative and 3.8G positive and the spin will not normally continue more than 1 to 1 1/2 turns, after which it tends to deteriorate into a high-speed spiral. Recovery can be made from either the spin or the spiral by neutralizing the controls and rolling out of the resulting inverted dive with aileron. Keep the canopy closed and avoid exceeding 150 knots while inverted.

FLIGHT CONTROL.

Control forces are moderate to light and response to controls is rapid and definite. Elevator and rudder control forces are very light and the aircraft is very sensitive to movement of these controls. Rudder feel is enhanced by the use of an anti-servo trim tab, which increases rudder pedal forces proportionate to the displacement of the rudder from neutral. Elevator tabs are conventional, their position being determined only by adjustment from the cockpit. Aileron forces are lightened by servo trim tabs and, although the aircraft is sensitive to aileron deflection and has a very high rate of roll, aileron stick forces remain high enough to provide excellent feel. Only very slight trim tab adjustment is needed for changes caused by landing gear position, fuel quantity or canopy position in the normal operating speed range and the aircraft can be trimmed for "hands-off" flight down to 77 knots IAS.

MANEUVERING FLIGHT.

The relatively light elevator and rudder forces and rapid response of the aircraft to control movement provide excellent acrobatic characteristics. Due to the light elevator forces, it is not recommended that the elevators be trimmed to reduce stick forces during maneuvers, as only slight additional stick forces would then be required to exceed the operating limits on acceleration loads. The aircraft is relatively clean and picks up speed rapidly with the nose down. Light rudder forces permit holding the aircraft straight in a dive without rudder trim.

DIVING.

Care should be exercised not to exceed the limit diving airspeed and maximum engine operating speed. Observe the following precautions in long or steep dives:

1. Canopy closed.

2. Mixture lever — full RICH. Retard throttle to avoid exceeding maximum allowable airspeed.

3. Observe tachometer to forestall possible engine overspeed. As the aircraft picks up speed, the governor has to continue increasing propeller pitch to hold a constant rpm. When the blades reach full high pitch, any increase in speed will then cause rpm to increase also regardless of the position of the propeller lever. The propeller pitch range is sufficient to keep the rpm within limits normally at speeds up to limit diving speed, but if an overspeed should occur, reduce airspeed either by reducing throttle or pulling out of the dive.

Altitude Loss in Dive Recovery.

The effect of initial altitude, dive speed and dive angle on altitude loss during dive recovery is shown in figure 6-2.

Section 7

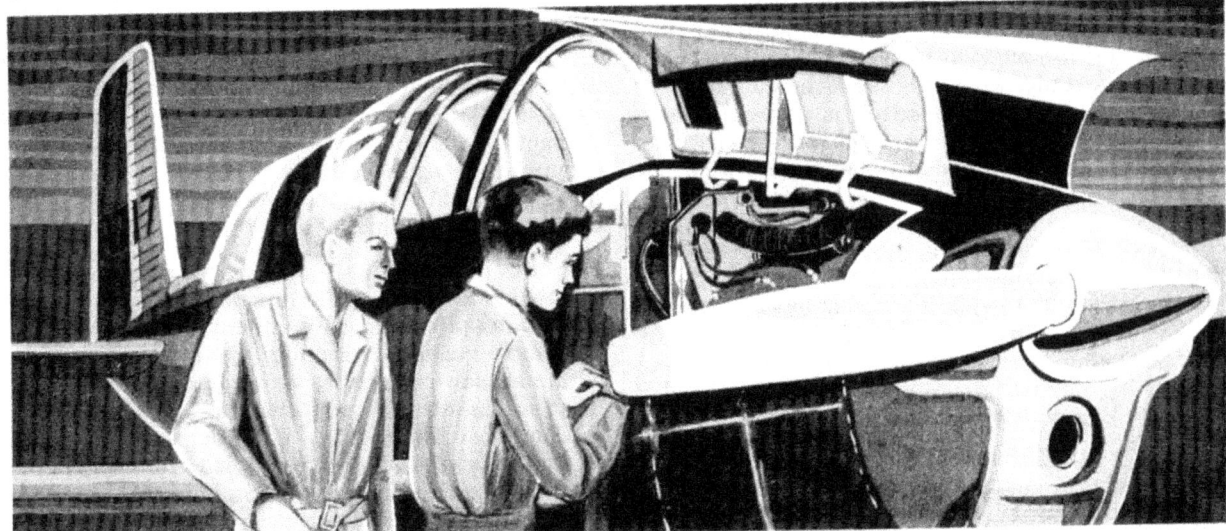

Systems Operation

TABLE OF CONTENTS

Introduction	7-1
Engine	7-1
Fuel System	7-3
Oil System	7-3
Electrical System	7-3
Landing Wheel Brake System	7-3

INTRODUCTION.

The following information on systems operation is designed to aid in proper understanding and operation of the aircraft. It should serve as a useful guide in establishing correct operating procedures with a resultant increase in service, operating economy and safety factor of the aircraft.

ENGINE.

Since the engine furnishes the motive power that enables the aircraft to fly, proper operation and consideration of the loads imposed on the engine are of prime importance in maintaining flight in a single-engine aircraft, where recourse to a second engine is not available. The power settings for take-off, climb and maximum continuous power for this engine are identical. This enables you to employ the maximum power available at any time for maximum rate of climb or for emergency cruise. This does not imply, however, that the engine is designed to operate "wide open" at all times. Continued use of extreme high power output materially shortens engine life by increasing wear. The prime factors to consider in maintaining greatest efficiency from the engine are proper lubrication and the loads imposed. Frequent attention to instruments, such as oil pressure and cylinder head temperature gages, will instill a habit of checking often on the existing operating conditions prevailing in the power plant. Faithful observation of good practices in the use of power will also preserve the dependability you expect from the engine. Some engine operation practices to keep in mind include the following: Change in power setting — When reducing power, always reduce throttle first, then reduce rpm, to avoid creating excessively high pressure in the cylinders. When increasing power, an inverse procedure is followed, i.e., increase the rpm first, then the throttle.

CAUTION

Maintain one inch manifold pressure for each 100 engine rpm as a standard rule.

Mixture lever — Practice will enable you to find the ideal mixture lever settings for maximum engine efficiency at different altitudes. Keep in mind that although mixture will tend to be over-rich at altitude, with mixture lever in full RICH, a somewhat over-rich mixture is preferable to an excessively lean one. Lean mixtures can cause overheating, valve sticking, detonation and, particularly at low power settings, sudden, partial or complete engine failure. Become particularly conscious of the mixture setting whenever it is leaned, and especially during descents at low power. Develop the habit, when starting a descent, of moving the mixture lever forward. If at any time during flight excessive operating temperatures or rough engine operation are encountered, move mixture lever to FULL RICH.

For a ground operational check of the idle rpm fuel air ratio mixture, move the propeller lever to FULL INCREASE and the mixture lever to FULL RICH, close the throttle to obtain engine idle speed (600 to 700 rpm) and check the oil temperature — NORMAL and cylinder head temperature — NORMAL (at least 150°C). Move the mixture lever slowly and evenly toward IDLE CUT-OFF.

NOTE

The term "slowly and evenly" may be defined as the rate of movement which would require 12 to 15 seconds to move the mixture control lever from FULL RICH to IDLE CUT-OFF position. This slow movement of the lever is necessary so that the engine can respond to the change in fuel air ratio and an accurate reading can be obtained as the best power mixture is reached.

If a rise of more than 10 rpm or a drop in manifold pressure exceeding 1/4 inch Hg is noted, the idle rpm mixture fuel air ratio is too rich. If no rise in rpm is noted, the idle rpm fuel air ratio is too lean. After maximum rpm rise has been obtained and rpm starts to decrease with further movement of the mixture control, return the mixture control to FULL RICH.

The idle rpm fuel air ratio must check according to the foregoing procedure to prevent spark plug fouling, which causes excessive magneto drop at ignition check, incorrect fuel air ratio in the cruise range and low torque oil pressure during take-off.

Carburetor icing — The possibility of carburetor icing is very remote since the temperature drop of induction air through this carburetor is less than usual, and fuel is not mixed with the air until after it is leaving the carburetor. However, when icing conditions exist, it is possible for ice, due to moist impact air, to collect on the air inlet filter at the front of the engine which will eventually shut off air flow to the carburetor. The use of carburetor heat will supply an alternate source of air but will have no effect on the ice accumulation on the filter. If icing conditions are severe enough to cause ice to form on the filter, wing and propeller icing will also occur, therefore, an attempt should be made to get out of the icing area or land immediately.

Spark plug fouling — A principal cause of ignition trouble and one of the most common aircraft engine maintenance and operating problems is spark plug fouling. Fouling may be defined as an accumulation of deposits which cause misfiring or prevents firing across the spark plug electrodes. The most common types of fouling are lead fouling and carbon fouling, with lead fouling the most predominant. In general, fouling involves a build-up of deposits through prolonged operation under a fixed set of conditions. Prevention and remedy for plug fouling, therefore, depend on taking action to vary these conditions, upset the chemistry of the fouling cycle, and restore good ignition.

Tetraethyl lead is the basic cause of lead fouling. During the fuel combustion process in a cylinder, this lead will condense out of the fuel onto the spark plug insulators as lead oxide or lead bromide compounds, in the presence of excess carbon which will form it into metallic lead particles. All such deposits can prevent ignition or firing.

Carbon fouling is usually due to prolonged ground running at idle, particularly when the idle mixture is richer than best power; excess carbon from the rich mixture plus engine oil in combustion tend to build up as fouling deposits. The symptoms of such fouling usually include excessive magneto drop at the power check at field barometric manifold pressure.

The importance of preventing plug fouling during ground running is obvious, since fouling is apt to cause flight delay either as a result of excessive magneto drop during the ground power check or engine malfunction during take-off. In some instances where plug fouling has occurred, the difficulty was not apparent at any stage of the engine check-out procedure.

It is generally more practical to prevent spark plug fouling than to attempt to remove fouling deposits, as a spark plug change is often the only satisfactory solution. However, as a partial remedy, after each 10 minutes of ground operation, run the engine up to field barometric manifold pressure for one minute. Additional running for short periods of time with manifold pressure changes of about two inches is sometimes effective. Due to generally poor engine cooling under such conditions, caution must be exercised to avoid any prolonged operation at or above field barometric manifold pressure.

FUEL SYSTEM.

During flight, fuel should be used from the left and right tanks alternately, at a safe and practical time, to check the proper functioning of the fuel tank selector valve and the valve handle. Alternate use of the fuel tanks to avoid wing heaviness may be accomplished as required. When switching from one tank to the other, use the "click-and-feel" method to determine valve position rather than depending on the exact location of the handle pointer; otherwise, a slight misalignment of the pointer could result in positioning the selector valve partially open, restricting fuel flow to the engine driven fuel pump and possibly inadvertent fuel transfer from the fuel tank being used to the other fuel tank when the fuel booster pump (for the fuel tank being used) is in operation. At such times that the fuel selector valve handle is repositioned, the fuel quantity gage for the tank not in use should be closely monitored to check for possible inadvertent fuel transfer from the tank being used to the other tank. However, for this fuel transfer action to occur, the fuel booster pump for the fuel tank in use must be in operation and the fuel tank selector valve must be improperly positioned. For this reason the use of fuel booster pumps is prohibited except during engine start and during flight when the fuel pressure gage indicates less than 9 psi. The fuel quantity gages provide an approximation of the fuel remaining in each tank, being calibrated in fractions of full capacity, but for more accurate determination of fuel remaining, use fuel consumption data based on known operating conditions — refer to the Performance Data, Section X for fuel consumption at various power settings and altitudes.

OIL SYSTEM.

A weighted flexible oil pick-up hose is installed in the oil tank to assure oil supply to the propeller during inverted flight. Inverted flight duration must not exceed 15 seconds.

Oil is not returned to the tank during inverted flight, therefore the aircraft must be maintained in normal attitude for approximately 30 seconds to allow complete scavenging of the oil from the crankcase sump.

ELECTRICAL SYSTEM.

The electrical loadmeter indicates total electrical load on the electrical system and is calibrated in terms of rated generator capacity. In flight, when all electrical power is normally being supplied by the generator, the loadmeter reading represents load actually imposed on the generator, including that used in charging the battery. Check the voltmeter occasionally for indication of proper generator voltage of 28 to 28.5 volts. When generator voltage drops to 4 volts below battery voltage (as during low rpm ground operation), the reverse current relay disconnects the generator, to prevent it from running as a motor.

LANDING WHEEL BRAKE SYSTEM.

To reduce maintenance difficulties and possible accidents due to wheel brake failure, it is absolutely necessary that the wheel brake system be treated with respect and that the importance of proper system usage be highly emphasized. To minimize brake wear, insofar as practicable, extreme care when applying brakes is the biggest factor in achieving long and useful service.

Careful application of the brakes immediately after touchdown or at any time when there is considerable lift on the wings, will prevent skidding the tires and causing flat spots. A heavy brake pressure can result in locking the wheel more easily if brakes are applied immediately after touchdown than if the same pressure is applied after the full weight of the aircraft is on the wheels. A wheel once locked in this manner will not become unlocked as the load is increased as long as brake pressure is maintained. Proper braking action cannot be expected until the tires are carrying heavy loads.

Brakes, themselves, can merely stop the wheel from turning, but stopping the airplane is dependent on the friction of the tires on the runway. For this purpose it is easiest to think in terms of coefficient of friction which is equal to the frictional force divided by the load on the wheel. It has been found that optimum braking occurs with approximately a 15 to 20 percent rolling skid; i.e., the wheel continues to rotate but has approximately 15 to 20 percent slippage on the surface so that the rotational speed is 80 to 85 percent of the speed which the wheel would have were it in free roll. As the amount of skid increases beyond this amount, the coefficient of friction decreases rapidly so that with a 75 percent skid the friction is approximately 60 percent of the optimum and, with a full skid, becomes even lower.

There are two reasons for this loss in braking effectiveness with skidding. First, the immediate action is to scuff the rubber, tearing off little pieces which act almost like rollers under the tire. Second, the heat generated starts to melt the rubber and the molten rubber acts as a lubricant.

NACA figures have shown that for an incipient skid, the coefficient of friction on dry concrete is approximately double the coefficient of a 75 percent skid. Therefore, if one wheel is locked during application of brakes there is a very definite tendency for the airplane to turn away from that wheel and further application of brake pressure will offer no corrective action. Since the coefficient of friction goes down when the wheel begins to skid, it is apparent that a wheel, once locked, will never free itself until brake pressure is reduced so that the braking effect on the wheel is less than the turning moment remaining with the reduced frictional force.

Normally, a full landing roll should be utilized to take advantage of aerodynamic braking and to use the brakes as little and as lightly as possible. However, if maximum braking is required after a touchdown, lift should first be decreased as much as possible by raising the flaps and dropping the nose before applying the brakes. This procedure will improve braking action by increasing the frictional force between the tires and the runway. For short landing rolls, a single, smooth application of the brakes with constantly increasing pedal pressure is most desirable.

If the brakes have been used excessively for an emergency stop and are in an over-heated condition, taxi operations should be conducted cautiously and at a reduced speed, especially in or around a congested parking area, since possible brake fading may occur.

CAUTION

To prevent brake disc warpage or other system damage, do not set the parking brake with the discs in an over-heated condition.

Section 8

Crew Duties (Not Applicable)

NOT APPLICABLE TO THIS AIRCRAFT

Section 9

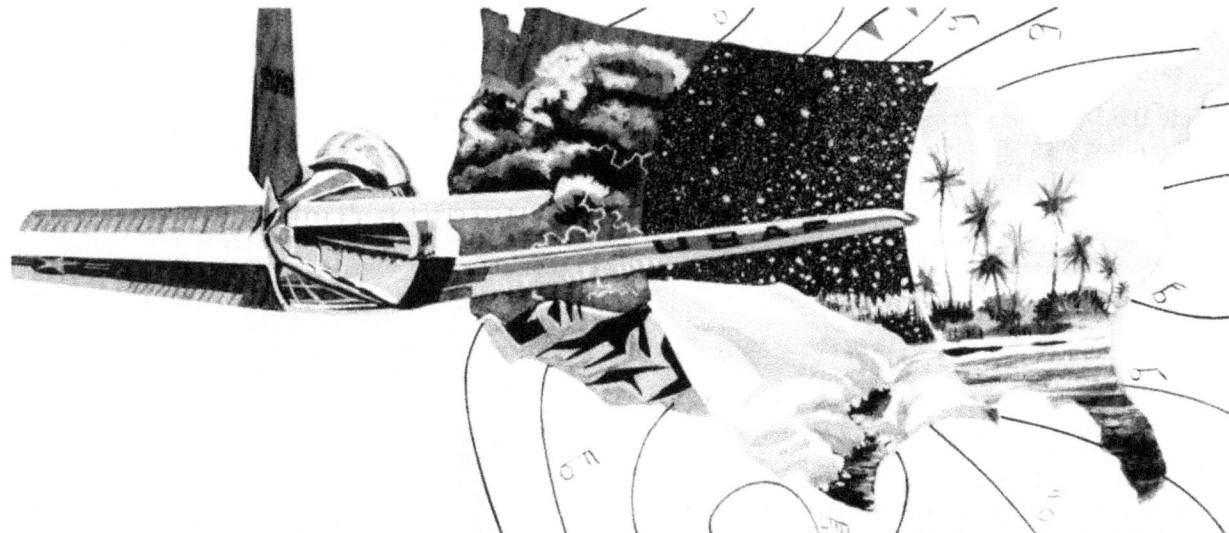

All-Weather Operation

TABLE OF CONTENTS

Introduction	9-1
Instrument Flight Procedures	9-1
Ice and Rain	9-4
Turbulence and Thunderstorms	9-4
Night Flight	9-4
Cold Weather Procedures	9-6
Hot Weather and Desert Operation	9-7

INTRODUCTION

Except for some repetition necessary for emphasis, clarity or continuity of thought this section contains only those procedures that differ or are in addition to the normal operation instructions covered in Section II. Systems operations are covered in Section VII.

INSTRUMENT FLIGHT PROCEDURES.

This airplane has the same stability and flight handling characteristics during Instrument Flight Conditions as when flown under VFR conditions. However, like most single-engine aircraft, it requires constant attention to the indications of the flight instruments. The stability, flight strength, instruments, and communications equipment are sufficient for instrument cross country flights under most weather conditions. Flight in icing conditions should not be attempted as there are no provisions for the wing and empennage deicing. The following techniques are recommended from take-off to touchdown under instrument and/or night flying conditions.

INSTRUMENT TAKE-OFF AND INITIAL CLIMB.

Complete the normal TAXI and PRE-TAKE-OFF checks as prescribed in Section II. If taxiing and take-off are to be made in visible moisture, a check for indication of carburetor icing should be made.

NOTE

A drop in manifold pressure and RPM and engine roughness are good indications of carburetor icing.

Adjust the carburetor heat handle to provide carburetor heat for deicing prior to take-off; return to normal just prior to starting take-off roll.

NOTE

When visible moisture is present, turn pitot heat switch ON just before taxiing into take-off position.

Rotate the Directional Indicator card to align runway heading with the index at the top of the dial.

NOTE

To be certain of proper operation of the gyro instruments, allow 8 minutes for them to reach full operating speed.

Apply power to approximately 20 inches Hg, release brakes and smoothly advance throttle to full OPEN. Use nose gear steering until rudder becomes effective at approximately 35 knots. During the take-off roll the Directional Indicator is the primary instrument for directional control; however, while runway markings remain visible they should be used as an aid in maintaining directional control. At approximately 55 knots IAS apply back pressure to the stick to establish a take-off attitude of about 2 horizon bar widths nose high on the Attitude Indicator. As the aircraft leaves the ground the Attitude Indicator is the primary instrument for pitch and bank and continues as such until the climb is established. When the Altimeter and Vertical Velocity Indicator indicate a climb, retract the gear and maintain a vertical velocity climb of approximately 500 FPM until the desired climb speed has been attained.

INSTRUMENT CLIMB.

When the aircraft is clear of the runway establish a definite climb by holding the miniature aircraft symbol in the attitude indicator approximately 2 bars width high and level. Check and see that the airspeed is increasing, and when the altimeter begins to indicate increasing altitude, retract the landing gear. Turns should not be attempted below 500 feet above the terrain and the angle of bank should not exceed 30° while establishing the climb. Maintain heading with the Directional Indicator and as soon as the airspeed indicates approximately 100 knots IAS, establish normal climb and maintain 100 knots IAS until the desired altitude has been attained. Adjust the carburetor heat as required throughout the climb.

DURING INSTRUMENT CRUISING FLIGHT.

After leveling off from the climb, it may be necessary to hold high power until cruising airspeed is established. It is seldom necessary in routine flight to exceed 30° of bank; however, the aircraft can be controlled in turns up to 60° of bank. For ease of crosscheck when flying constant headings for a prolonged period, placing the selected reading under the top index of the Direction Indicator is recommended.

NOTE

Resetting the compass card and pointer by use of the right reset knob should be accomplished in straight flight to eliminate any error of the pointer induced by a change of aircraft heading during the caging process.

The use of pitot heat and alternate air should be used liberally when conditions are such that icing is possible. For windshield defrosting it may be necessary to adjust the cold and hot air handles for maximum heat even though the temperature may become slightly warm in the cockpit. No other adjustment for windshield defrosting is provided since this equipment is installed primarily for defogging.

WARNING

Icing conditions should be avoided due to the fact that no wing and empennage deicing equipment is provided.

RADIO AND NAVIGATION EQUIPMENT.

The ARC-12 VHF set is the only radio equipment provided for enroute navigation. The R-11A radio range receiver portion of the ARC-12 enables the pilot to navigate and make approaches utilizing LF radio range facilities. DF steers may be obtained with the VHF transmitter-receiver.

DESCENT.

Slow the aircraft to the desired descent airspeed before the descent is initiated since it is difficult to slow the aircraft once the descent is established. Check mixture full rich; adjust carburetor, pitot, and windshield heat as necessary, and perform the normal pre-traffic pattern checks prior to descending.

CAUTION

Maintain one inch manifold pressure for each 100 engine rpm as a standard rule.

NOTE

The cabin and windshield should be kept as warm as possible before and during descents to eliminate fogging conditions on the transparent areas of the cockpit.

HOLDING.

Slow the aircraft to 110 knots clean configuration and complete descent check list. For best control and ease of handling never exceed 30° of bank in turns.

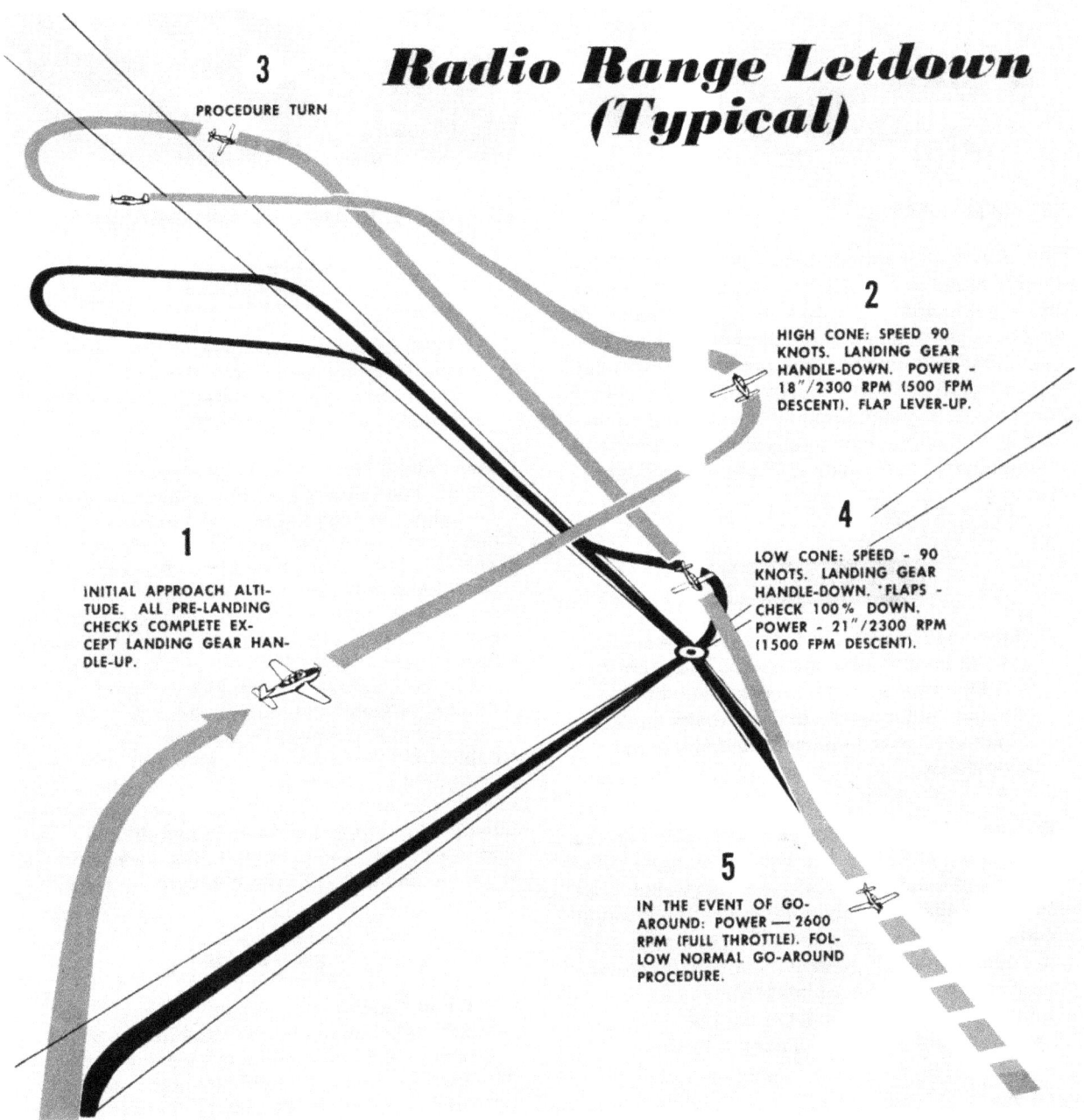

Figure 9-1

INSTRUMENT APPROACHES.

Since there is no radio compass installed on the airplane, instrument approaches must be accomplished on basic radio equipment (VHF transmitter and receiver and range receiver). Either radio range or GCA approaches may be made. Flying the aircraft on instrument approaches is not difficult due to the excellent stability and low stalling speeds. Always reduce the airspeed well in advance of necessary airspeed reductions; think and act ahead if at all possible. The proper trim technique is very important during approaches. With each change of power, attitude, configuration, or airspeed it is necessary to retrim the aircraft to eliminate the need for holding control pressures.

RADIO RANGE APPROACH.

See Figure 9-1 for radio range letdown and approach procedure.

GROUND CONTROLLED APPROACH.

See Figure 9-2 for GCA procedure and typical GCA pattern.

ICE AND RAIN.

When flying in weather, the possibility of engine or air frame ice is often present. If icing conditions are encountered, remember these two serious aspects. First, engine or carburetor ice may seriously affect engine operation. Second, the accumulation of air frame ice destroys lift and increases drag resulting in abnormally high stalling speeds. Structural damage also may result due to vibrations induced by unbalanced loads of ice accumulations.

WARNING

Heavy air frame ice accumulations can greatly increase stalling speed. Therefore extreme caution must be exercised when making approaches and landings and airspeed should be increased under such conditions.

Installations on the aircraft, for combating the various icing problems, are pitot heat, carburetor heat and windshield defogging. Entering anything other than very light icing conditions might become hazardous and since light icing conditions can rapidly change to heavy icing, it is important that icing conditions be avoided. If ice is encountered, attempt to get out of the icing area by turning back and/or changing altitude.

NOTE

Ice accumulation on the propeller usually results in rough engine operation. It can sometimes be eliminated by rapidly increasing and decreasing propeller RPM.

Ice and snow accumulated on the aircraft while on the ground can also result in serious aerodynamic and structural effects when flight is attempted, especially during take-off and climb-out operations. These hazards, however, can be eliminated by removing the snow and ice from the wings, fuselage, and tail before flight is attempted.

TURBULENCE AND THUNDERSTORMS.

CAUTION

Flight in heavy turbulence or thunderstorms should be avoided if at all possible to eliminate the hazard of aircraft damage and loss of control.

Under night or instrument flight conditions, avoiding these turbulent areas may be difficult. The following techniques are recommended for flight into turbulent or thunderstorm areas. Throttle setting and attitude are the keys to turbulent flight conditions. The throttle setting and pitch attitude required for the desired penetration airspeed, 120 to 130 knots IAS, should be established before entering the storm. Maintaining this throttle setting and keeping close watch of the Attitude Indicator for proper attitude will result in a constant airspeed, regardless of any false readings of the airspeed indicator and other pressure reading instruments due to pressure variations within the storm area. Loose equipment should be secured, safety belt and shoulder harness tightened, and cockpit lights turned to full bright to minimize blinding caused by lightning.

CAUTION

When operating in these conditions, do not make turns unless absolutely necessary, and when making pitch corrections, use the least control pressure necessary to avoid overstressing the aircraft structure.

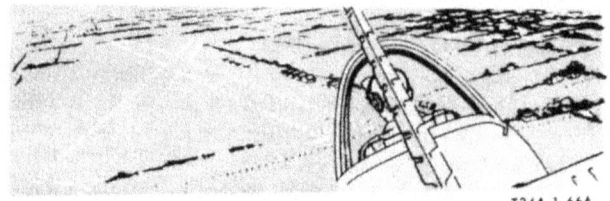

NIGHT FLIGHT.

When night flying, check the lighting equipment thoroughly and be familiar with the location of all switches in the cockpit during the pre-flight

Ground Controlled Approach (G.C.A.) (Typical)

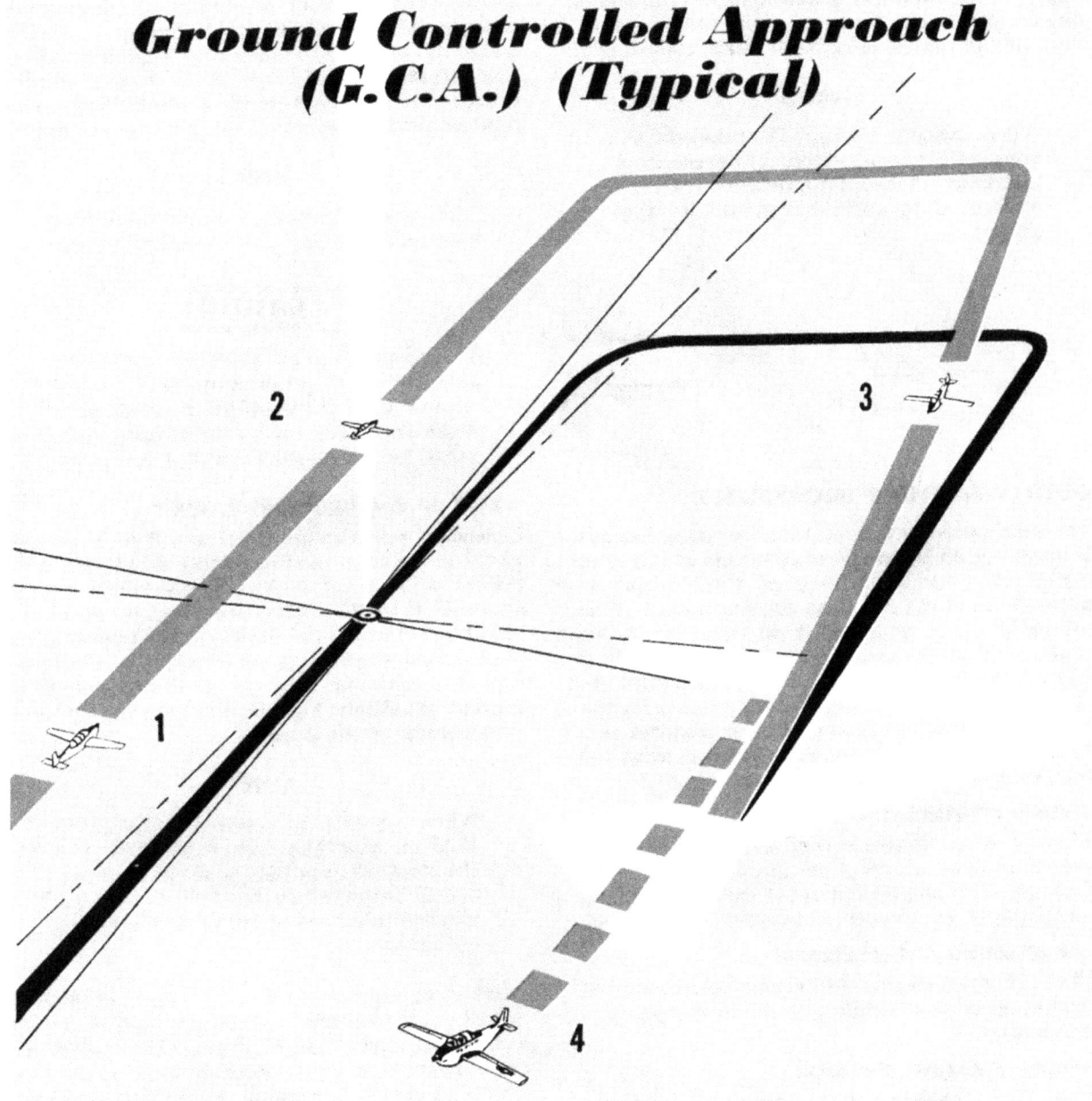

1. WHEN SIGNALS INDICATE APPROXIMATELY FIVE MINUTES FROM HIGH CONE, CONTACT APPROACH CONTROL, SLOW THE AIRCRAFT TO THE DESIRED AIRSPEED FOR MANEUVERING DESCENT AND COMPLETE THE NORMAL PRE-TRAFFIC PATTERN CHECK LIST.

2. MAKE GCA CONTACT AND LOWER THE GEAR (IF AIRSPEED IS AT OR BELOW MINIMUM GEAR DOWN AIRSPEED) AND IF THE GCA OPERATOR'S INSTRUCTIONS ARE SUCH.

3. CONTINUE FOLLOWING GCA OPERATOR'S INSTRUCTIONS WHICH WILL NORMALLY BE TO COMPLETE THE TRAFFIC PATTERN CHECK LIST AND LOWER FLAPS TO THE AMOUNT DESIRED FOR LANDING.

4. FOR MISSED APPROACH PROCEDURE, FOLLOW THE NORMAL GO-AROUND PROCEDURE; POWER ON . . . GEAR UP . . . HOLD FORWARD ELEVATOR PRESSURE TO PREVENT TOO STEEP A CLIMB. ON REACHING SAFE AIRSPEED RAISE FLAPS AND CONTINUE A NORMAL CLIMB, FOLLOWING THE MISSED APPROACH PROCEDURE AS OUTLINED FOR THAT PARTICULAR AIRFIELD.

Figure 9-2

stage. Be sure to carry a flashlight. Night flights essentially present the same problems as instrument flight and should be treated accordingly.

NOTE

When making night VFR take-offs in areas of limited horizon references, the instrument take-off procedures are recommended to avoid flying back to the ground.

COLD WEATHER PROCEDURES.

The success of low temperature operation depends primarily upon the preparations made during post flight and ground handling of the airplane in anticipation of the following day's operation. This aircraft is not equipped with an oil dilution system. Therefore, it should be hangared in a warm area if possible. To expedite pre-flight inspection and insure satisfactory operation for the next flight, the normal operating procedures outlined in Section II should be adhered to with the following additions and exceptions.

BEFORE ENTERING THE AIRCRAFT.

Remove all protective covers and check that the entire airplane is free from ice, snow and frost. Check all fuel and oil drains for free flow of fluid, and battery for proper installation, if removed.

ON ENTERING THE AIRCRAFT.

Check flight controls for complete freedom of movement and complete the other normal procedures.

BEFORE STARTING ENGINE.

Have the propeller pulled through at least two blades before using the starter and complete all normal procedures prior to starting the engine.

NOTE

Prior to attempting a start at temperatures below 0°F (−18°C) the engine should be heated sufficiently to obtain fuel vaporization, permit proper engine valve clearance and seating and to insure proper engine lubrication.

STARTING ENGINE.

The normal engine starting procedures should be used with the possible exception of priming and use of carburetor heat. Use priming rather steadily until the engine starts firing, then intermittently enough to keep the engine running. Cold starts normally require a more retarded throttle. If any warm air is reaching the engine compartment, carburetor heat may then be useful.

NOTE

Moisture forms quickly on the spark plug electrodes during cold weather starts.

CAUTION

If there is no oil pressure within 30 seconds, or if pressure drops to below normal after the engine is running, shut down and check for blown oil lines, radiators, or congealed oil or ice in drains.

WARM-UP AND GROUND CHECK.

Generally, warm-up procedures will be the same as those under normal operating conditions with the following exceptions: Use external power, if available, to supply electrical current for operation of the gyros and other electrical equipment being used during warm-up, so the engine rpm may be held to a minimum until the oil warms enough to prevent extremely high oil pressure encountered at generator cut-in speed.

NOTE

When aircraft is serviced with grade 1100 oil that has been exposed to low temperature weather, ground warm-up of oil temperature to 40°C is recommended to assure warm-up of the entire oil supply.

After external power, if used, has been disconnected, turn battery switch ON and maintain sufficient engine speed for generator operation. It is possible under extremely cold conditions, after the engine is running, to get better vaporization of fuel with the use of carburetor heat, resulting in smoother engine operation during warm-up. Operate the propeller control through several complete cycles to replace the oil in the propeller system with warm engine oil.

TAXIING.

WARNING

Make sure all instruments have warmed up sufficiently to insure normal operation. Normally it takes 5 to 8 minutes for the Directional Indicator to reach proper operating speed.

Do not taxi through water or slush if it can be avoided. Water or slush splashed on the wing and tail surfaces will freeze, increasing weight and drag and perhaps limiting control surface movement. If taxiing behind other aircraft maintain a greater interval to prevent ice and slush being blown on the aircraft from aircraft ahead. Taxi slowly, use nose gear steering and make brake applications easy and sparingly. For information on the use of the landing wheel brake system, refer to Section VII.

BEFORE TAKE-OFF.

Run up engine, using carburetor heat to eliminate any possible carburetor ice then return to IN position for take-off.

TAKE-OFF.

Make a normal take-off using caution against cold engine operation. Do not utilize carburetor heat during take-off.

CAUTION

Exercise extreme caution when steering with the brakes during take-off from an icy runway, as this may cause a skidding condition.

AFTER TAKE-OFF — CLIMB.

Use carburetor heat as soon as full power is no longer required. If take-off is made under VFR conditions from a snow or slush covered field, operate the landing gear and flaps through several cycles to prevent their freezing in the retracted position. If take-off is made under IFR conditions, delay raising the gear and flaps to allow as much slush and water to drain as possible.

CAUTION

Do not exceed the gear and flap down limit airspeed during this operation.

DURING FLIGHT.

Use carburetor heat as needed and cycle the propeller periodically to maintain a warm supply of oil in the propeller system.

DESCENT.

Use caution against engine overcooling by making a gradual descent within gear and flaps operating airspeed. Slow the aircraft by retarding throttle and maintaining a nose high attitude prior to starting a descent. While in the descent, if overcooling demands, the gear and flaps may be lowered and the rpm increased. Keep as much power applied as possible in descending if overcooling is a problem. Use carburetor heat as needed until reaching the landing pattern or, if severe freezing conditions prevail, just prior to flare-out or just prior to advancing throttle for a go-around.

BEFORE LANDING — LANDING.

Make a normal landing pattern and complete the normal checks and procedures. Use pitot heat as needed.

WARNING

Carburetor icing could be severe enough to demand the use of carburetor heat in the traffic pattern. Do not use carburetor heat on final approach. Return carburetor heat handle to IN (cold) immediately after turning off base leg onto final approach.

As soon as the aircraft is on the ground retract the flaps and use the brakes sparingly on icy runways.

AFTER LANDING.

Use carburetor heat while taxiing.

BEFORE LEAVING THE AIRCRAFT.

When use of the aircraft the following day is contemplated, it should be hangared in a warm area when possible.

With the wheel chocks in place release brakes and lock the control surfaces.

Cover the wings, empennage, engine and both cockpits for protection against freezing rain, frost and snow.

HOT WEATHER AND DESERT OPERATION.

BEFORE TAKE-OFF.

Check the aircraft thoroughly for dust and sand and clean such from any parts or operating mechanisms where it could cause damage.

TAKE-OFF.

Under extremely hot conditions, aircraft require a longer take-off run. Consider this in loading and choice of runways. The performance of both aircraft and engine is dependent upon the density of the air in which they are operating. Since the density of the air varies with atmospheric conditions, the performance of aircraft and engines can be analyzed objectively only if operating and performance data are reduced to certain standard conditions. Density of the air varies with the temperature and barometric pressure. These varying conditions can be corrected to standard, and expressed as density altitude. Density altitude is the altitude at which air of a given density exists in the standard atmosphere.

BEFORE LEAVING THE AIRCRAFT.

Leave at least one canopy open when parking in the sun so temperatures inside will not become excessive.

High temperatures can cause fluid in the compasses to boil away, dry out electrical insulation and cause inside paint to pull away from the skin.

Whenever possible, protect all airscoops, vents, operating mechanisms and the cockpits from blowing sand and dust.

NOTE

Sand and dust in the airscoops and vents might restrict airflow during subsequent operation.

Appendix

Performance Data

TABLE OF CONTENTS

Introduction	A-1
Glossary of Terms and Abbreviations	A-1
Temperature Conversion	A-2
Density Altitude Curve	A-2
Engine Power Schedules	A-2
Fuel Flow Per Engine	A-3
Take-Off Distance	A-3
Take-Off, Approach and Touch-Down Velocity	A-3
Climb at "METO" Power	A-3
Nautical Miles Per Pound of Fuel	A-3
Long-Range Prediction — Distance	A-3
Long-Range Prediction — Time	A-3
Maximum Endurance	A-4
Landing Distance	A-4
Use of the Charts	A-4

INTRODUCTION

A series of charts is provided on the following pages to furnish the pilot with sufficient data to make an intelligent and safe flight plan. The charts include data on take-off, climb, and landing, and operating instructions for cruising flight from Maximum Endurance through 99 percent best economy to "METO" power. Because the number of variables involved makes precise predictions impossible, the emphasis in these charts has been on conservation. No allowance has been made for navigational error, formation flight, or other contingencies. Appropriate allowances for these items should be dictated by local regulations and should be accounted for when the fuel available for cruise is determined. The charts are arranged to give maximum facility to use for pre-flight and in-flight planning.

GLOSSARY OF TERMS AND ABBREVIATIONS

The following terms may be found in the Appendix and are defined as follows:

AIRSPEED

    IAS — indicated airspeed corrected for instrument error.

Appendix

CAS — calibrated airspeed; IAS corrected for installational error in the pitot system.

TAS — true airspeed; CAS corrected for relative density.

V$_S$ — stalling speed.

V$_{td}$ — touch-down speed.

V$_{to}$ — take-off speed.

V$_{50}$ — speed to clear a 50-foot obstacle.

CEILINGS

Absolute — the altitude at which the rate-of-climb is zero at stated weight and engine power.

Cruise — the altitude at which the rate-of-climb is 300 ft/min at stated weight and engine power.

Service — the altitude at which the rate-of-climb is 100 ft/min at stated weight and engine power.

C.G. — center-of-gravity (aircraft).

CAT — carburetor air temperature.

DENSITY ALTITUDE

The altitude in a standard atmosphere at which the density of the air is the same as the air density at a given location.

DEWPOINT

The temperature at which, under ordinary conditions, condensation begins in a cooling mass of air. This temperature is used as the basis of calculating the effect produced by humidity on the output of the engines.

FAT — free air, ambient, or outside air temperature (OAT)

FR — full rich carburetor mixture

GS — ground speed

LIMIT BHP

The maximum brake horsepower which the engine is capable of developing without damage to the engine.

MAP — Engine absolute manifold pressure measured in inches of mercury (in. Hg.)

ML — Manual lean carburetor mixture

"METO" POWER

The maximum power available from the engine for continuous operation. Using 80 octane fuel, set FULL RICH mixture, 2600 RPM. No time limit.

PRESSURE ALTITUDE

The altitude in a standard atmosphere at which the air pressure is the same as the pressure of the air at a given location.

RPM — engine speed in revolutions per minute.

SFC — specific fuel consumption lb/hr/hp.

TAKE-OFF POWER

The same as "METO" power.

ρ (rho) = air density at some specific altitude.

ρ_0 = air density at sea level.

σ (sigma) = ρ/ρ_0 = density ratio.

$1/\sqrt{\sigma}$ = reciprocal of the square root of density ratio; used in converting airspeeds to TAS at altitude.

°C — degree Centigrade.

°F — degree Fahrenheit

TEMPERATURE CONVERSION

A temperature conversion chart (figure A-1) is included to facilitate the conversion of either Fahrenheit temperatures to Centigrade or Centigrade temperatures to Fahrenheit.

DENSITY ALTITUDE CURVE

A Density Altitude Chart (figure A-2) is provided to determine the density altitude for free air temperature and pressure altitude combinations. Many of the performance charts are based on density altitude rather than pressure altitude to compensate for temperature variations at any altimeter reading. Along the right side of the chart, the reciprocal square root of the density ratio is given to provide a means of computing true airspeed at any density altitude from the indicated airspeed read on the airspeed indicator. For example, at a pressure altitude of 2000 feet and a free air temperature of +28°C, the density altitude is 4000 feet and the reciprocal square root of the density ratio $1/\sqrt{\sigma}$ is 1.061. Assuming an indicated airspeed of 180, the airspeed relationships are as follows:

IAS — 180 kts

CAS — 180 kts

TAS = CAS x $1/\sqrt{\sigma}$

TAS = 180 x 1.061 = 191 kts

ENGINE POWER SCHEDULES

For any selected brake horsepower, the power schedule curves (figures A-3 through A-9) will define the permissible RPM and corresponding MAP for best power operation. A method of adjusting MAP for variations from standard CAT is included on each curve. Each schedule contains the manifold pressure and RPM necessary to establish the BHP noted in the heading, under various conditions of pressure altitude and carburetor air temperature.

FUEL FLOW PER ENGINE

Fuel flow corresponding to any selected brake horsepower may be determined by reference to the Fuel Flow per Engine Chart (figures A-10 and A-11). Curves for best power at various altitudes are provided. Standard day conditions are assumed.

TAKE-OFF DISTANCE

The Take-Off Distance Chart (figure A-12) predicts ground roll distance required and approximate total distance required to clear a 50-foot obstacle when density altitude (or pressure altitude and free air temperature), engine power, and gross weight are known. Facilities to modify the result for headwind and tailwind, and tables indicating take-off speed, and speed to clear a 50-foot obstacle for gross weights at 100-pound increments are included. The Standard Take-Off Distance Chart presupposes a hard surface runway.

TAKE-OFF, APPROACH AND TOUCH-DOWN VELOCITY

The indicated take-off, approach and touch-down speeds are shown (figure A-13) for weights from minimum to maximum gross weight at various flap settings.

CLIMB AT "METO" POWER

A Climb Chart (figure A-14) is provided for operation at "METO" power. The chart is entered with a known gross weight and altitude at the start of the climb and a desired altitude to be achieved. The reduced gross weight after climb resulting from fuel consumption, the length of time required to complete the climb, the climb power schedule, the best climb speed, and the distance in nautical miles (no wind) traversed during the climb is indicated on the graph. A reference line also included on the chart, shows the conditions at which the rate-of-climb is 300 feet per minute.

NAUTICAL MILES PER POUND OF FUEL

The Nautical Miles Per Pound of Fuel Charts (figures A-15 through A-21) illustrate graphically the cruise performance of the aircraft at various gross weights ranging from 2500 to 2900 pounds, in terms of airspeed (TAS and CAS) and fuel consumption (Air Nautical Mi/Lb). In addition, the power setting necessary to obtain a desired speed or fuel consumption may be read in terms of BHP. Recommendations for maximum endurance performance are indicated by a dashed line intersecting the "gross weight" and "power setting" lines at the low speed extremities. Similarly, the recommended power settings and speeds for 99-percent Best Economy in various wind conditions are indicated by dashed lines crossing the "gross weight" lines slightly on the high speed side of peak fuel economy. It should be noted that the fuel consumption read from the scales at the left is always expressed as air nautical miles per pound, or air nautical miles per gallon — even when a known wind condition is used for 99-percent Best Economy recommendations. A formula for converting air nautical miles per pound to ground nautical miles per pound is given under "NOTE" on each chart. Since the charts cover selected density altitude levels in increments of 2000 feet, it is necessary to interpolate the readings from two separate charts for intermediate altitudes.

NOTE

To obtain the times and distances shown on the Long-Range Predictions Charts (figures A-22 and A-23), the recommended power settings for 99-percent Best Economy given on the Nautical Miles Per Pound of Fuel Charts should be used and powers should be reset for each significant decrease in gross weight throughout the mission.

LONG-RANGE PREDICTION — DISTANCE

A chart is provided for Long-Range Prediction — Distance operation (figure A-22). This chart is composed of separate curves showing cruise distance plotted versus change in gross weight (due to fuel consumption) at various density altitudes ranging from sea level to 15,000 feet. Notice that the distance in air nautical miles may not be read directly from the scale at the left but is represented by the difference between two readings which correspond to the initial and final cruising weights.

NOTE

Flight tests were limited to 15,000 feet, therefore, range data is not shown up to service ceiling.

LONG-RANGE PREDICTION — TIME

A chart is also provided (figure A-23) for Long-Range Prediction — Time operation. This chart is composed of separate curves showing time plotted versus change in gross weight (due to fuel consumption) at various density altitudes ranging from sea level to 15,000 feet. Notice that the time required may not be read directly from the scale at the left, but is represented by difference between two readings which correspond to the initial and final cruising gross weights.

Appendix T.O. 1T-34A-1

MAXIMUM ENDURANCE

The Maximum Endurance Chart (figure A-24) provides CAS, power settings, and fuel flow versus gross weight. The altitude perimeters are from sea level to 15,000 feet.

LANDING DISTANCE

The Landing Distance Chart (figure A-25) is provided for landing with brakes only during the ground roll. For any selected gross weight the landing distance is indicated when either density altitude or pressure altitude and free air temperature is known. Additional refinement of the landing distance is possible if velocity of the headwind is known or if the landing must be accomplished over a 50-foot obstacle. Touch-down speeds, and speeds for 50-foot obstacle clearance for gross weights at 100-pound increments are given in an accompanying table. The Standard Landing Distances Charts presuppose a hard surface runway and 100 percent flaps.

USE OF THE CHARTS

The following sample problems, based on a typical mission and employing actual graphic values, demonstrates the proper use of the graphs.

PROBLEM: It is required that you fly to a base 600 nautical miles away. The first 200 miles will be flown at 6000 feet altitude and the remainder at 10,000 feet altitude due to terrain.

KNOWN FACTORS:

Required Range — 600 Nautical Miles
Weather — Clear — Zero Winds Aloft — Standard Day
Basic Weight 2174 Pounds
Personnel Weight — 400 Pounds (2 Men at 200 Pounds Per Man)
Fuel Weight — 300 Pounds (50 Gallons at 6 Pounds Per Gallon)
Oil Weight — 23 Pounds (3 Gallons at 7.5 Pounds Per Gallon)
Total Weight — 2950 Pounds
Take-Off Air Field — 2000 Feet Pressure Altitude — Temperature 11°C — 10-knot headwind
Landing Air Field — 4000 Feet Pressure Altitude — Temperature 7°C — 10-knot headwind

In completing the actual flight plan, each separate flight condition should be treated as a separate problem.

From the Take-Off Curve (Figure A-12):

Take-Off:

Initial weight .... 2950 lbs

Warm-up (5 minutes at
"METO" power) .... 12 lbs
Take-Off weight .... 2938 lbs
Take-Off distance (ground roll) .... 900 ft
Take-Off distance over 50 feet .... 1125 ft

With the weight determined at start of cruise from the climb graph (figure A-14) and the distance to be covered, the fuel used during mission may be found by using long-range prediction — distance graph (figure A-22). With this information, the time can be found from long-range prediction — time (figure A-23).

From the Climb Curve (figure A-14):

CLIMB — LEG 1

Start climb weight .... 2938 lbs
Climb fuel (one gallon) .... 6 lbs
Altitude .... 2000 to 6000 ft
End climb weight .... 2932 lbs
Climb distance .... 7 naut mi
Climb time .... (4.3 min) .07 hr

From the Power Schedule Chart (Figures A-4, A-5, and A-6):

Power setting .... 2600 rpm
(BHP 212) .... 26.5 in. Hg at 2000 feet
(BHP 193) .... 25.0 in. Hg at 4000 feet
(BHP 177) .... 23.0 in. Hg at 6000 feet

NOTE: RPM, MP, and Mixture.

These items are read directly from the Power Schedule Chart. The fuel used in climb was read directly from climb curve (figure A-14). This value plus 2 gallons for warm-up and take-off is equal to 3 gallons.

CRUISE — LEG 2

Start cruise weight 2932
Fuel in gallons 50 − (2+1) 47
Distance to travel .... 200 naut mi

From long-range prediction — distance — 6000 ft (figure A-22):

Fuel used .... 72 lb = 12 gal
End cruise weight (2932 − 72) .... 2860 lbs
Average cruise weight .... 2896 lbs

The cruise speed power settings were based on 99 percent maximum miles per pound calculations. From nautical miles per pound of fuel — 6000 feet (figure A-18):

True air speed .... 114.5 kts
Power setting .... 1920 rpm
(BHP 91) .... 18.2 in. Hg
                                                    Manual lean
Time (200/114.5) .... 1.75 hr

CLIMB — LEG 3

Start climb weight (2932 − 72) .... 2860 lbs
Fuel in gallons 50 − (2+1+12) 35
Altitude .... 6000 to 10,000 ft

A-4

From the Power Schedule (Figures A-6, A-7, and A-8):

    Power setting ....2600 rpm
      (BHP 177) ....23.0 in. Hg at 6000 ft
      (BHP 165) ....21.6 in. Hg at 8000 ft
      (BHP 152) ....20.0 in. Hg at 10,000 ft

From the Climb Curve (Figure A-14):

    Fuel used (36 lbs) ....6 gal
    Climb distance ....8 naut mi
    Climb time ....(4.5 min) .08 hr
    End climb weight (2860 — 36) ....2824 lbs

CRUISE — LEG 4

    Start cruise weight ....2824 lbs
    Fuel in gallons 50 — (2 + 1 + 12 + 6)........29 gal
    Distance ....385 naut mi

From long-range prediction — distance 10,000 feet (Figure A-22):

    Fuel used ....136 lbs
    End cruise weight (2824 — 136) ....2688 lbs
    Average cruise weight ....2756 lbs

From nautical miles per pound — 10,000 feet (Figure A-20):

    True airspeed ....118 kts
    Power setting ....1900 rpm
      (BHP 88) ....17.5 in. Hg
                               Manual Lean
    Time (385/118) ....3.26 hr

Fuel Used:

    Fuel used was the change in weight starting at 2824 pounds and traveling 385 nautical miles as determined by the use of the long-range prediction-distance curve.

Fuel Remaining at End of Mission:

    Initial fuel minus fuel used in Legs 1, 2, 3, and 4 gives 50 — (2 + 1 + 12 + 6 + 23) = 6 gallons.

TOTAL MISSION

    Distance to climb 6000 feet .... 7 naut mi
    Cruise at 6000 feet ....200 naut mi
    Distance to climb from 6000 ft to
      10,000 ft .... 8 naut mi
    Cruise at 10,000 ft ....385 naut mi
      TOTAL ....600 naut mi
    Time to climb 6000 ft ....(4.3 min) .07 hr
    Cruise time at 6000 ft ....1.75 hr
    Time to climb from 6000 ft to
      10,000 ft ....(4.5 min) .08 hr
    Cruise time at 10,000 ft ....3.26 hr
      TOTAL TIME ....5.16 hr

From the Landing Curve (Figure A-25):
Landing:

    Final weight ....2688 lbs
    (No fuel or distance allowance
      for let-down)
    Landing distance (ground roll) ....280 ft
    Landing distance over 50 feet ....490 ft

Appendix T.O. 1T-34A-1

TEMPERATURE CONVERSION

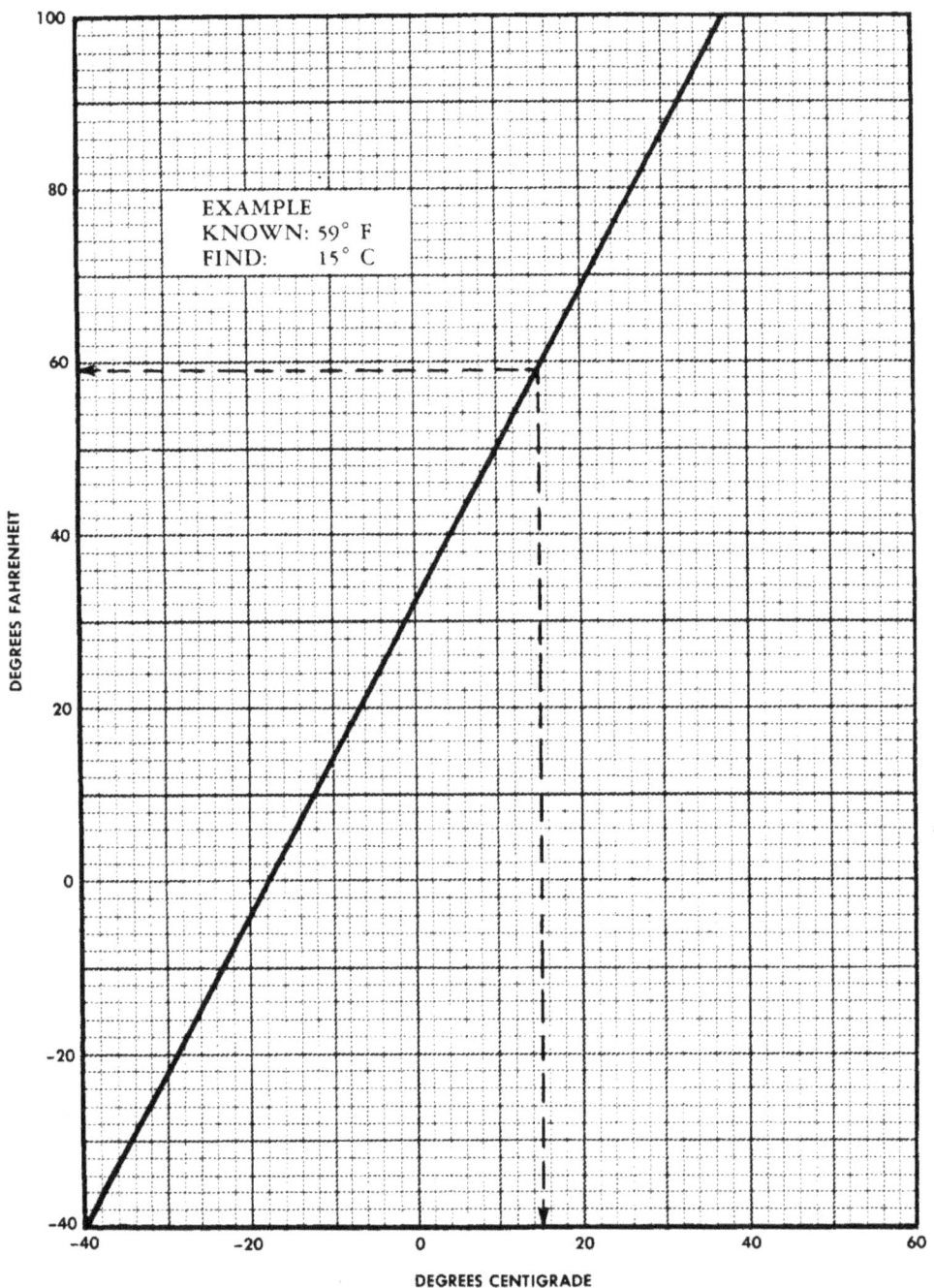

Figure A-1

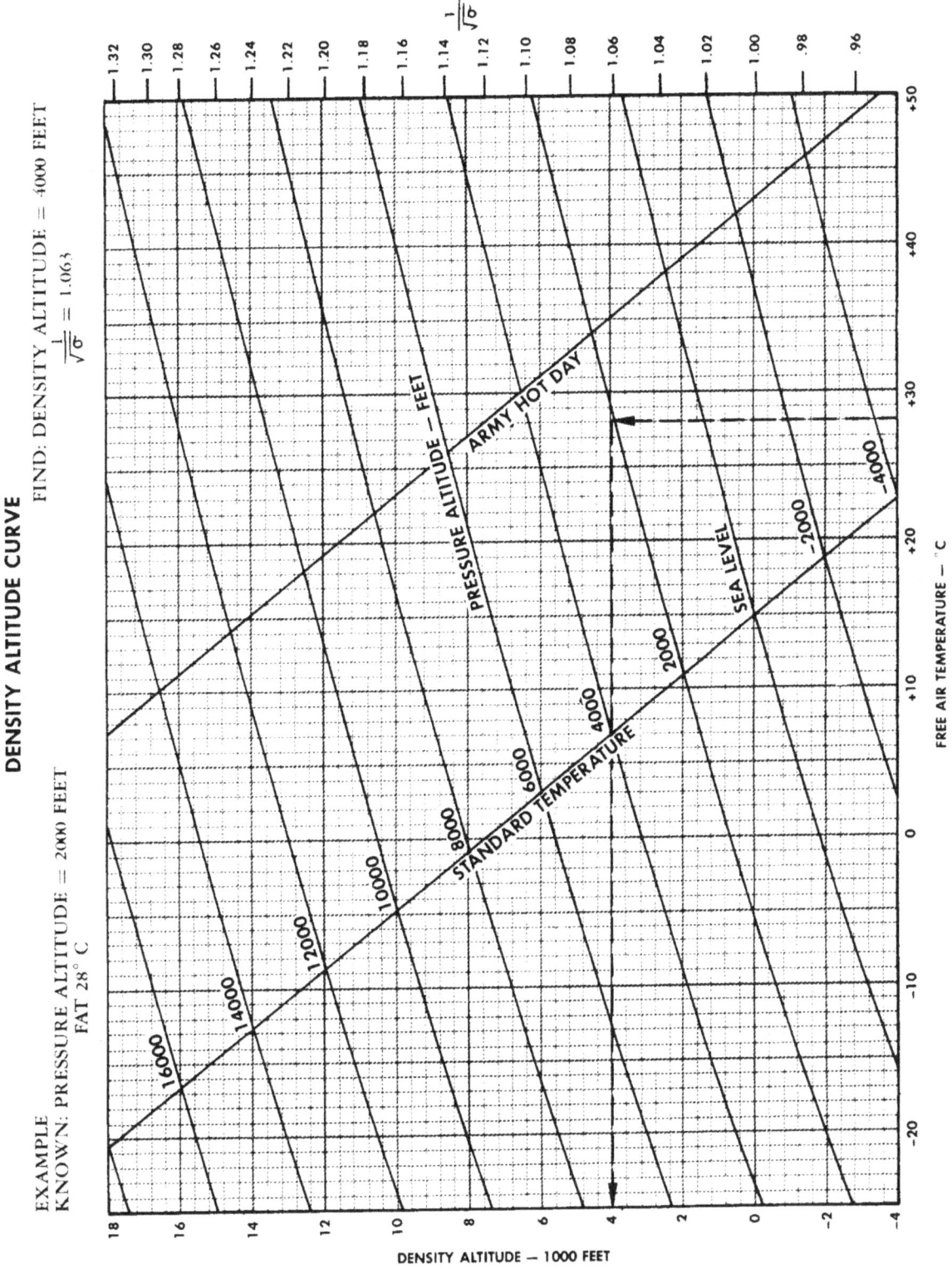

Figure A-2

Appendix T.O. 1T-34A-1

POWER SCHEDULE
SEA LEVEL
BEST POWER MIXTURE

MODEL T-34A ENGINE: O-470-13

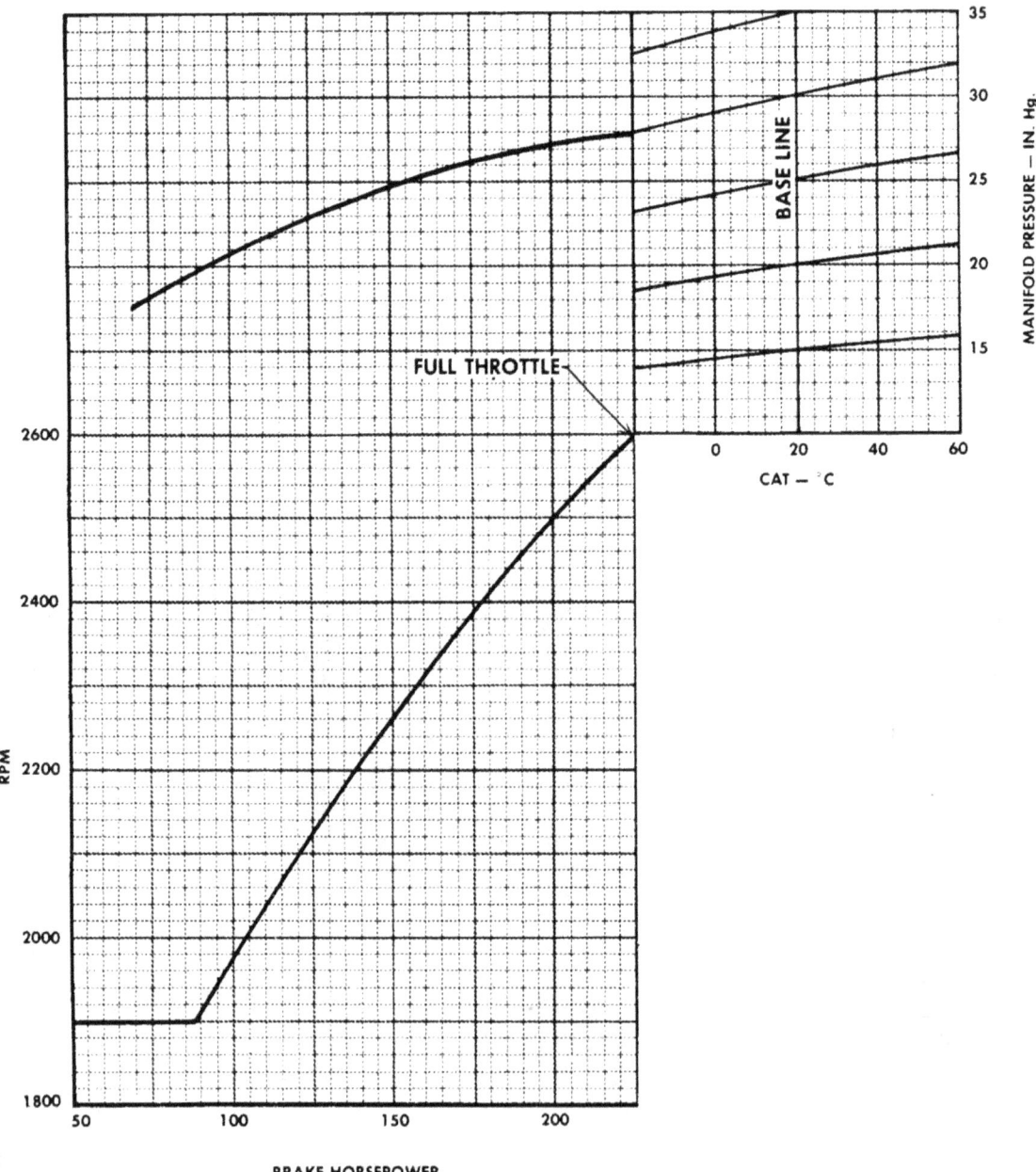

DATA AS OF: FEBRUARY 1954 FUEL GRADE: 80
DATA BASED ON: FLIGHT TEST FUEL DENSITY: 6.0 LBS/GAL

Figure A-3

T.O. 1T-34A-1 — Appendix

POWER SCHEDULE
2000 FEET
BEST POWER MIXTURE

MODEL T-34A
ENGINE: O-470-13

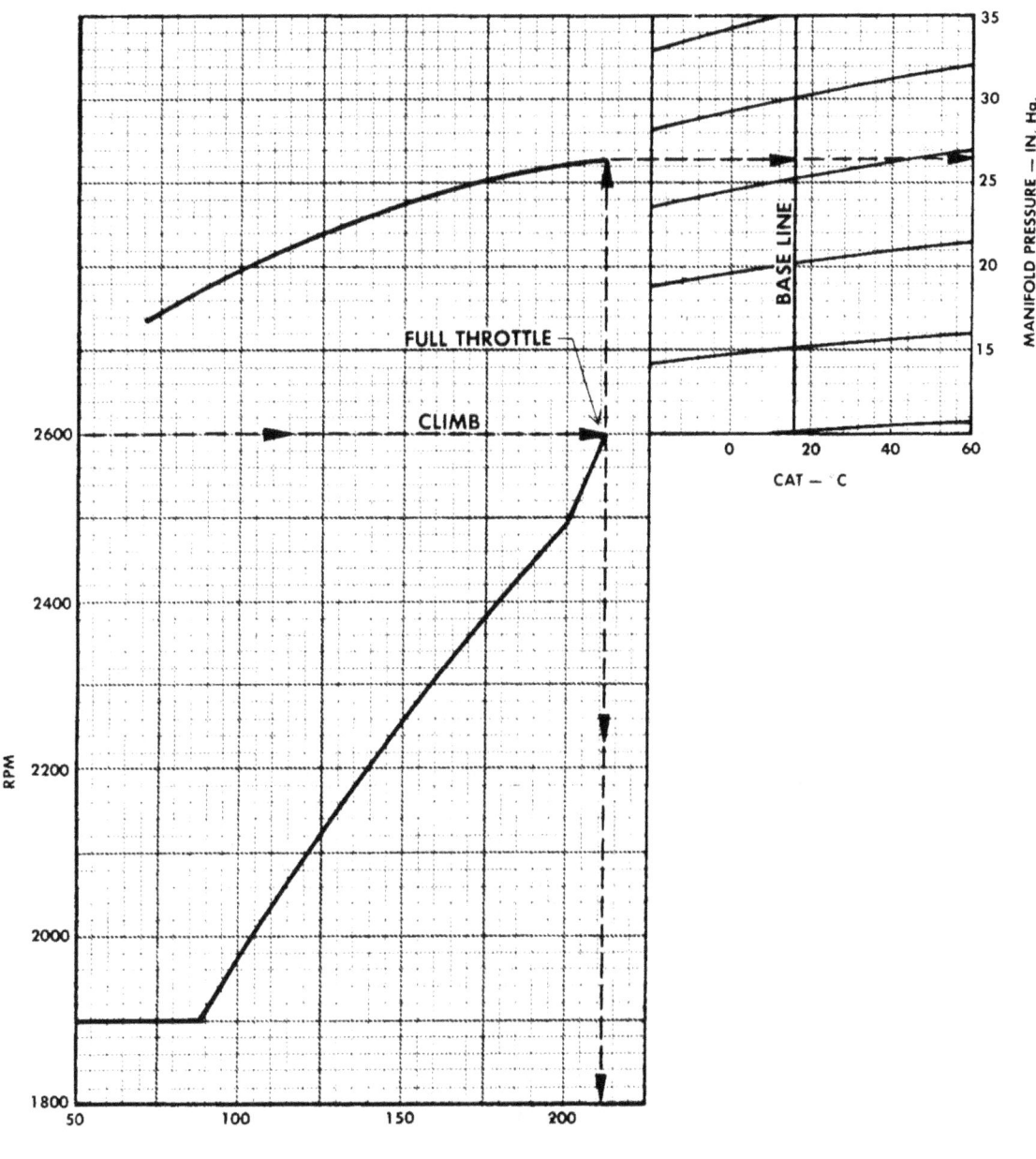

DATA AS OF: FEBRUARY 1954
DATA BASED ON: FLIGHT TEST
FUEL GRADE: 80
FUEL DENSITY: 6.0 LBS/GAL

Figure A-4

Appendix T.O. 1T-34A-1

POWER SCHEDULE
4000 FEET
BEST POWER MIXTURE

MODEL T-34A

ENGINE: 0-470-13

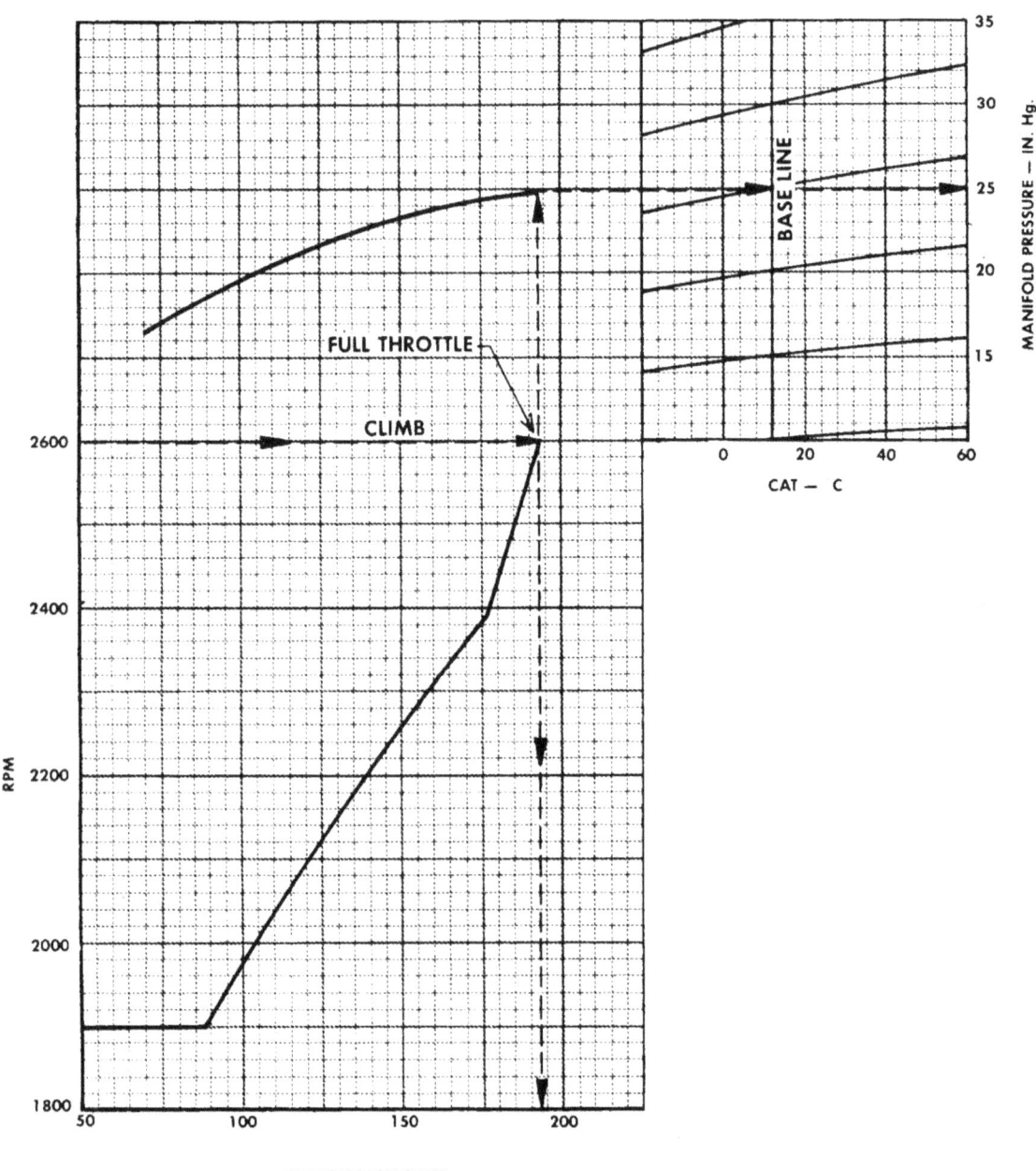

DATA AS OF: FEBRUARY 1954
DATA BASED ON: FLIGHT TEST

FUEL GRADE: 80
FUEL DENSITY: 6.0 LBS/GAL

Figure A-5

POWER SCHEDULE
6000 FEET
BEST POWER MIXTURE

MODEL T-34A

ENGINE: O-470-13

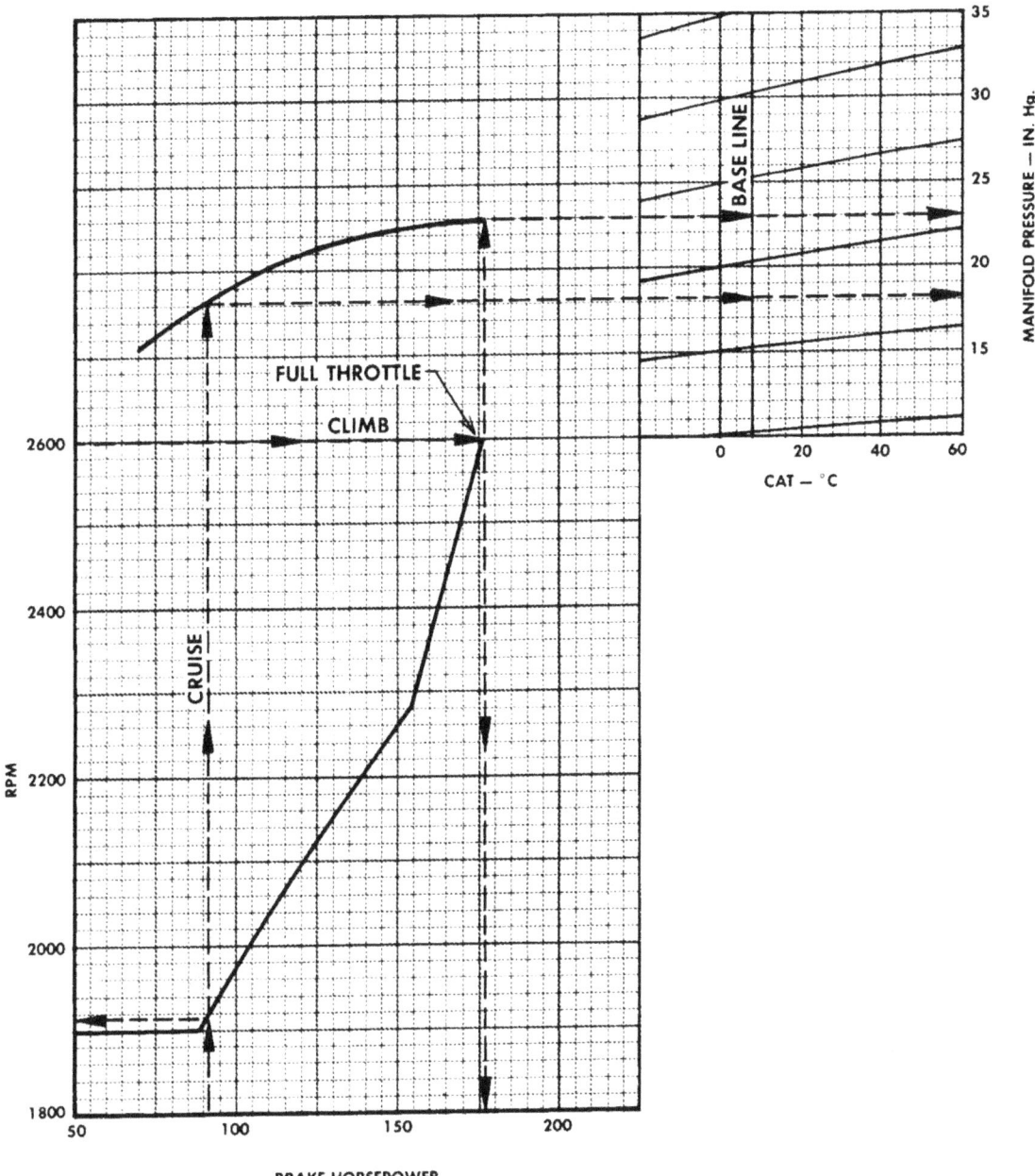

DATA AS OF: FEBRUARY 1954
DATA BASED ON: FLIGHT TEST

FUEL GRADE: 80
FUEL DENSITY: 6.0 LBS/GAL

Figure A-6

Appendix T.O. 1T-34A-1

POWER SCHEDULE
8000 FEET
BEST POWER MIXTURE

MODEL T-34A

ENGINE: O-470-13

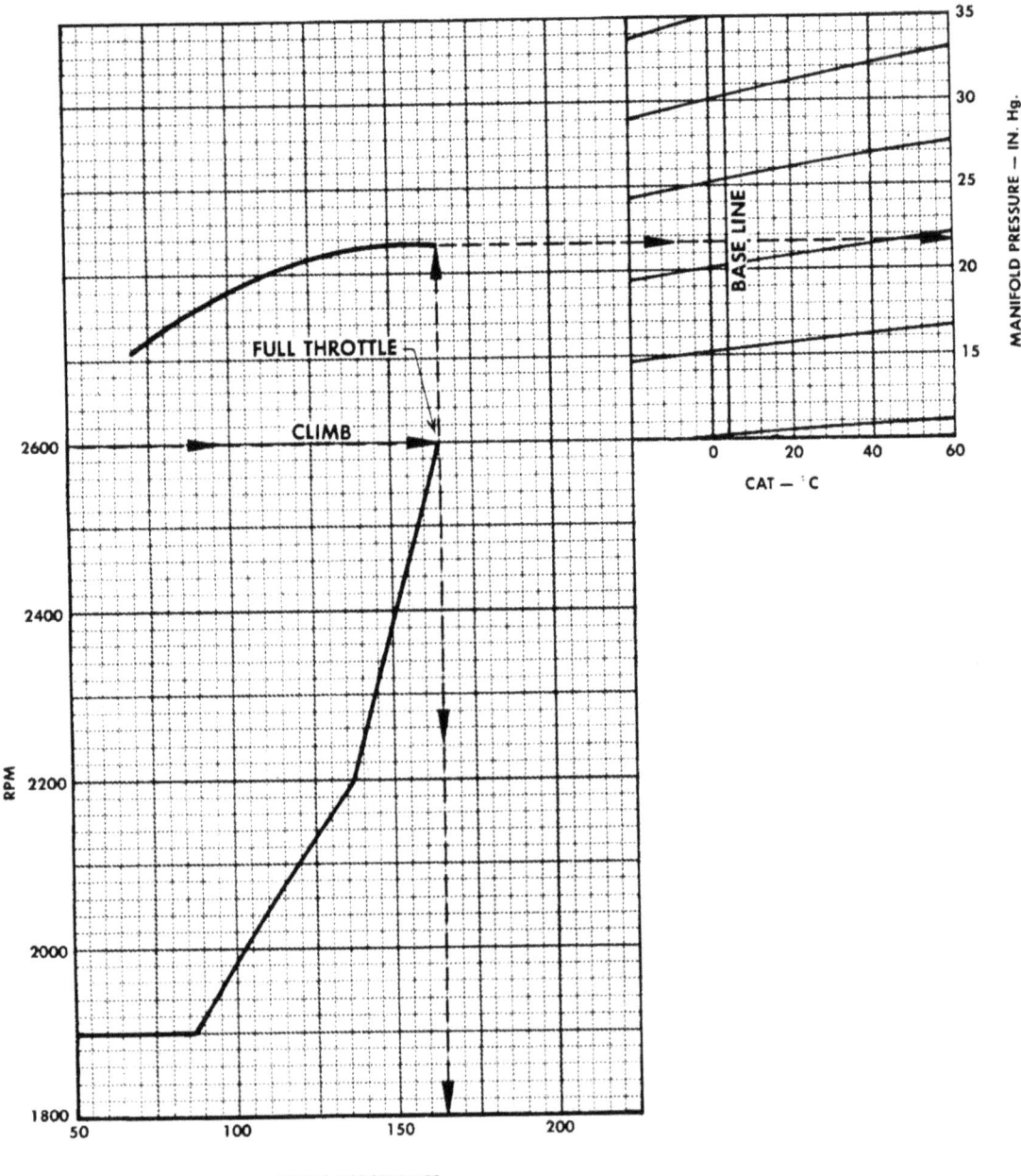

DATA AS OF: FEBRUARY 1954
DATA BASED ON: FLIGHT TEST

FUEL GRADE: 80
FUEL DENSITY: 6.0 LBS/GAL

Figure A-7

T.O. 1T-34A-1

Appendix

POWER SCHEDULE
10000 FEET
BEST POWER MIXTURE

MODEL T-34A

ENGINE: O-470-13

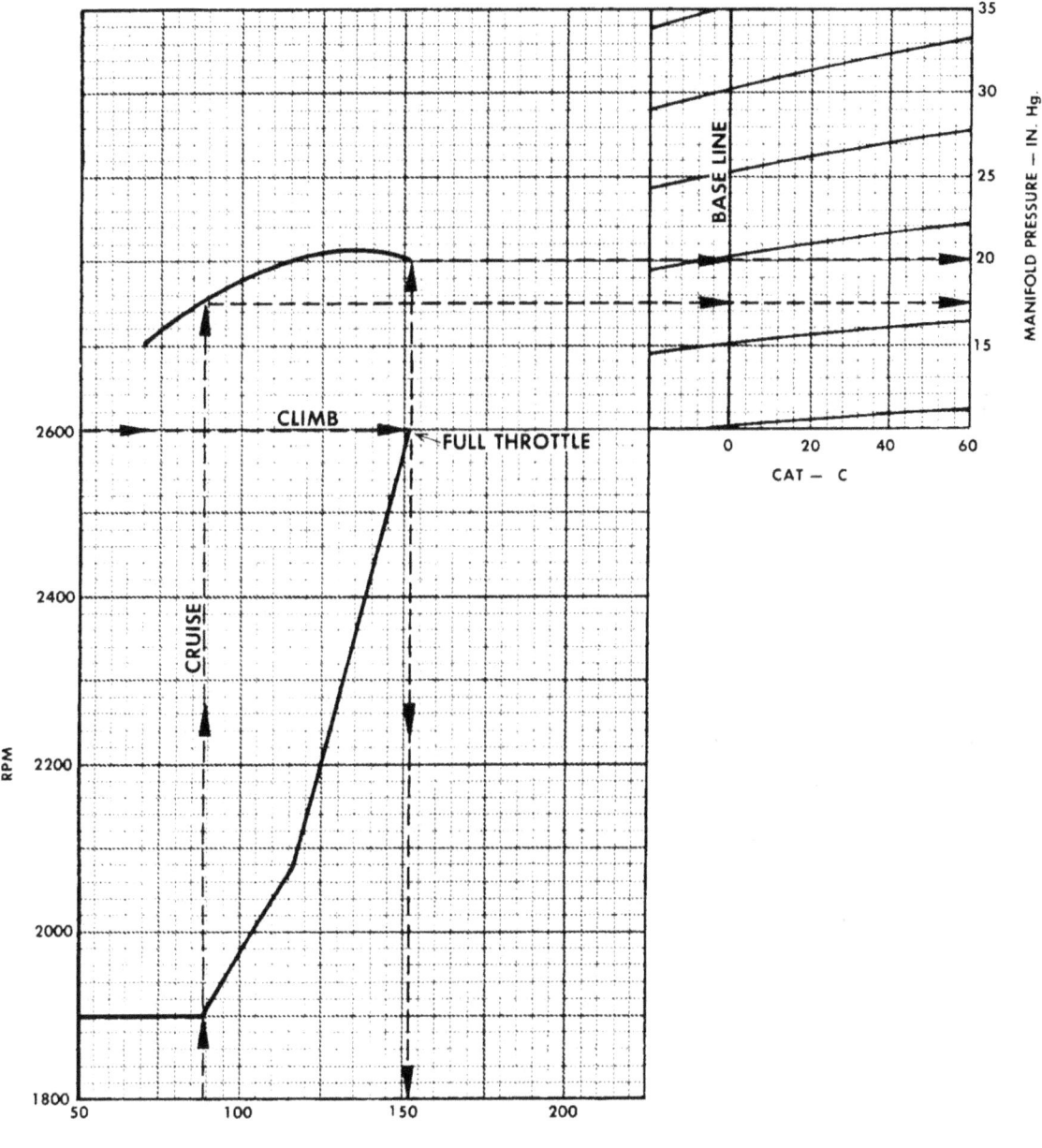

DATA AS OF: FEBRUARY 1954
DATA BASED ON: FLIGHT TEST

FUEL GRADE: 80
FUEL DENSITY: 6.0 LBS/GAL

Figure A-8

Appendix

T.O. 1T-34A-1

POWER SCHEDULE
15000 FEET
BEST POWER MIXTURE

MODEL T-34A

ENGINE: 0-470-13

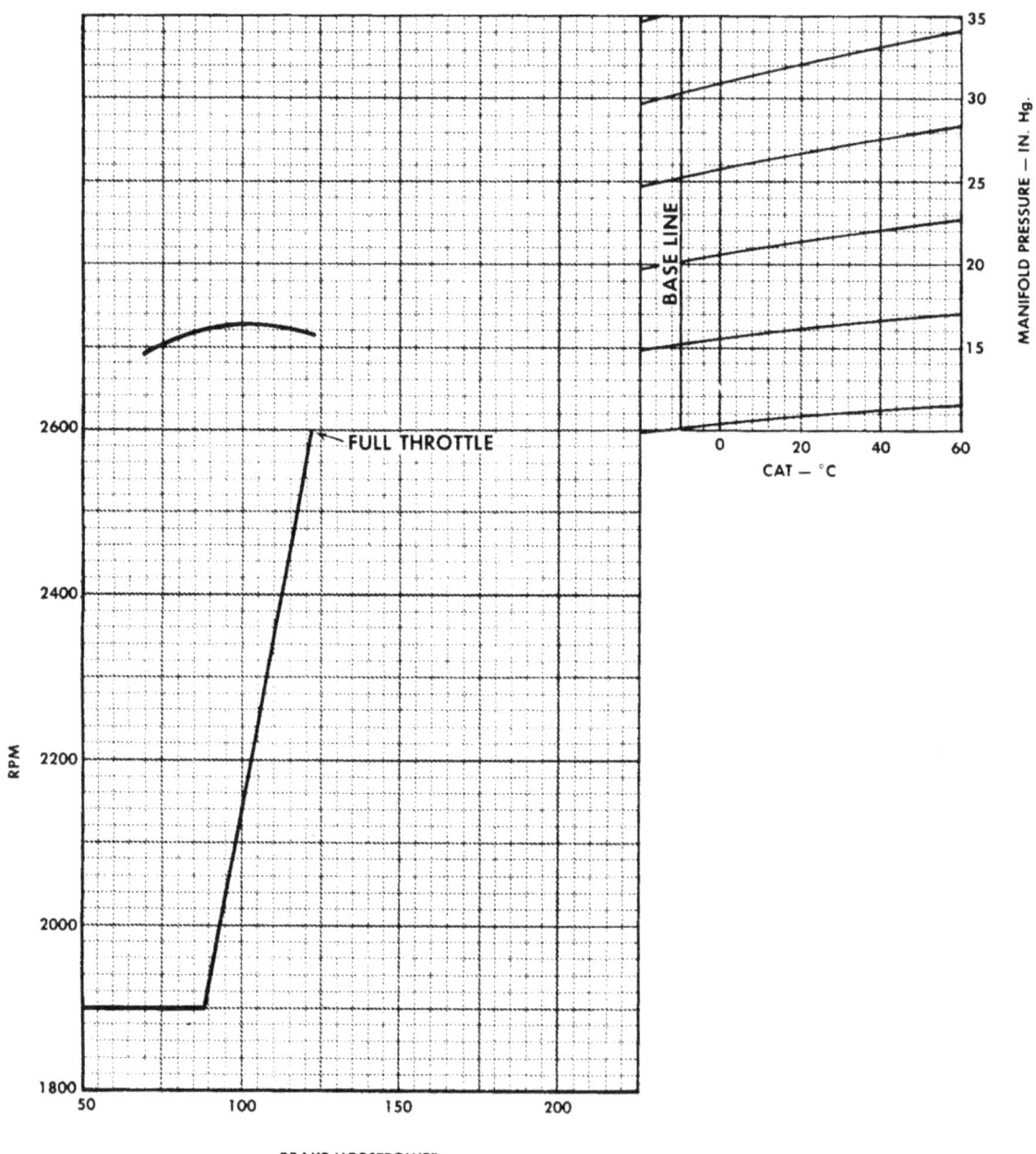

DATA AS OF: FEBRUARY 1954
DATA BASED ON: FLIGHT TEST

FUEL GRADE: 80
FUEL DENSITY: 6.0 LBS/GAL

Figure A-9

FUEL FLOW PER ENGINE
BEST POWER MIXTURE

MODEL T-34A

ENGINE: O-470-13

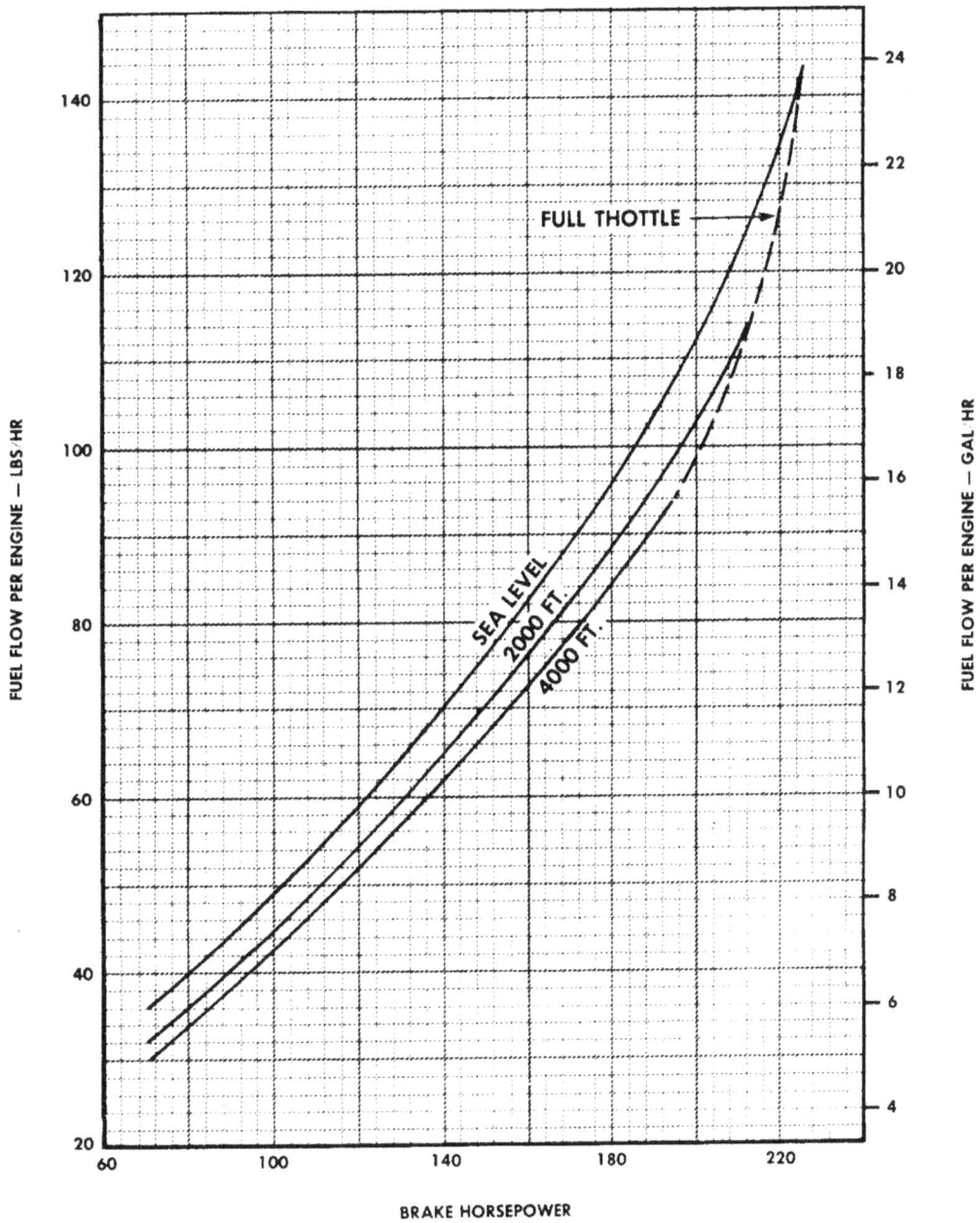

DATA AS OF: FEBRUARY 1954
DATA BASED ON: FLIGHT TEST

FUEL GRADE: 80
FUEL DENSITY: 6.0 LBS/GAL

Figure A-10

FUEL FLOW PER ENGINE
BEST POWER MIXTURE

MODEL T-34A

ENGINE: O-470-13

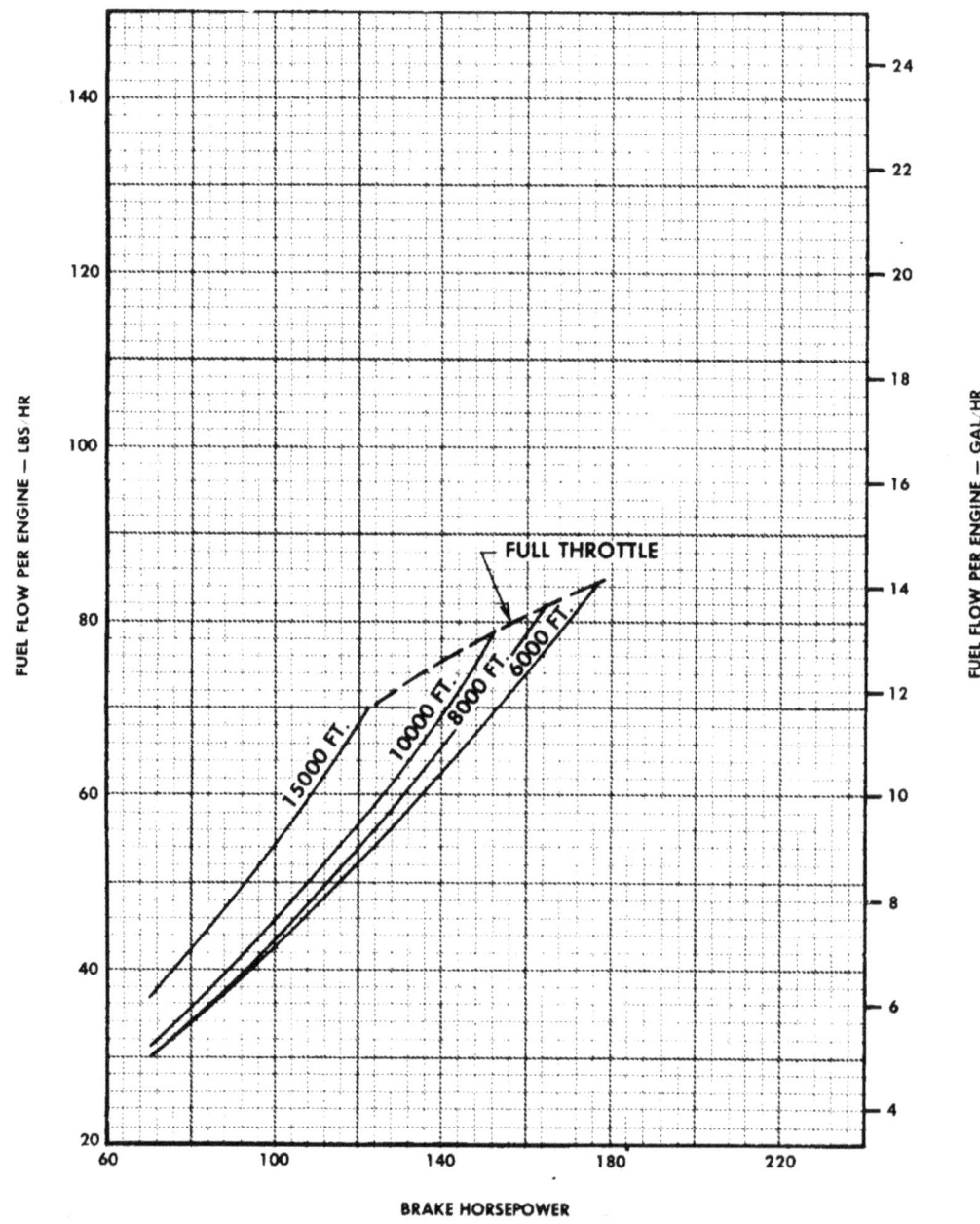

DATA AS OF: FEBRUARY 1954
DATA BASED ON: FLIGHT TEST

FUEL GRADE: 80
FUEL DENSITY: 6.0 LBS/GAL

Figure A-11

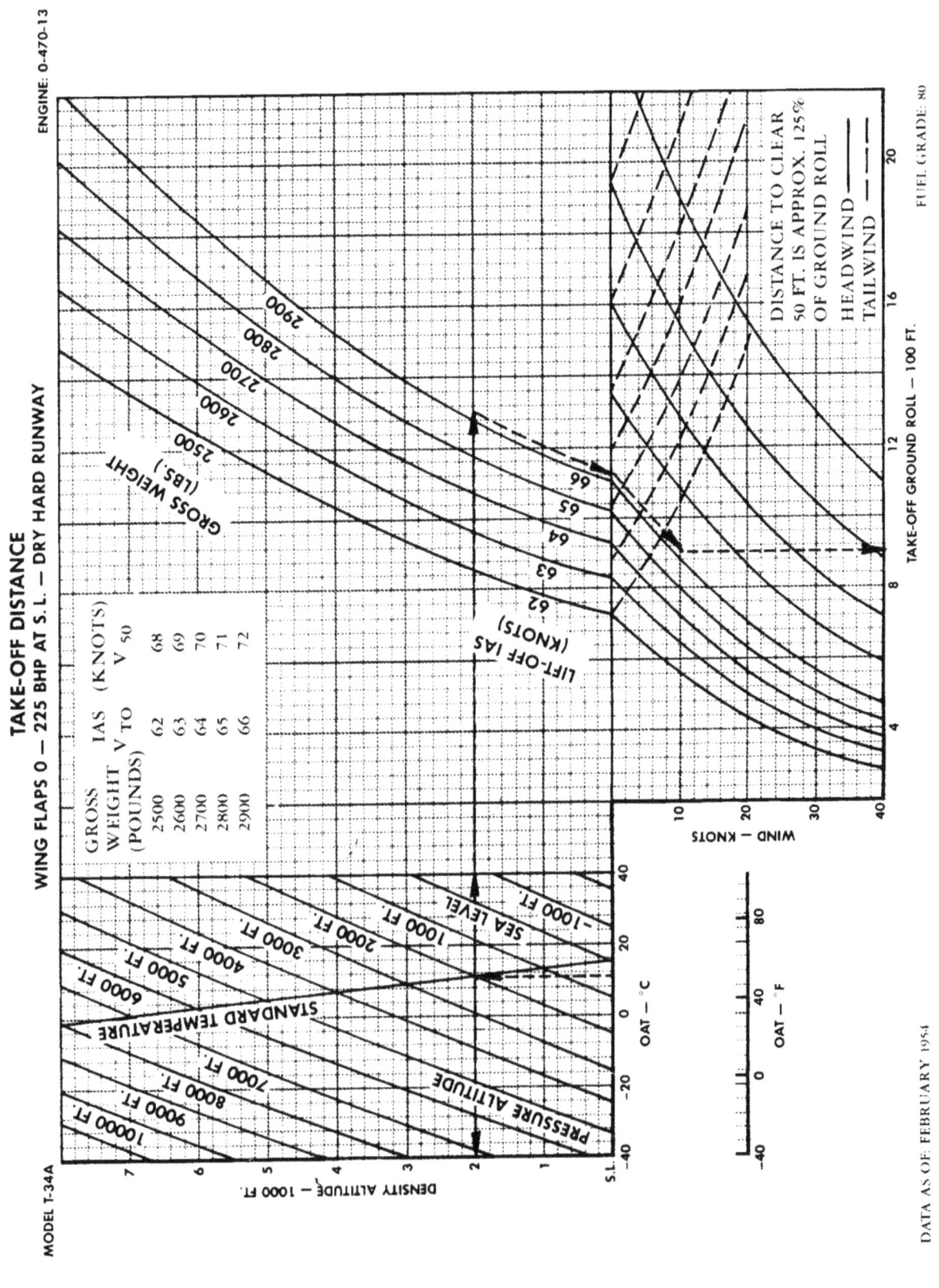

Figure A-12

Appendix

T.O. 1T-34A-1

TAKE-OFF, APPROACH AND TOUCHDOWN VELOCITY

MODEL T-34A

ENGINE: O-470-13

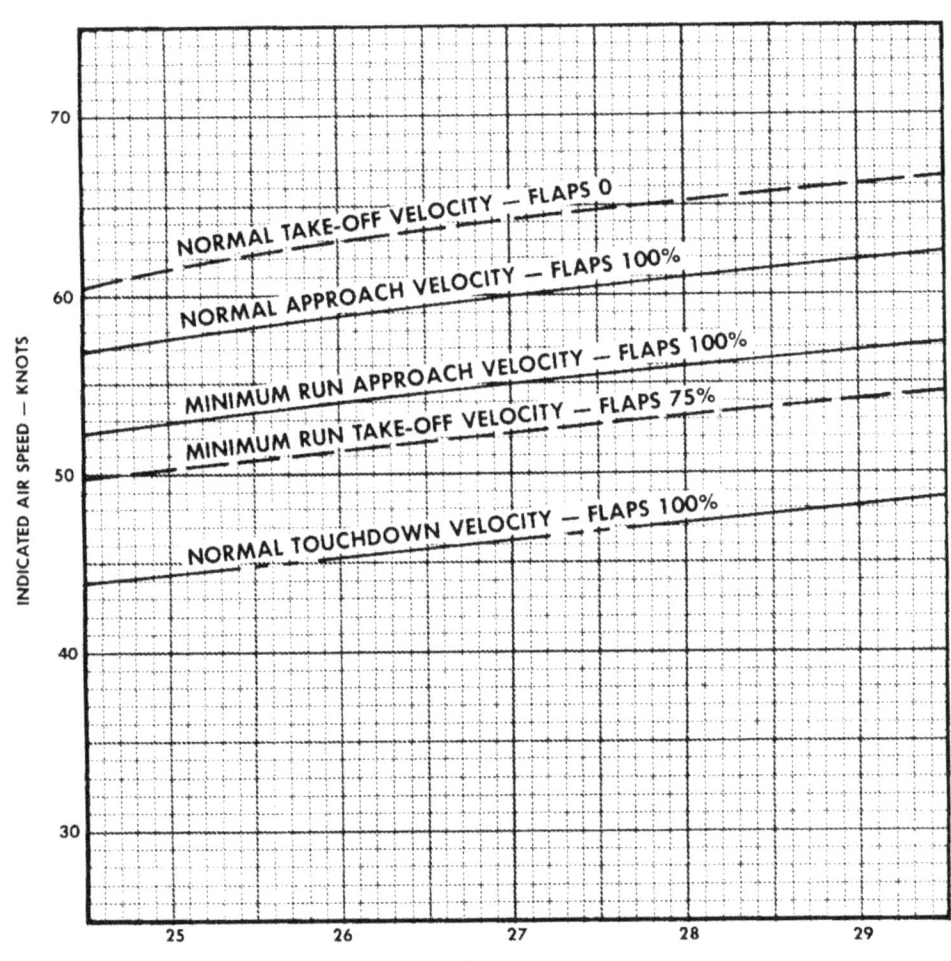

DATA AS OF: FEBRUARY 1954
DATA BASED ON: FLIGHT TEST

FUEL GRADE: 80
FUEL DENSITY: 6.0 LBS/GAL

Figure A-13

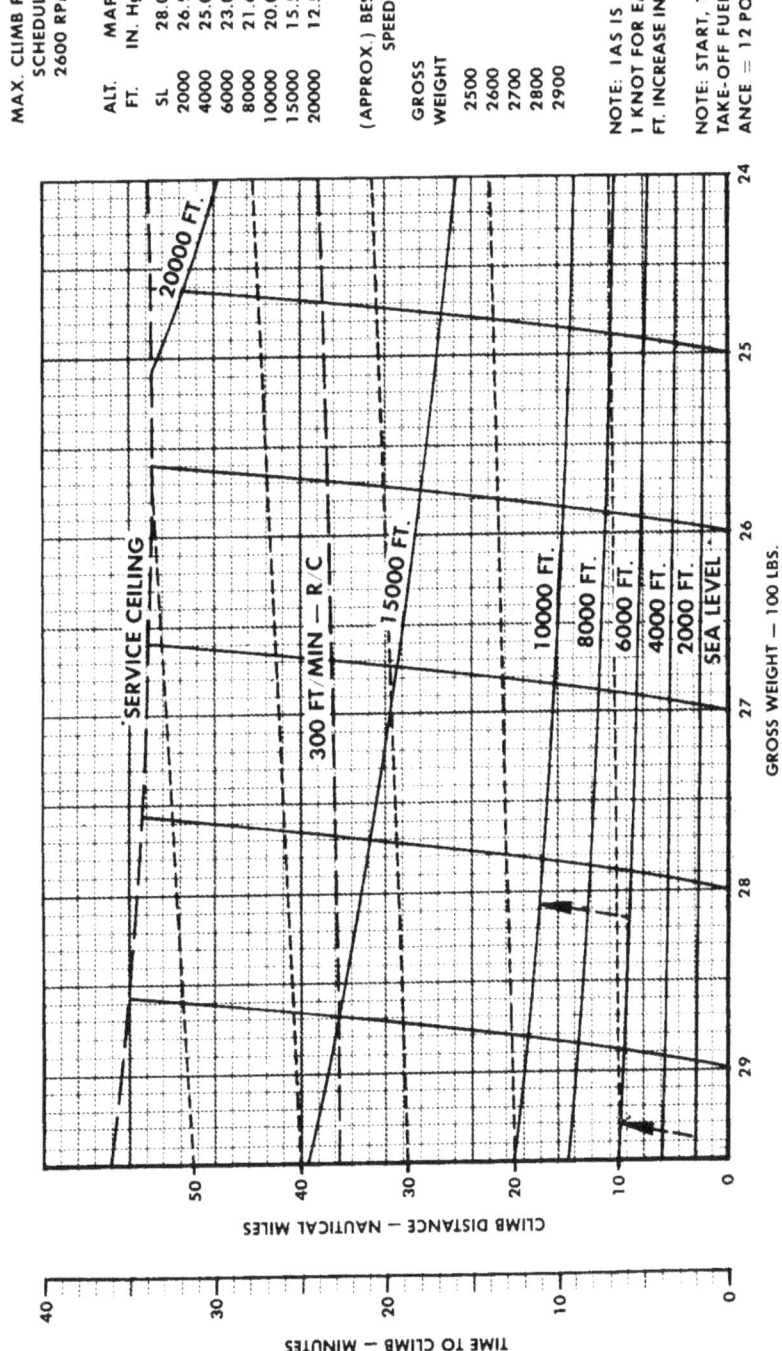

Figure A-14

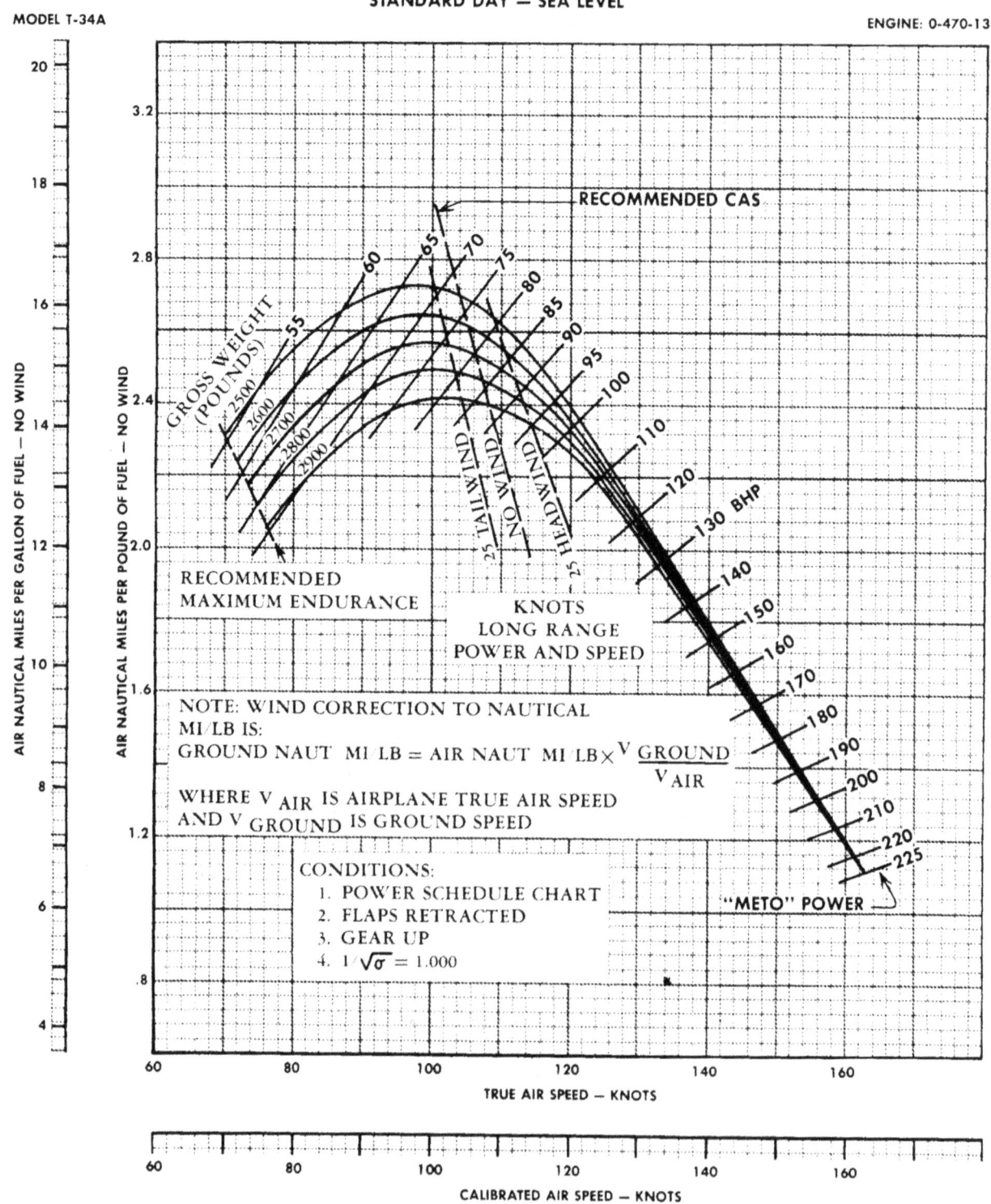

Figure A-15

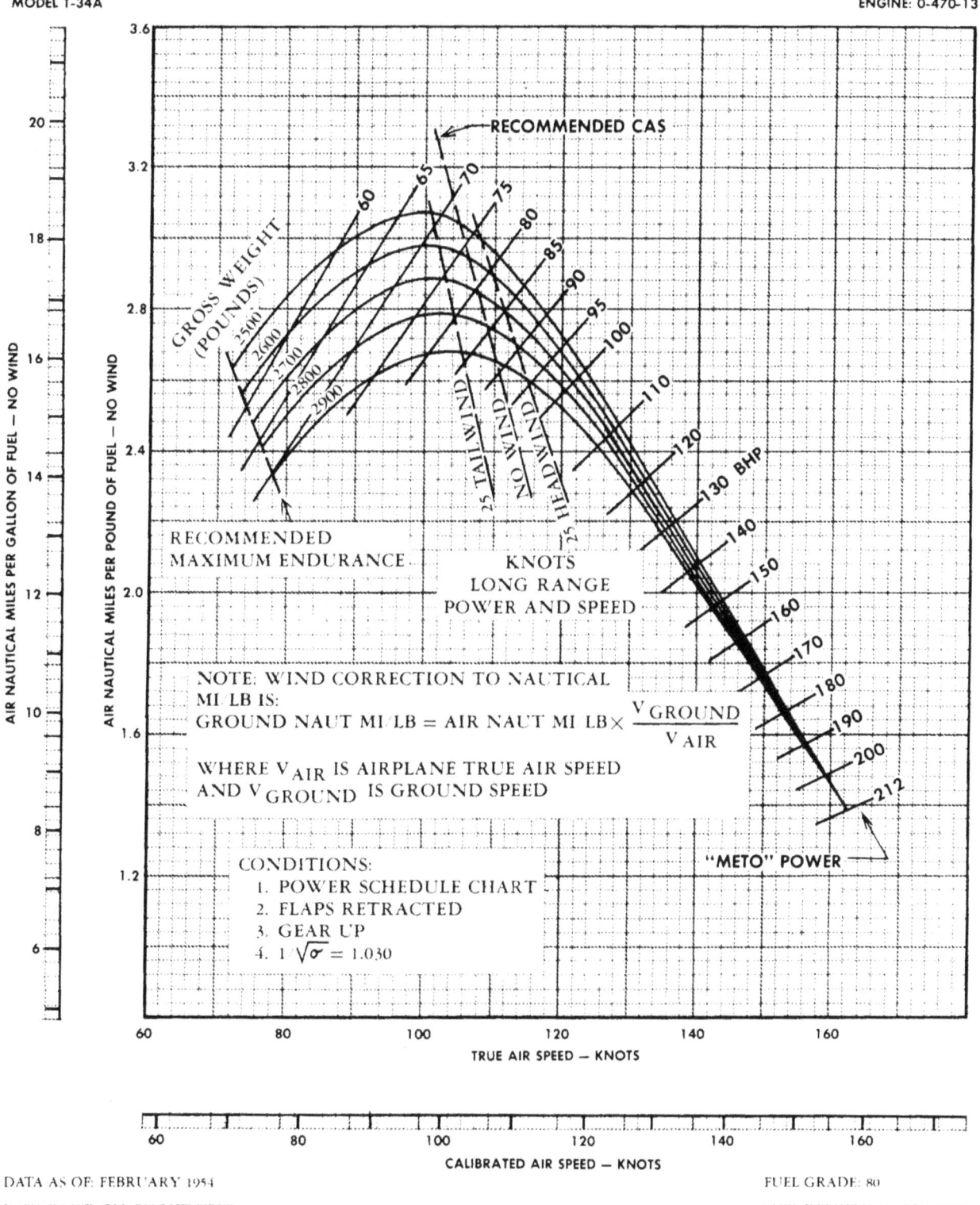

Figure A-16

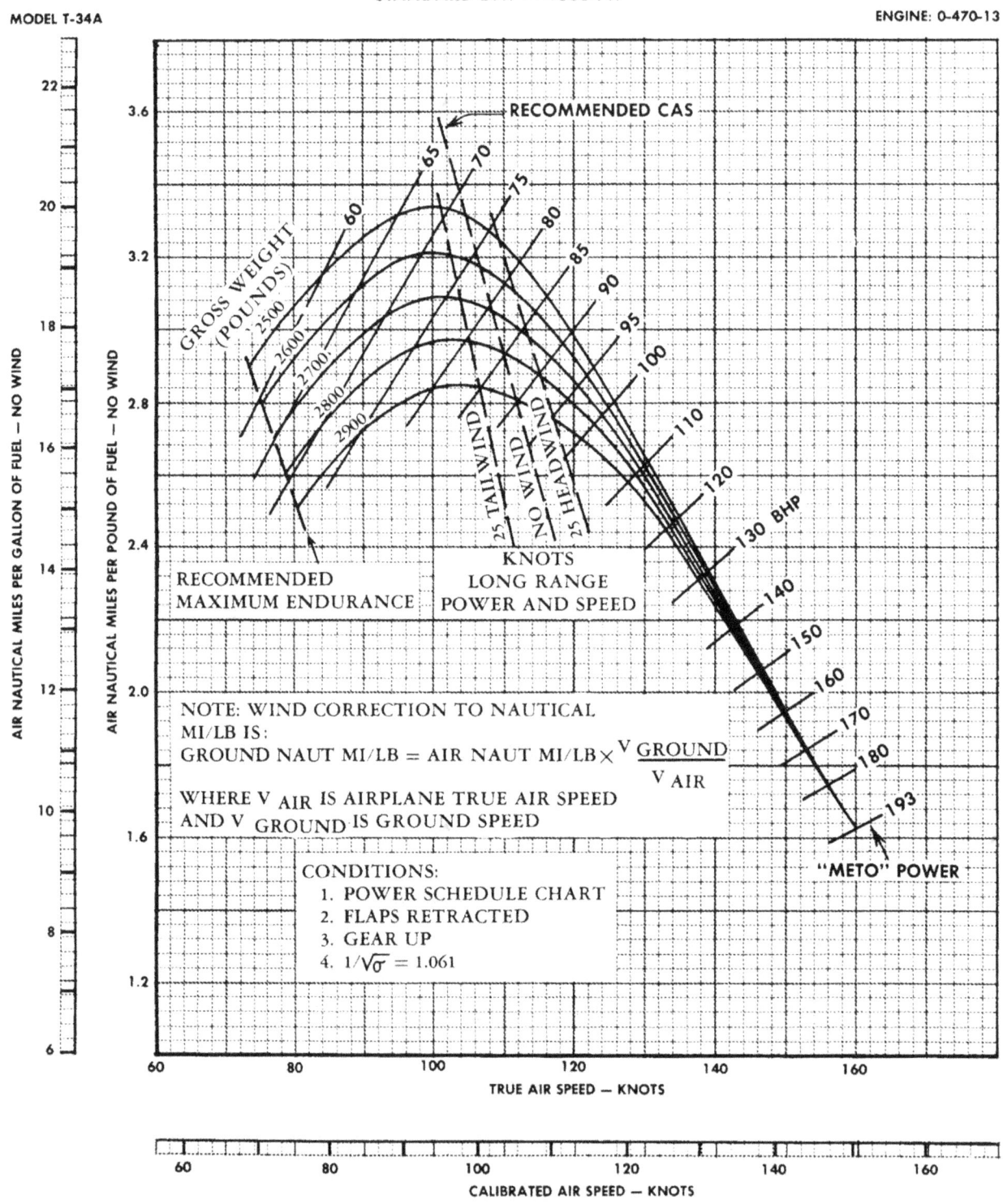

Figure A-17

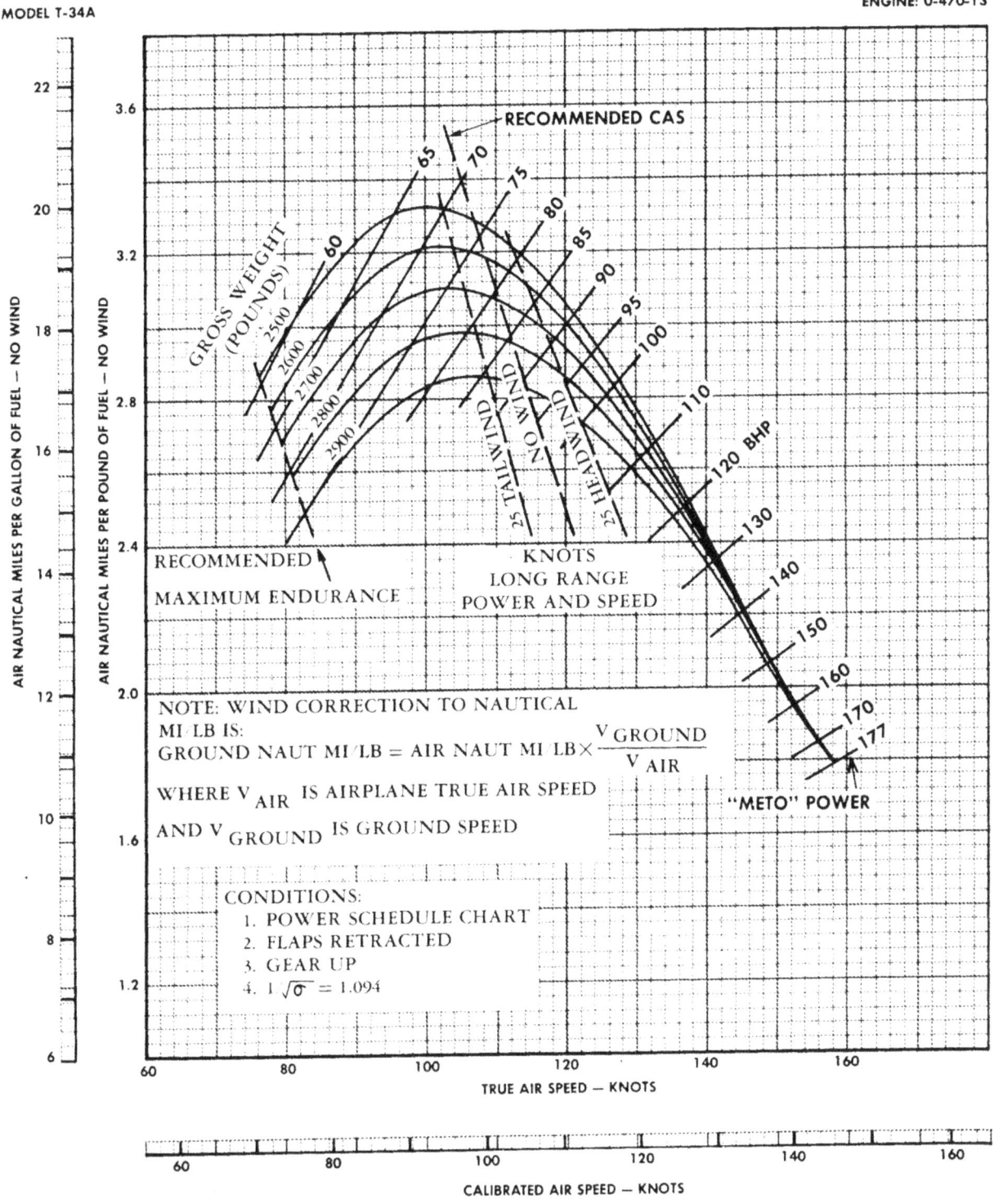

Figure A-18

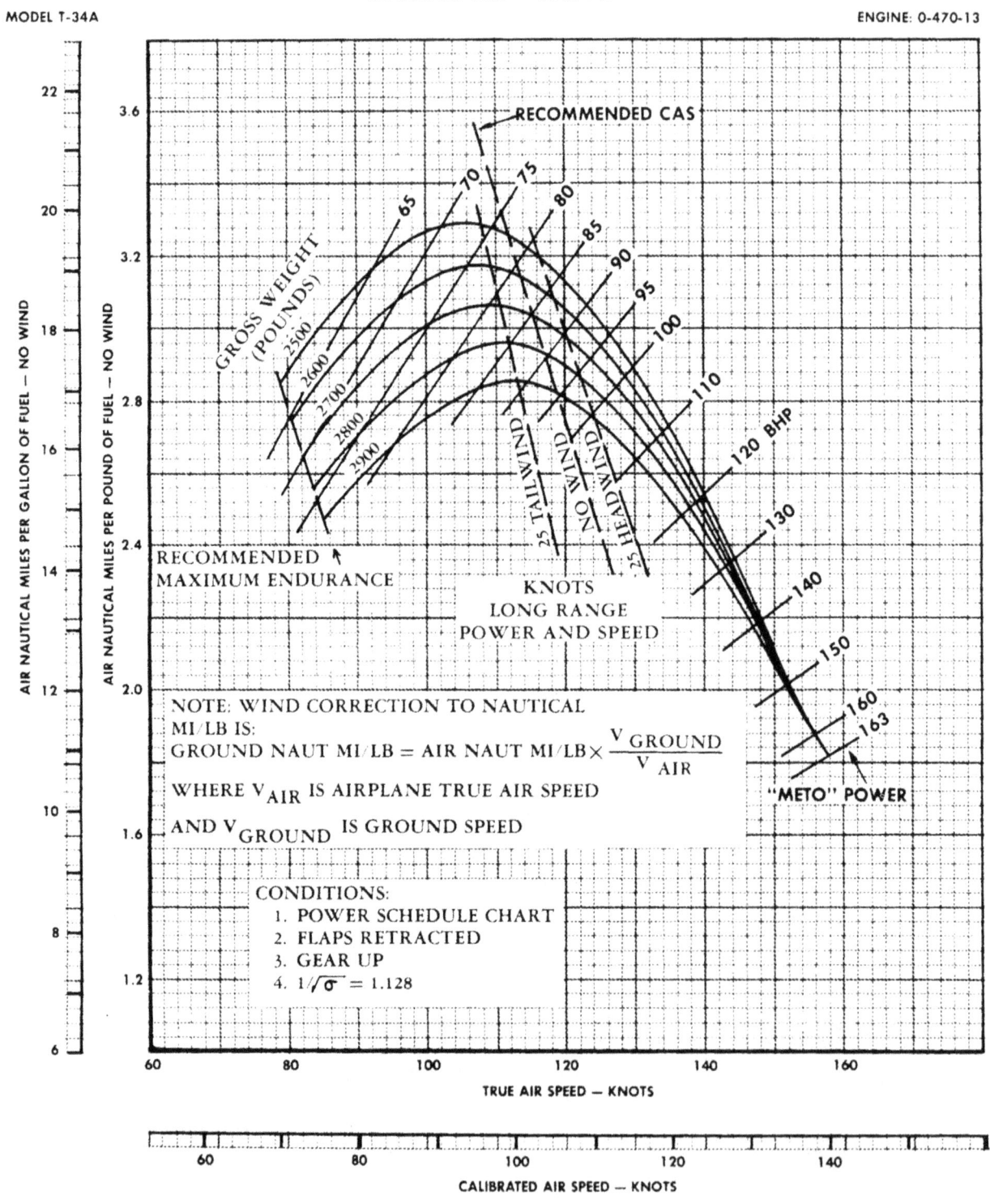

Figure A-19

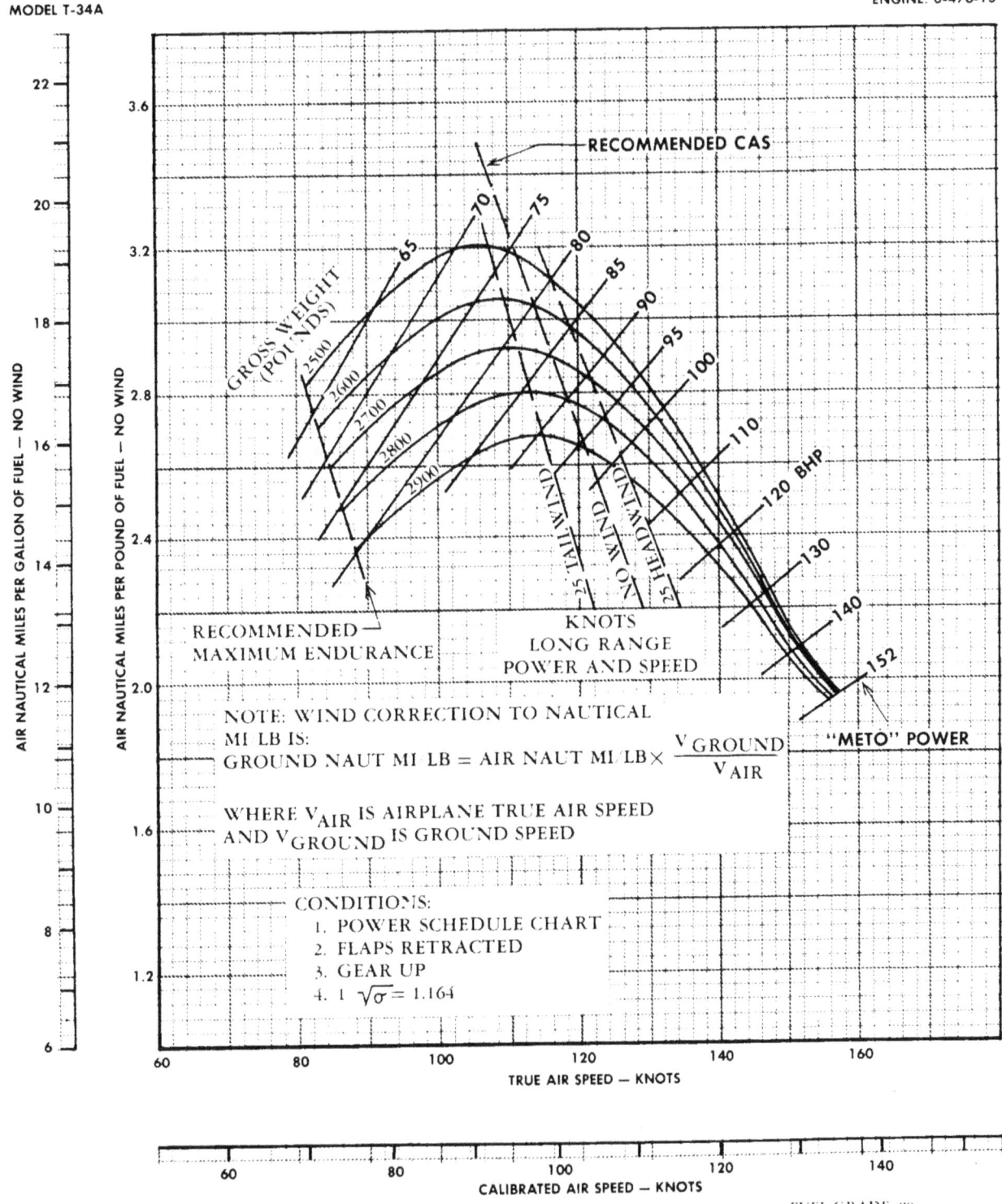

Figure A-20

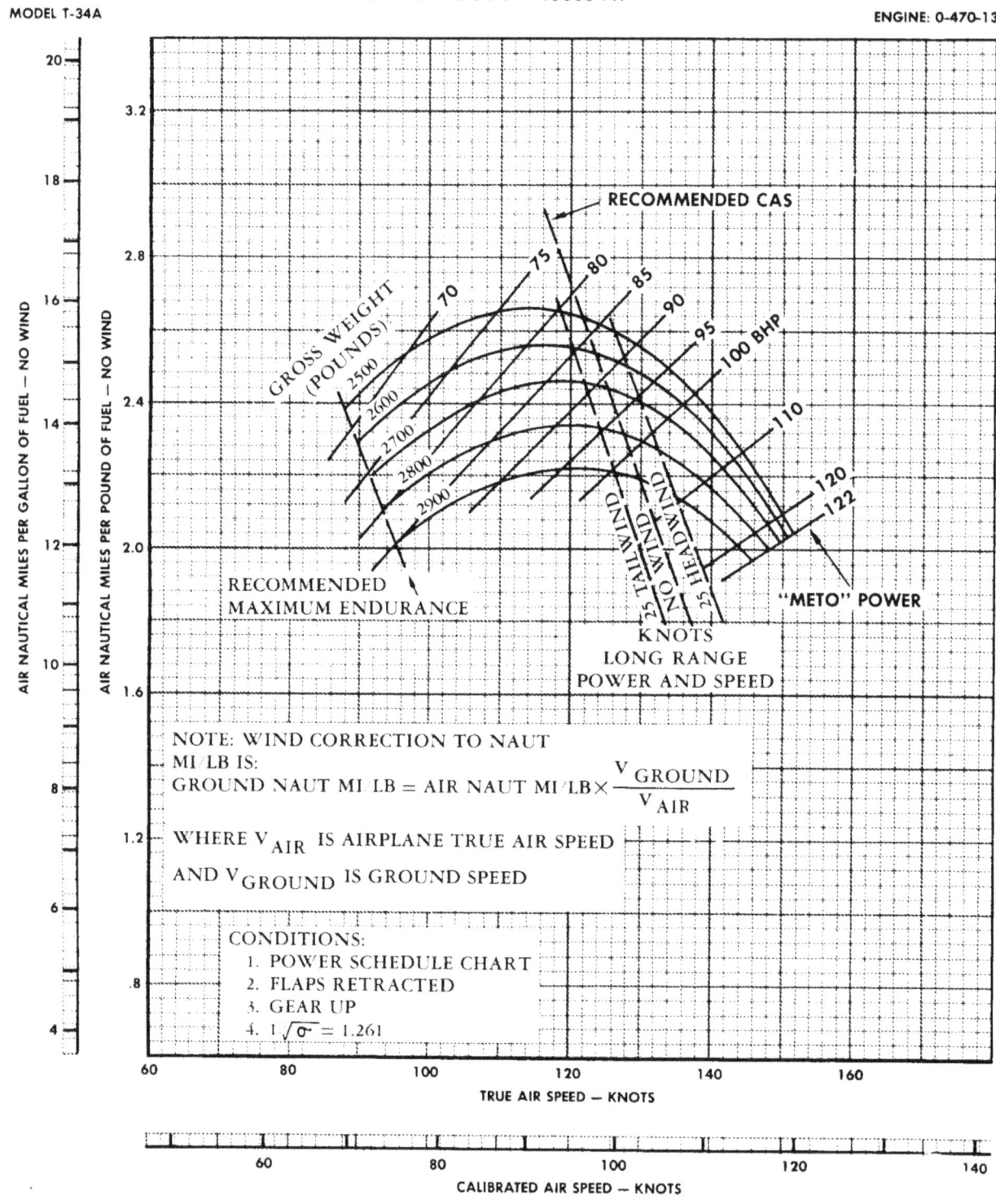

Figure A-21

LONG RANGE PREDICTION — DISTANCE (NO WIND)
STANDARD DAY

MODEL T-34A ENGINE: 0-470-13

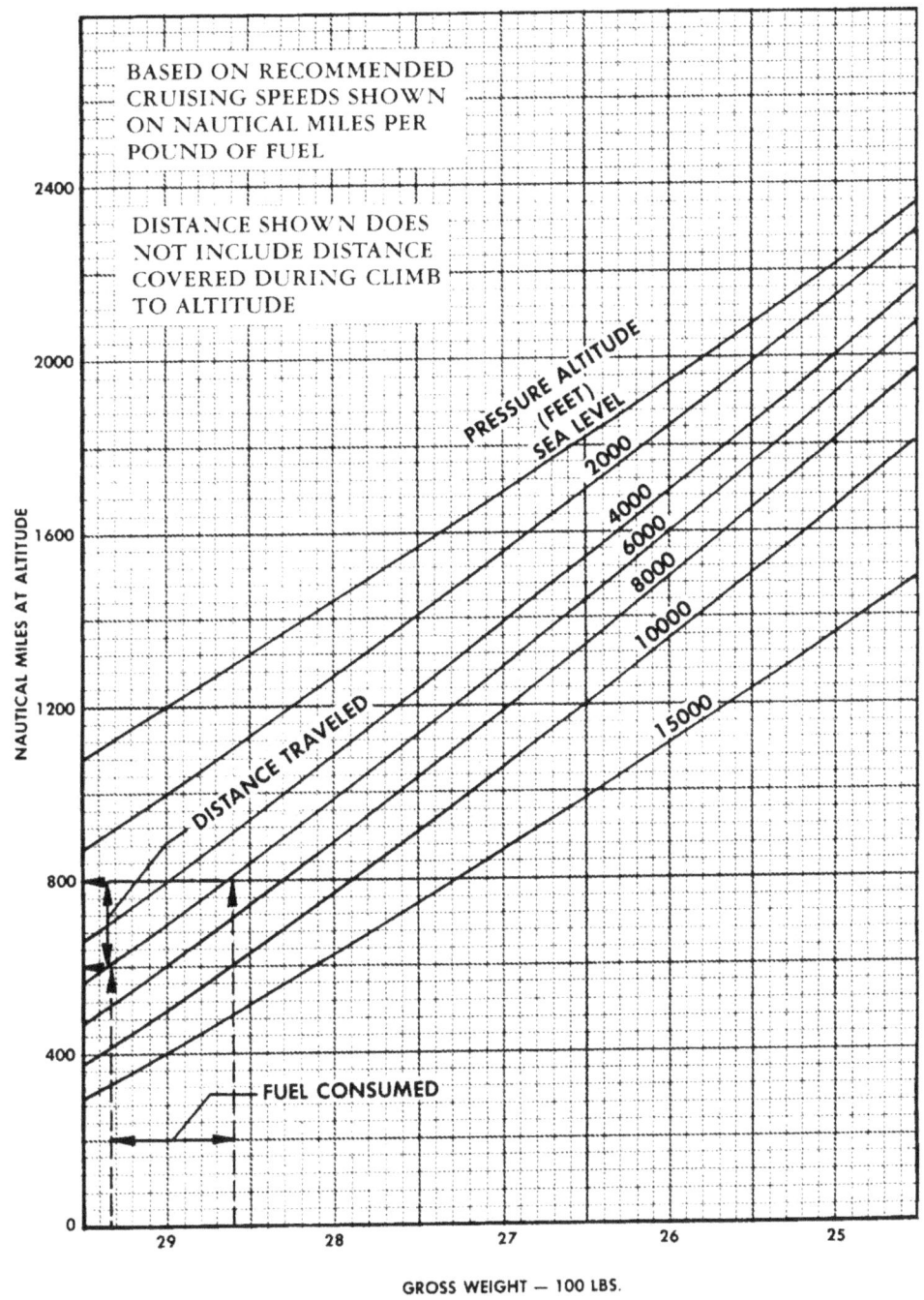

DATA AS OF: FEBRUARY 1954
DATA BASED ON: FLIGHT TEST

FUEL GRADE: 80
FUEL DENSITY: 6.0 LBS/GAL

Figure A-22

Appendix T.O. 1T-34A-1

LONG RANGE PREDICTION — TIME (NO WIND)
STANDARD DAY

MODEL T-34A
ENGINE: O-470-13

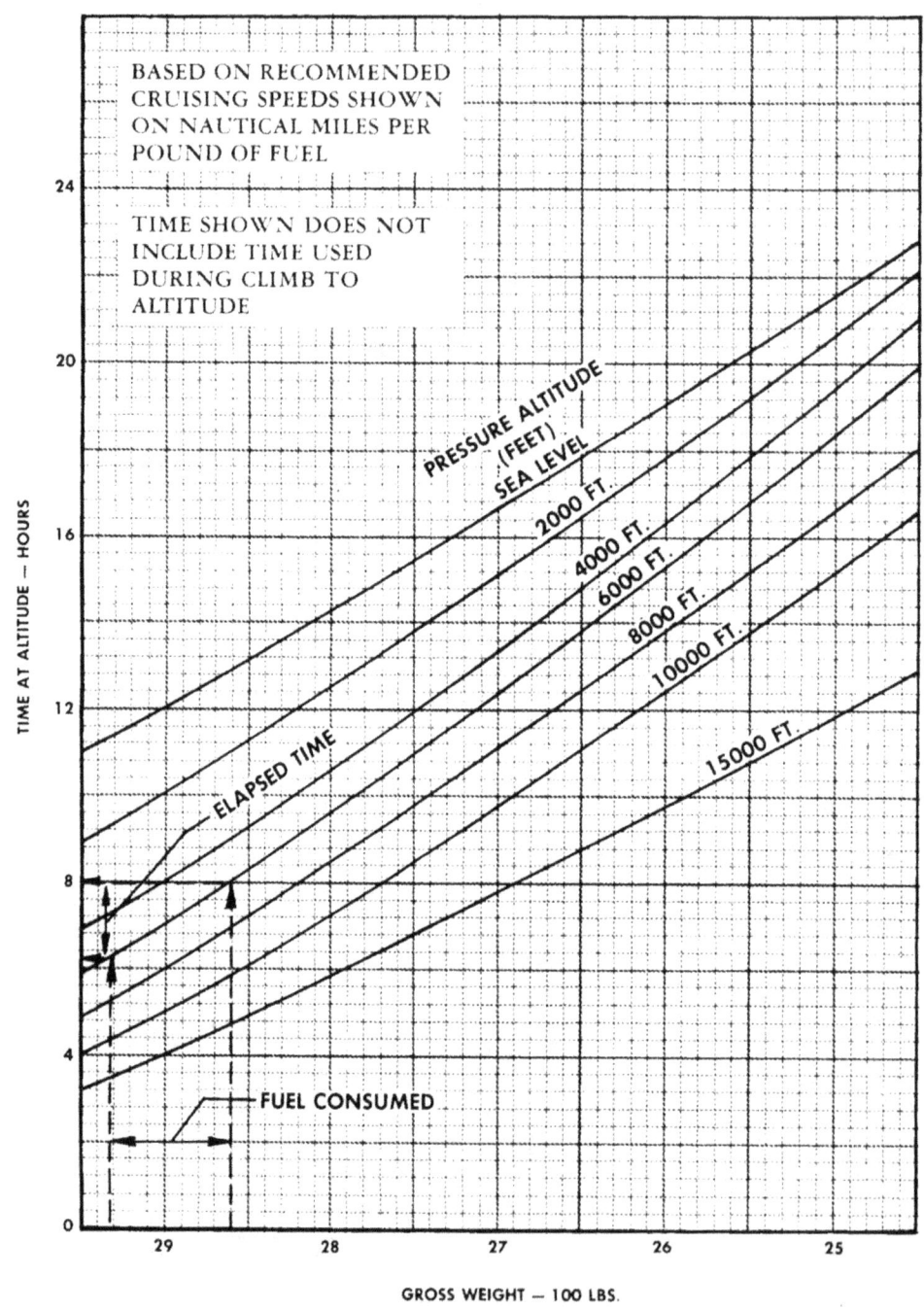

DATA AS OF: FEBRUARY 1954
DATA BASED ON: FLIGHT TEST

FUEL GRADE: 80
FUEL DENSITY: 6.0 LBS/GAL

Figure A-23

T.O. 1T-34A-1 Appendix

MAXIMUM ENDURANCE

MODEL T-34A ENGINE: O-470-13

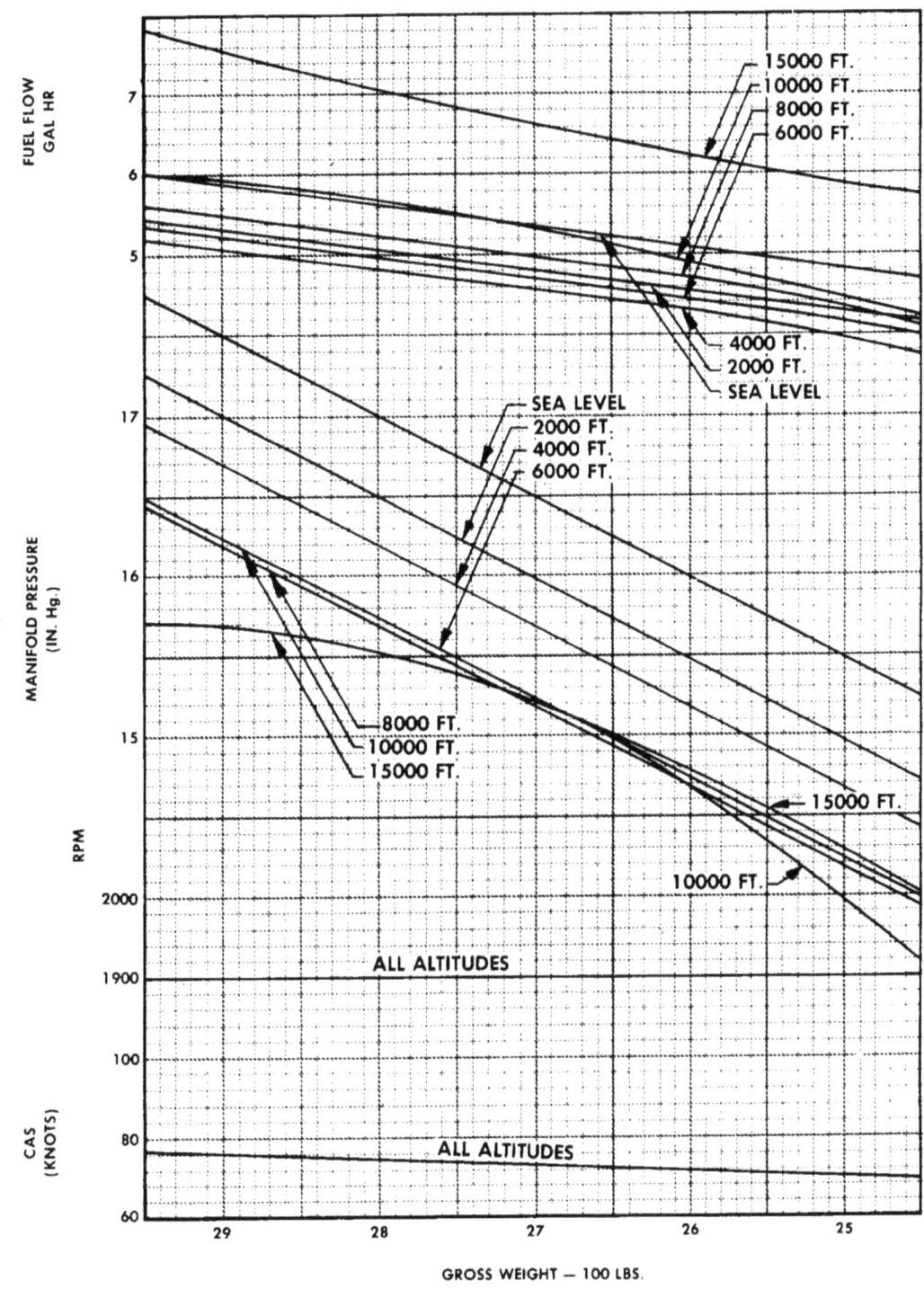

DATA AS OF: FEBRUARY 1954
DATA BASED ON: FLIGHT TEST

FUEL GRADE: 80
FUEL DENSITY: 6.0 LBS/GAL

Figure A-24

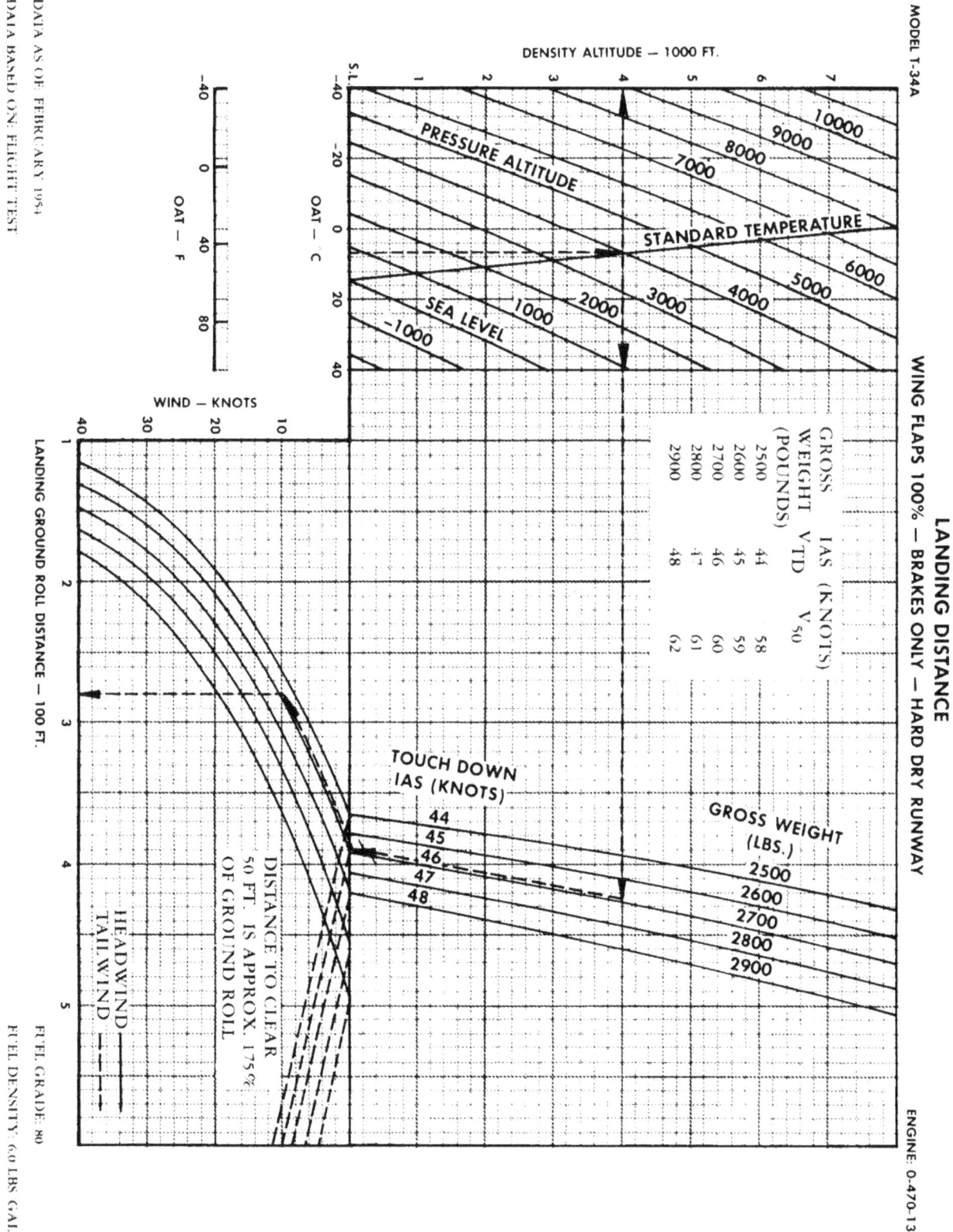

Figure A-25

Alphabetical Index

PAGE NUMBERS APPEARING IN BOLD FACE DENOTE ILLUSTRATIONS

A

Abbreviations	A-1
AC Power Failure	3-10
AC Power Supply	1-16
Accelerated Stall	6-3
Acceleration Limits	5-5
After — Landing	2-12, 9-7
— Take-Off	2-9, 9-7
Aileron Trim Tab Wheel	1-20, **1-20**
Aileron Trim Tab Position Indicator	1-20
Aircraft — Dimensions	1-1
— Entrance	2-2
— General	1-1
— Gross Weight	1-2
Airspeed	A-1
— Indicator	1-25
— Limitations	5-4
Altimeter	1-25
Altitude — Density	**A-7**
— Loss in Dive Recovery	**6-4**, 6-6
— Pressure	A-2
Appendix	A-1
Approaches — Ground Controlled	**9-2**, 9-3
— Instrument	9-3
— Radio Range	9-3, **9-3**
Arrangement — Front and Rear Cockpit	**1-3**
— General	**1-2**
Auxiliary Equipment	1-28

B

Baggage Compartment	4-7, **4-7**
Bail-Out	3-7, **3-7**
Base Leg	2-10
Battery Switch	1-14
Before — Entering Aircraft (Cold Weather)	9-6
— Exterior Inspection	2-2
— Landing	2-9, 9-7
— Leaving Aircraft	2-12, 9-7, 9-8
— Starting Engine	2-4, 9-6
— Take-Off	2-7, 9-7
— Taxiing	2-6
Brake Failure — Emergency Landing	3-8
Brake System — Landing Wheel	7-3
Button — Horn Silencing	1-23
— Interphone and Transmitter	**4-4**
— Landing Gear Warning Light Test	1-23
— Manifold Pressure Purge Valve	1-4
— Push for Control	4-4

C

Canopy	1-26
— Emergency Release Handle	**1-25**, 1-26
— Exterior Emergency Release Handle	1-28
— Locking Handles	**1-25**, 1-26
— Jettison Procedure	**3-10**
— Overhead Assist Closing Handle	**1-26**

X-1

PAGE NUMBERS APPEARING IN BOLD FACE DENOTE ILLUSTRATIONS

Carburetor 1-7
    — Air Temperature Gage 1-5
    — Heat Handle 1-7
Ceilings A-2
Center-of-Gravity Limitations 5-5
Characteristics — Flight 2-9
    — General Flight 6-1
Checks — Before Landing 2-9
    — Interior (All Flights) 2-4
    — Post Flight Engine 2-12
    — Preflight 2-2
    — Rear Cockpit for Solo Flights .. 2-2
    — Traffic Pattern 2-10
Circuit Breaker Panel **1-18**
Climb 9-2, **A-19**
    — Instrument Flight 9-1
Clutch Knob — Landing Gear Emergency
    Hand Crank 1-22
Cockpit — Cold Air Handle 4-1
    — Front — Left Side **1-10**
    — Right Side **1-11**
    — Hot Air Handle 4-1
    — Rear — Left Side **1-12**
    — Right Side **1-13**
Cold Weather Procedures 9-6
Communications and Associated Electronics
    Equipment **4-3**, 4-4
Compartment — Baggage 4-7, **4-7**
Control — Engine Quadrant 1-2, **1-4**
    — Flight 6-5
    — Heating and Ventilation
        System 4-1, **4-2**
    — Interior Lighting Rheostats 4-7
    — Lock Installation **1-19**
Conversion — Temperature **A-6**
Cooling **1-5**
Crew — Minimum 5-1
Cross Wind — Landing 2-10
    — Take-Off 2-9
    — Taxiing 2-6
Cruise 2-9
    — Instrument Flight 9-2
Cylinder Head Temperature Gage 1-5

D

Data Card — Take-Off and Landing 2-2
DC Power — Failure 3-10
    — Supply 1-14
Density Altitude **A-7**
Descent — Normal 2-9
    — Instrument Flight 9-2
Desert and Hot Weather Operations 9-7
Dewpoint A-2

Dimensions 1-1
Ditching 3-9
Dive — Altitude Loss in Recovery **6-4**, 6-6
Diving 6-5
Down-Wind Leg 2-10
    — Taxiing 2-6
During Flight — (Cold Weather) 9-7

E

Electrical — Fire 3-7
    — Power Supply Emergency
        Operation 3-10
    — Power Supply System 1-14, **1-17**, 7-3
Elevator Trim Tab — Wheel 1-19, **1-19**
    — Position Indicator 1-19
Elimination — Smoke 3-7
Emergency — Ditching 3-9
    — Electrical Power Supply System
        Operation 3-10
    — Entrance **1-25**, 3-9, **3-9**
    — Equipment 1-26, **3-4**
    — Fuel System Operation 3-10
    — Landings 3-8
    — Landings — Flat Tire 3-8
    — Landing Gear Extension 3-11, **3-11**
    — Landing Gear Operation 3-11
    — Wing Flap Operation 3-10
Endurance — Maximum **A-29**
Engine 1-2, 7-1
    — Before Starting 2-4, 9-6
    — Control Quadrant 1-2, **1-4**
    — Control Quadrant Friction Lock ... 1-4
    — Cooling **1-5**, 1-7
    — Failure and Procedures 3-1, 3-2, 3-2
    — Fire Access Door **3-5**
    — General 1-2
    — Ground Operation and Tests ... 2-5
    — Instruments 1-4
    — Limitations 5-1
    — Run Up 2-6
    — Starting 2-4, 9-6
    — Stopping 2-12
Entrance to Aircraft 2-2, **2-2**
Entry to Pattern 2-9
Equipment — Auxiliary 1-28
    — Communications and Associated
        Electronic **4-3**, 4-4
    — Emergency 1-26, **3-4**
    — Miscellaneous 4-7
    — Radio and Navigation 4-7
    — VHF Communications and
        Receiving, Operation 4-4
Extension — Landing Gear Emergency .. 3-11

PAGE NUMBERS APPEARING IN BOLD FACE DENOTE ILLUSTRATIONS

Exterior — Inspection 2-2, **2-3**
    — Lighting 4-5
External — Gear Down Indicator Lights 1-23
    — Switch 4-5
    — Power Receptacle 1-16

F

Failure — AC Electric Power 3-10
    — DC Electric Power 3-10
    — Engine 3-1, 3-2, 3-3
    — Engine During Take-Off Run
        and Take-Off 3-1, 3-2
    — Engine During Flight 3-2
    — Engine Failure Procedures 3-1, 3-2
    — Generator Failure Light 1-16
    — Fuel Pump 3-10
    — Inverter Failure Light 1-16
    — Landing with Brake Failure 3-8
    — Propeller 3-5
Fire 3-5
    — Electrical 3-7
    — Engine — During Flight 3-7
        — After Starting 3-5
        — During Start 3-5
    — Fuselage in Flight 3-7
    — Wing 3-7
First Aid Kit 1-26, 3-4
Flaps — Wing 1-20
Flat Tire — Emergency Landing 3-8
Flight — Characteristics 2-9
    — Control 6-5
    — Controls Lock 1-18
    — Control System 1-18
    — General 6-1
    — Instrument Flight Radio and
        Navigation Equipment 9-2
    — Instrument Procedures 6-1
    — Maneuvering 6-5
    — Night 9-4
    — Planning 2-1
    — Preparation 2-1
    — Restrictions 2-1
    — In Turbulence and Thunderstorms ... 9-4
Forced Landings — No Power Available 3-4, **3-6**
        — Simulated 3-4
Friction Lock — Engine Control Quadrant 1-4
Fuel — Booster Pump Switch 1-9
    — Booster Pump Indicating Lights 1-14
    — Booster Pump Override Panel **1-14**
    — Booster Pump Override Switches ... 1-9
    — Flow **A-15, A-16**
    — Pressure Drop — In Flight 3-3
        — On the Ground 3-3

    — Pressure Gage 1-7
    — Pump Failure 3-10
    — Quantity Gages 1-14
    — Quantity Table **1-16**
    — Selector Valve Handle 1-9
    — System 1-9, **1-15**, 7-3
    — System Emergency Operation 3-10
Fuselage Fire in Flight 3-7

G

Gage — Free Air Temperature 1-25
Gear-Up Landing 3-8
General — Arrangement **1-2**
    — Front and Rear Cockpit **1-3**
    — Flight Characteristics 6-1
    — Limitations 5-1
Generator — Failure Light 1-16
    — Switch 1-14
Glide — Maximum **3-3**, 3-4
Glossary of Terms and Abbreviations A-1
Go-Around 2-12, **2-13**
Gross Weight 1-1
    — Limitations 5-5
Ground Controlled Approach 9-3, **9-5**

H

Handcrank — Landing Gear Emergency 1-21
    — Clutch Knob 1-22
Heat — Pitot 4-3
Heating and Ventilating System 4-1, **4-2**
    — Controls 4-1
Holding — Instrument Flying 9-2
Hot Weather and Desert Operation 9-7
Hood — Instrument Flying 4-7, **4-7**
    — Release 4-7
Horn — Landing Gear Warning 1-23
    — Silencing Button 1-23

I

Ice and Rain 9-4
Ignition System 1-7
    — Switch 1-7
Indicators — Aileron Trim Tab Position 1-20
    — Airspeed 1-25
    — Attitude 1-24
    — Directional 1-24
    — Elevator Trim Tab Position 1-19
    — Engine 1-4
    — Landing Gear Position 1-22, **1-22**
    — Rudder Trim Tab Position 1-19
    — Turn and Slip 1-23
    — Vertical Velocity 1-25
    — Wing Flap Position 1-20

PAGE NUMBERS APPEARING IN BOLD FACE DENOTE ILLUSTRATIONS

Inertia Reel Lock Handle **1-26**, 1-28
Inspection — Before Exterior 2-2
— Exterior 2-2, **2-3**
— Interior 2-4
— On Entering the Aircraft 2-4
Instrument — Flight 9-1
— Flying Hood 4-7, **4-7**
— Approaches 9-3
— Climb 9-2
— Cruising Flight 9-2
— Markings **5-2, 5-3**
— Panel 1-6
— Take-Off 9-1
Instruments 1-23
Interior Lighting and Control Rheostats 4-7
Interphone Button 4-4, **4-4**
Inverted Spins 6-5
Inverter Switch 1-16
Inverter Failure Light 1-16

J

Jettison Procedure — Canopy **3-10**

K

Kit — First Aid 1-26
Knob — Rudder Trim Tab 1-19

L

Landing 2-10
— After 2-12
— Before 2-9
— Cross Wind 2-10
— Emergency 3-8
— Forced 3-4, **3-6**
— Light Switches 4-5
— Minimum Run 2-10
— Night 2-10
— Normal 2-10, **2-11**
— On Unprepared Runway 3-8
— With Brake Failure 3-8
— With Flat Tire 3-8
— With Gear Up 3-8
— With Nose Gear Retracted 3-8
— With One Main Gear Retracted 3-9
Landing Distance Chart **A-30**
Landing Gear — Emergency Extension 3-11, **3-11**
— Emergency Handcrank 1-21
— Emergency Operation 3-11
— Emergency Retract 3-11

— Emergency Retract Switch 1-21
— Handle 1-21
— Position Indicators 1-22, **1-22**
— System 1-21
— Warning Horn 1-23
— Warning Light 1-22
— Warning Light Test Button 1-23
Landing Light Switches 4-5
Landing Wheel Brake System 7-3
Levers — Mixture 1-4
— Propeller 1-4, 1-9
— Wing Flaps 1-20, 1-21
Lighting Controls **4-6**
Lights — External Gear Down Indicator 1-23
— Fuel Booster Pump Indicator 1-14
— Generator Failure 1-16
— Inverter Failure 1-16
— Landing Gear Warning 1-22
Lighting — Exterior 4-5
— Interior 4-6
Limits — Acceleration 5-5
— Brake Horsepower A-2
Limitations — Airspeed 5-4
— Center-of-Gravity 5-5
— Engine 5-1
— General 5-1
— Gross Weight 5-5
— Loading 5-5
— Propeller 5-1
Loadmeter 1-16
Loading Limitations 5-5
Lock — Flight Controls 1-18
— Mixture Lever Idle Cut-Off 1-4
Long Range Prediction — Distance **A-27**
— Time **A-28**
Loss — Altitude in Dive Recovery **6-4**, 6-6

M

Maneuvering — Flight 6-5
Maneuvers — Prohibited 5-5
Manifold Pressure Gage 1-4
Manifold Pressure Purge Valve Button 1-4
Maximum — Endurance Chart **A-24**
— Glide 3-4
Minimum — Crew 5-1
— Run Landing 2-10
— Run Take-Off 2-7
— Turning Radius **2-5**
Miscellaneous Equipment 4-7
Mixture Lever 1-4
Mixture Lever Idle Cut-Off Lock 1-4

PAGE NUMBERS APPEARING IN BOLD FACE DENOTE ILLUSTRATIONS

N

Nautical Miles per Pound of Fuel
— Sea Level **A-20**
— 2000 Ft. **A-21**
— 4000 Ft. **A-22**
— 6000 Ft. **A-23**
— 8000 Ft. **A-24**
— 10000 Ft. **A-25**
— 15000 Ft. **A-26**
Navigation Lights Intensity Switch 4-5
Navigation Lights Switch 4-5
Night — Flight 9-4
— Landing 2-10
— Take-Off 2-9
Normal — Landing 2-10
— Take-Off 2-7, **2-8**
Nose Wheel Steering 1-23

O

Obstacle Clearance Take-Off 2-7
Oil — Pressure Gage 1-7
— System 1-9, 7-3
— Temperature Gage 1-7
On Entering the Aircraft 2-4
Operating — Flight Strength **5-4**, 5-5
Operations — Cold Weather 9-6
— Landing Gear Emergency 3-11
— Propeller With No Power 3-5
— Range Receiver 4-5
— Systems 2-9
— VHF Communications Equipment 4-4
— Wing Flap Emergency 3-10

P

Panel — Instrument **1-6**
Panels — Sub — Right and Left **1-8**
Parking — Before Leaving Aircraft
(Cold Weather) 9-7
(Hot Weather) 9-8
— Brake Handle 1-23
Partial Engine Failure 3-2
Passing Light Switch 4-5
Pitot Heat 4-3
Pitot Heater Switch 4-3
Pitot-Static System 1-25
Post Flight Engine Check 2-12
Power — AC Electric Supply 1-16
— DC Electric Supply 1-14
— M.E.T.O. A-2

Power-off Stall — Gear and Flaps Down 6-3
— Gear and Flaps Up 6-3
— in a Turn, Gear and Flaps Up 6-3
Power-off Stalls 6-2
Power-on Stall — Gear and Flaps Down 6-3
— Gear and Flaps Up 6-3
— in a Turn, Gear and Flaps Up 6-3
Power-on Stalls 6-1
Power Schedule — Sea Level **A-8**
— 2000 Ft. **A-9**
— 4000 Ft. **A-10**
— 6000 Ft. **A-11**
— 8000 Ft. **A-12**
— 10000 Ft. **A-13**
— 15000 Ft. **A-14**
Practice Stalls 6-3
Pre-Flight Check 2-2
Pressure Altitude A-2
Pre-Take-Off (Hot Weather) 9-7
Primer — Switch 1-7
— System 1-7
— Cold Weather 9-6
Procedures — Engine Failures 3-1, 3-2, 3-3
— G.C.A. Letdown 9-2
— Hot Weather and Desert 9-7
Prohibited Maneuvers 5-5
Propeller 1-8
— Failure 3-5
— Lever 1-4, 1-9
— Limitations 5-1
— Operation — No Power 3-5
— Uncontrollable 3-5
Push For Control Button 4-4

Q

Quadrant — Engine Control 1-2, 1-4

R

Radio and Navigation Equipment 9-2
Radio — Push for Control Button 4-4
— Range Approach 9-3, **9-3**
— Switch 4-4
Rain and Ice 9-4
Range Receiver 4-5
Receptacle — External Power 1-16
Recovery — Altitude Loss in Drive ... **6-4**, 6-6
— Spin 6-5
— Stall 6-2
Release Handle — Canopy Emergency **1-25**, 1-26
Release — Instrument Flying Hood 4-6
Rudder Pedals 1-18

X-5

PAGE NUMBERS APPEARING IN BOLD FACE DENOTE ILLUSTRATIONS

Rudder Trim Tab Knob 1-19, **1-20**
Rudder Trim Tab Position Indicator 1-19
Run Up — Engine 2-6

S

Seat Adjustment Handles **1-26**, 1-28
Seats 1-28
Servicing Diagram 1-27
Smoke Elimination 3-7
Spins — Inverted 6-3
 — Recovery 6-5
Stalling Speeds 6-2
Stalls — Accelerated 6-1
 — Power-off 6-2
 — Power-on 6-1
 — Practice 6-3
 — Recovery 6-2
Starter Switch 1-8
Starting Engine 2-4, 9-6
Steering — Nose Wheel 1-23
Stopping Engine 2-12, 9-6
Strength — Operating Flight **5-4**, 5-5
Sub-Panels, Right and Left **1-8**
Switches — Battery 1-14
 — External Gear Down Indicator
   Lights 4-5
 — Fuel Booster Pump 1-9
 — Fuel Booster Pump Override 1-9
 — Generator 1-14
 — Ignition 1-7
 — Inverter 1-16
 — Landing Gear Emergency
   Retract 1-21
 — Landing Light 4-5
 — Navigation Lights 4-5
 — Passing Light 4-5
 — Pitot Heater 4-3
 — Primer 1-7
 — Radio 4-4
 — Starter 1-8
Systems — Electrical Power
   Supply 1-14, **1-17**, 7-3
 — Flight Control 1-18
 — Fuel 1-9, **1-15**, 7-3
 — Heating and Ventilating 4-1, **4-2**
 — Ignition 1-7
 — Landing Gear 1-21
 — Oil 1-9, 7-3
 — Operation 2-9
 — Pitot-Static 1-25
 — Priming 1-7
 — Wheel Brake 1-23, 7-3

T

Table of Communications and Associated
   Electronic Equipment 4-4
Tabs — Trim 1-18, **1-19, 1-20**
Tachometer 1-5
Take-Off 2-7, 9-6
 — After 2-9
 — Approach, and Touchdown
   Velocity **A-18**
 — Before 2-7, 9-6
 — Cold Weather 9-7
 — Cross Wind 2-9
 — Distance Chart A-17
 — Instrument 9-1
 — Hot Weather 9-7
 — Minimum Run 2-7
 — Normal 2-7, **2-8**
 — Obstacle Clearance 2-7
 — Power A-2
Taxiing 2-6, 9-6
 — Cross Wind 2-6
 — Down Wind 2-6
Temperature Conversion Chart **A-6**
Temperature Gage — Free Air 1-25
Throttle 1-2
Thunderstorms and Turbulence 9-4
Traffic Pattern Check 2-10
Transmitter Button 4-4, **4-4**
Trim Tabs 1-18, **1-19**
Turbulence and Thunderstorms 9-4

U

Use of Charts A-4

V

Vertical Velocity Indicator 1-25
VHF Communications Equipment 4-4
Voltmeter 1-16

W

Warm-Up and Ground Check 9-6
Weight and Balance 2-2
Weight — Gross 1-2
Wheel — Aileron Trim Tab 1-20
 — Brake System 1-23, 7-3
 — Elevator Trim Tab 1-19
Wing Flaps 1-20
Wing Flap Emergency Operation 3-10
Wing Flap Lever 1-20, 1-21
Wing Flap Position Indicator 1-20

X Y Z

f. Fuel quantity — check, cap secure.
g. Air intake — check, screen clean.
2. Left main gear.
   a. Wheel chocks — in place.
   b. Tire — check.
   c. Wheel brake — check puck, hydraulic line, adjusting pin recessed $3/16$ inch maximum.
   d. Strut — check.
   e. Landing gear doors — check.
   f. Wheel well — unobstructed.
3. Nose section.
   a. Left augmentor tube — unobstructed.
   b. Left cowling — secure.
   c. Propeller — check.
   d. Passing light — secure.
   e. Air intake — check, unobstructed.
   f. Strut — check.
   g. Tire and static wire — check.
   h. Nose landing gear doors — check.
   i. Wheel well — unobstructed.
   j. Right cowling — secure.
   k. Battery and battery retainer bar — secure.
   l. Battery sump jar — check.
   m. Exterior canopy emergency release handle — undisturbed.
   n. Right augmentor tube — unobstructed.
4. Right main gear — check same as left main gear.
5. Right wing.
   a. Air intake — check, screen clean.
   b. Fuel quantity — check, cap secure.
   c. Leading edge and landing light — check.
   d. Wing tip and navigation light — check.
   e. Aileron — check; trim tab for servo action.
   f. Wing flap — check.

11. Engine control quadrant friction lock knob — adjusted.
12. Mixture lever — IDLE CUT-OFF.
13. Propeller lever — FULL INCREASE.
14. Throttle — cracked ¼ inch.
15. Ignition switch — OFF.
16. Landing gear handle — DOWN.
17. Landing gear emergency retract switch — guard safetied.
18. Carburetor heat handle — IN and LOCKED.
19. Clock and altimeter — set.
20. Attitude indicator and directional indicator — uncaged.

21. Primer switch — OFF.
22. Starter switch — OFF.
23. Battery switch — OFF.
24. Generator switch — ON.
25. Cockpit air handles — as desired.
26. Landing gear emergency handcrank — disengaged (clutch knob up and LOCKED).

27. Inverter switch — OFF.
28. Light switches and rheostats — OFF.
29. Radio switch — OFF.
30. Pitot heater switch — OFF (guard down).
31. Circuit breakers — IN.
32. Battery switch — ON.
33. Landing gear position indicators — check.
34. Landing gear warning light — test.
35. Fuel quantity gages — check.
36. Fuel pressure (booster pump) — check.
37. Generator and inverter warning lights — check illuminated.

38. Navigation lights — check, STEADY and FLASH positions.
39. External gear down indicator lights — check illuminated.

T.O. 1T-34A-1
10 February 1958

4

9. Ignition switch — check (grounded).
10. Radio — check operation.

TAXIING.
1. Area — check clear for taxi.
2. Wheel chocks — removed.
3. Brakes — check.

ENGINE RUN-UP.
1. Fuel selector valve handle — fullest tank.
2. Propeller lever — FULL INCREASE.
3. Mixture lever — FULL RICH.
4. Engine instruments — check.
5. Propeller governor — check at 1800 rpm. Note 150-200 rpm drop.
6. Ignition system — check at 2000 rpm, 75 rpm maximum drop.
7. Carburetor heat system — check at 2000 rpm.
8. Engine power check (2475 ±75 rpm).

BEFORE TAKE-OFF.
1. Wing flaps — up (lever — NEUTRAL).
2. Trim tabs — repeat 10, interior inspection.
3. Friction lock knob — adjusted.
4. Mixture lever — FULL RICH.
5. Propeller lever — FULL INCREASE.
6. Engine instruments — check.
7. Flight controls — freedom of movement and proper response.
8. Canopy — position optional.
9. Safety belt and shoulder harness — adjusted.
10. Inertia reel — LOCKED.

T.O. 1T-34A-1
10 February 1958

6

NOTES:

T.O. 1T-34A-1
10 February 1958

BLANK

10

NOTES:

Blank

4. Throttle — advance ½ inch beyond present setting.
5. Mixture lever — FULL RICH.
6. Propeller lever — FULL INCREASE.
7. Ignition switch — check BOTH.
8. Battery switch — check ON.
9. Generator switch — check ON.
10. Carburetor heat handle — climatic.

If Complete Engine Failure Is Encountered, Proceed as Follows:
11. Airspeed — Maintain 90 knots.

Attempt to Restart Engine if Altitude Permits:
12. Mixture lever — IDLE CUT-OFF.
13. Fuel selector valve handle — OFF.
14. Throttle — FULL OPEN.
15. Fuel selector valve handle — ON (fullest tank).
16. Fuel booster pump switch — ON.
17. Throttle — ¼ inch OPEN.
18. Mixture lever — FULL RICH.
19. Primer switch — ON (intermittently as required to start engine).
   a. If engine fires, primer switch — ON (as required to reach field).

If Engine Fails to Restart:
20. Mixture lever — IDLE CUT-OFF.
21. Throttle — CLOSED.
22. Ignition switch — OFF.
23. Fuel selector valve handle — OFF.
24. All switches — OFF.
25. Shoulder harness — locked.

T.O. 1T-34A-1
10 February 1958

2

If Propeller Is Uncontrollable:
    4. Wing flap lever — DOWN.
    5. Airspeed — approximately 60 knots.

FIRE.

FIRE DURING ENGINE START.

If Fire Is Other Than Exhaust or Induction — Discontinue Starting Attempt.
    1. Mixture lever — IDLE CUT-OFF.
    2. Battery switch — OFF.
    3. Ignition switch — OFF.
    4. Generator switch — OFF.

If Fire Is Exhaust or Induction — Continue Starting Attempt; if Fire Persists:
    1. Mixture lever — IDLE CUT-OFF.
    2. Throttle — FULL OPEN, continue cranking.
    3. Fuel control valve handle — OFF.
    4. Ignition switch — OFF.
    5. Starter switch — OFF.
    6. Battery switch — OFF.
    7. Generator switch — OFF.

ENGINE FIRE DURING FLIGHT.
    1. Mixture lever — IDLE CUT-OFF.
    2. Fuel selector valve handle — OFF.
    3. Ignition switch — OFF.
    4. Battery switch — OFF.
    5. Throttle — CLOSED.

FUSELAGE FIRE IN FLIGHT.
    1. Canopy position — closed.
    2. Cockpit air handles — FULL OUT.
    3. Battery switch — OFF.
    4. Generator switch — OFF.

T.O. 1T-34A-1
10 February 1958

4

LANDING WITH ONE MAIN GEAR RETRACTED.
 1. Canopy position — open.
 2. Throttle — CLOSED.
 3. Mixture lever — IDLE CUT-OFF.
 4. Fuel selector valve handle — OFF.
 5. Ignition switch — OFF.
 6. Battery switch — OFF.
 7. Generator switch — OFF.

LANDING WITH NOSE GEAR RETRACTED.
 1. Canopy position — open.
 2. Throttle — CLOSED.
 3. Mixture lever — IDLE CUT-OFF.
 4. Elevator trim tab wheel — full nose down.
 5. Ignition switch — OFF.
 6. Battery switch — OFF.
 7. Generator switch — OFF.
 8. Fuel selector valve handle — OFF.

DITCHING.
 1. Landing gear handle — check UP.
 2. Canopy position — open.
 3. Battery switch — OFF.
 4. Safety belt — fastened.
 5. Life raft or life preserver — check.
 6. Wing flap lever — DOWN.
 7. Ignition switch — OFF.
 8. Inertia reel — LOCKED.

T.O. 1T-34A-1
10 February 1958

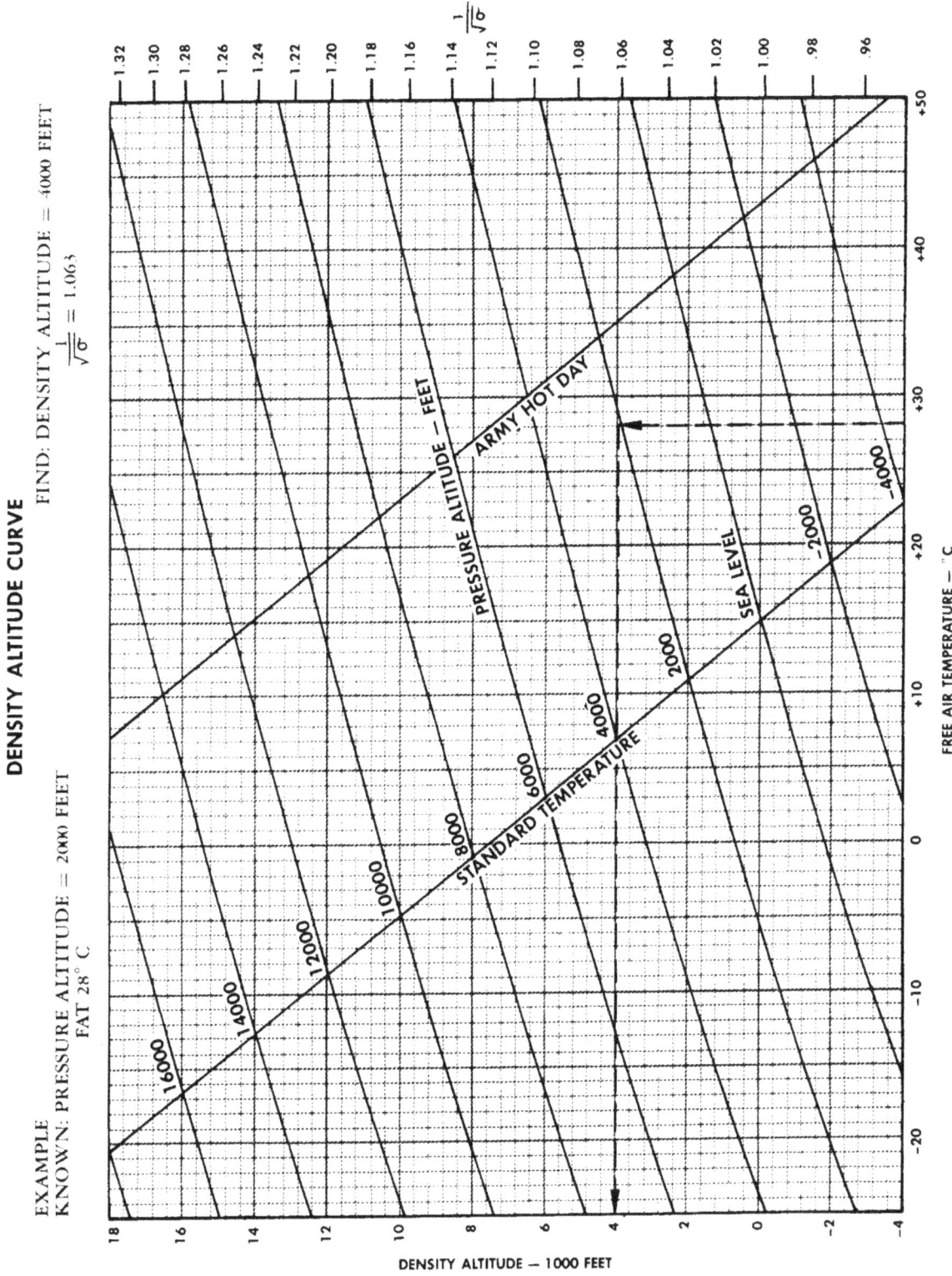

Figure A-2

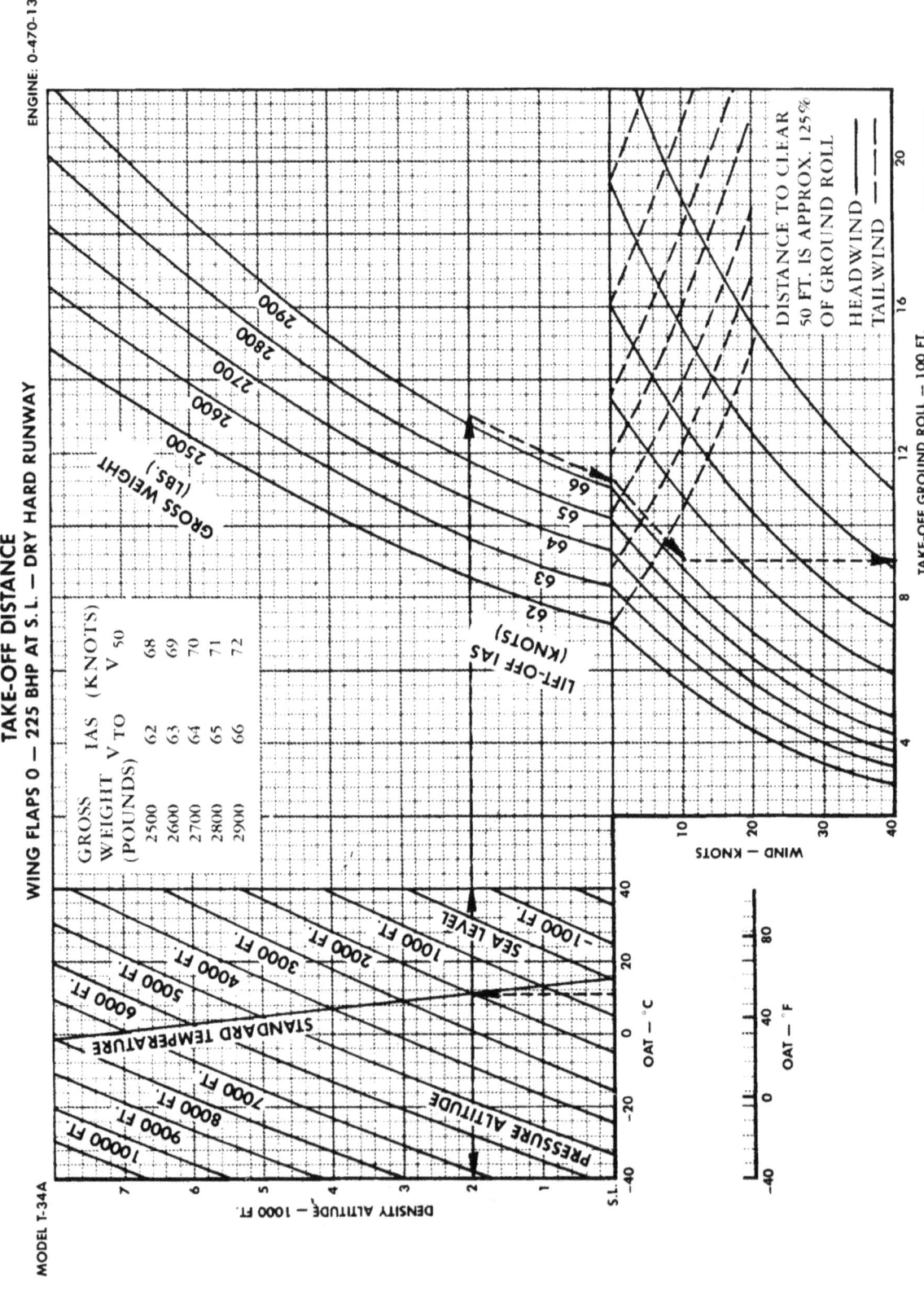

Figure A-12

T.O. 1T-34A-1 Appendix

CLIMB
STANDARD DAY – NO WIND
"METO" POWER

MODEL T-34A

ENGINE: O-470-13

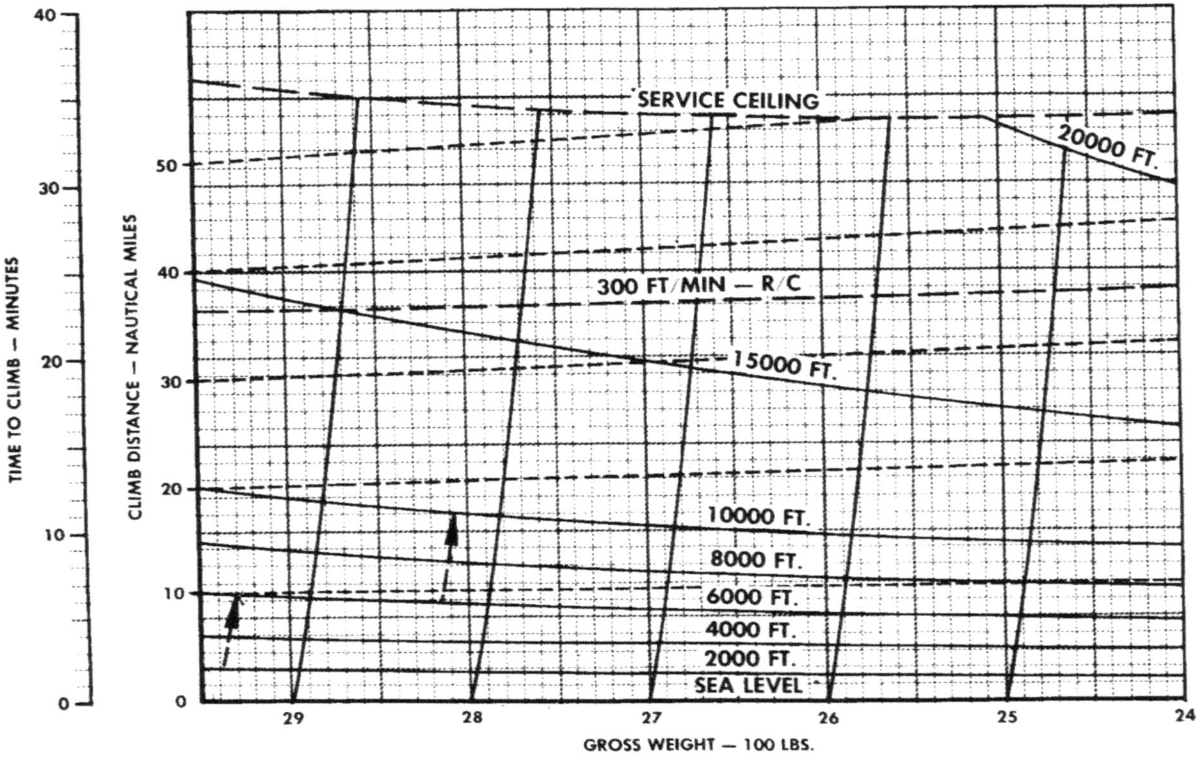

MAX. CLIMB POWER SCHEDULE 2600 RPM

ALT. FT.	MAP IN. Hg.	CARB. MIX.
SL	28.0	FR
2000	26.5	FR
4000	25.0	ML
6000	23.0	ML
8000	21.6	ML
10000	20.0	ML
15000	15.5	ML
20000	12.5	ML

(APPROX.) BEST CLIMB SPEED

GROSS WEIGHT	IAS KNOTS
2500	87
2600	88
2700	90
2800	91
2900	93

NOTE: IAS IS REDUCED 1 KNOT FOR EACH 1000 FT. INCREASE IN ALTITUDE.

NOTE: START, TAXI AND TAKE-OFF FUEL ALLOWANCE = 12 POUNDS

NOTE: FOR EACH 1° C HOTTER THAN STANDARD FAT, ADD 25 LBS. TO ACTUAL AIRPLANE GROSS WEIGHT TO OBTAIN AN EQUIVALENT WEIGHT FOR CLIMB DETERMINATION.

DATA AS OF: FEBRUARY 1954
DATA BASED ON: FLIGHT TEST

FUEL GRADE: 80
FUEL DENSITY: 6.0 LBS/GAL

Figure A-14

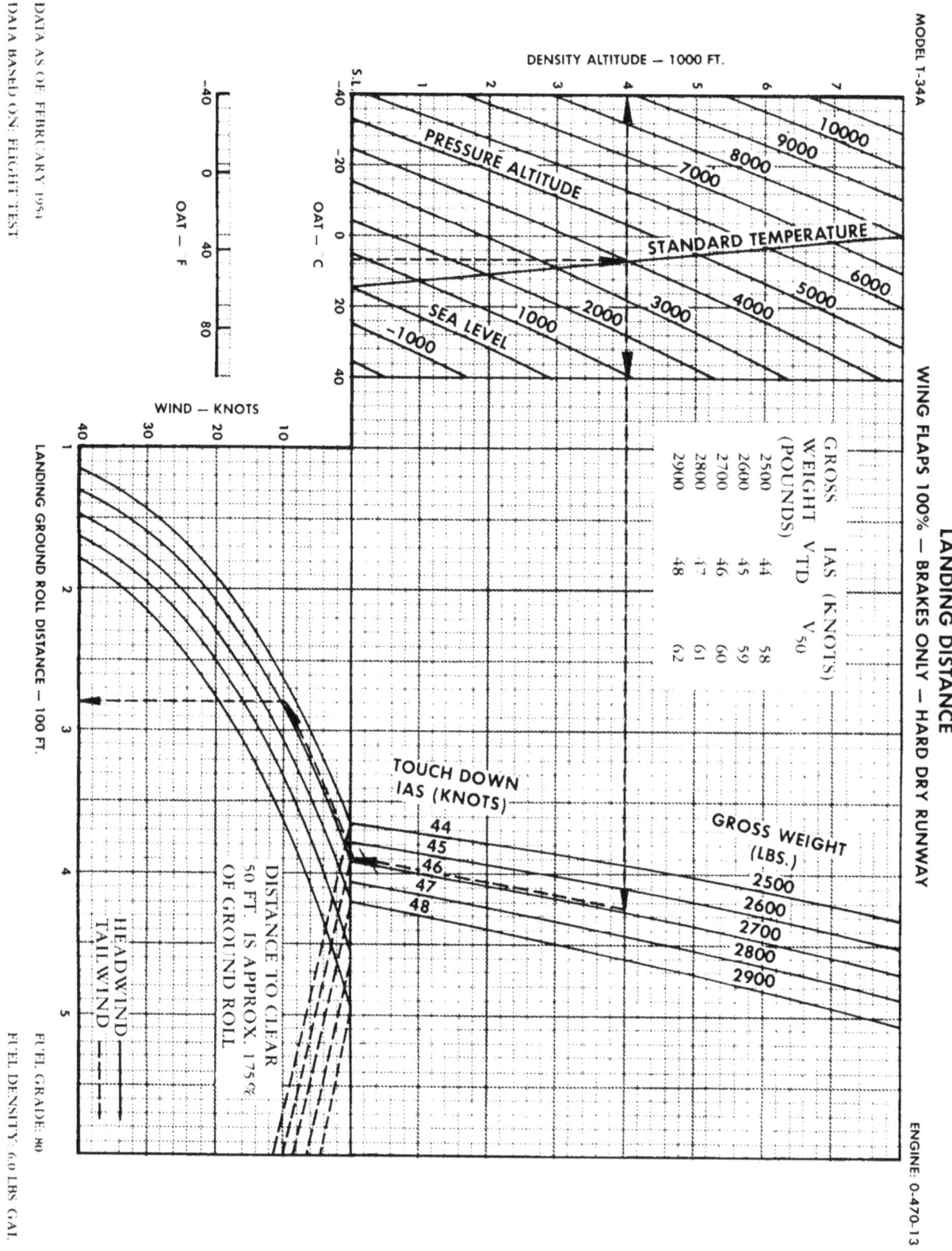

Figure A-25

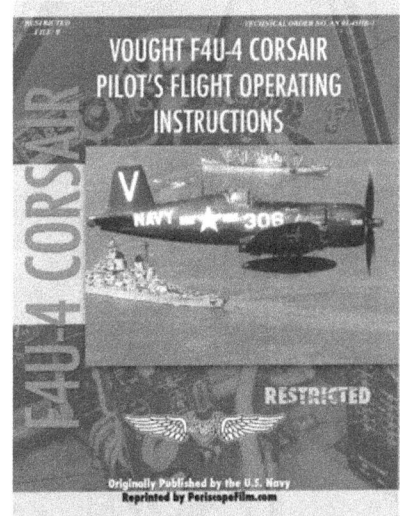
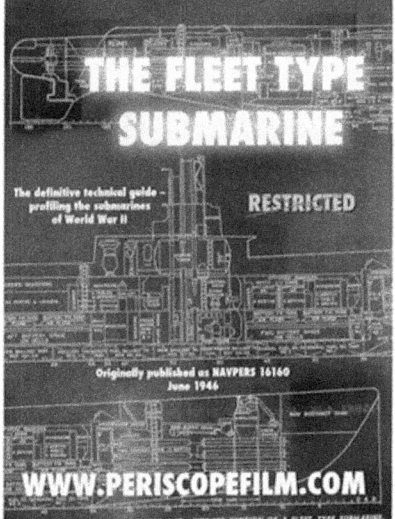

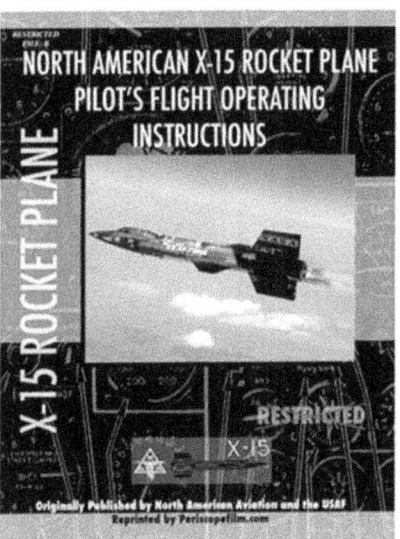

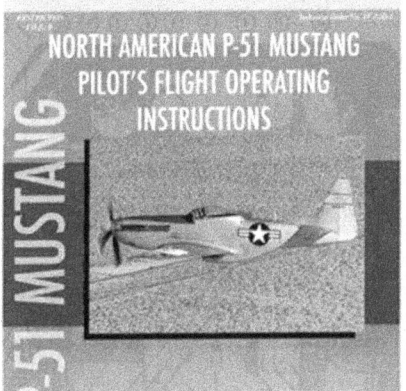

ALSO NOW AVAILABLE FROM PERISCOPEFILM.COM

2013 Periscope Film LLC
All Rights Reserved
ISBN #978-1-937684-62-4

www.ingramcontent.com/pod-product-compliance
Lightning Source LLC
Chambersburg PA
CBHW080508110426

42742CB00017B/3042